Tausee

CW00472196

Who misleads you about money

And what you can do about it

Paul Claireaux

Independently published
Bristol, United Kingdom

Who misleads you about money?

copyright © 2015 Paul Claireaux

The moral rights of the author have been asserted.

Cover design and formatting www.jdsmith-design.com

Published by irate investment

First published 2015

ISBN: 978-0-9927748-4-4

For
Harry, George and Edward

The golden rule is that there are no golden rules.

~ George Bernard Shaw

About Paul Claireaux

Paul Claireaux is an author, educator and the consumer champion of the personal finance world. And he's on a mission – to turn our ideas about money management upside down.

With a diploma in financial planning and 25 years' experience on the inside of the financial services industry (heading up investment product developments for a leading provider), he's more than qualified to be a financial adviser – but chooses not to sell financial products.

Ask him why and he'll tell you **they're the last thing you need** to develop your financial life plan.

What he *does* offer is education and ideas to help you understand your money, take control of it, and protect it from those who want to steal it or expose it to crazy risks. He also helps us to understand our own, irrational behaviours (the 'enemies inside our heads' if you like) which can lead to our biggest money mistakes.

His first book, *Who Can You Trust About Money?* was described as *"One of the best-written and most engaging books of its kind"* by Moira O'Neill, award winning journalist and personal finance editor of *Investor's Chronicle*.

Through books, blogs and workshops, Paul teaches a powerful process to help us connect our money to our life – which is why he's called his educational business www.yourmoney-yourlife.com

Paul is father to three adult boys (Harry, George and Ed) who inspired him to start writing and focus his efforts on helping younger people aged 25 to 45 make better choices about money.

Two other interesting things about Paul. He held a private pilot's licence for 25 years until he had to undergo surgery to replace collapsed discs in his neck with titanium joints. So, if he looks at you with his head on one side, it's not *necessarily* because he doesn't believe what you're saying.

Foreword

In his two-book series *Who misleads you about money* and *How we mislead ourselves about money,* Paul Claireaux uses his natural skill as an educator to teach his readers important lessons about personal finance. Paul avoids the trap of filling pages with dry charts of stock prices and statistical tables and instead turns his insight into a simple, often humorous narrative that people can really learn from.

Paul's focus on our relationship with money is especially important. The latest research in behavioural science has shown that we humans are far removed from the perfectly rational calculating machines that economic and finance theory assumes us to be. When it comes to making decisions about money and investing, we humans are deeply flawed; our instinctive behaviour is often far from rational and rarely optimal.

Over this series you will learn both how our behavioural biases undermine the foundational ideas of economics and finance, and why this renders some financial advice worse than useless. You will also learn how marketers and salesmen are able to turn our emotions against us: Paul's characterisation of the financial salesman as a rhinoceros – thick skinned and prone to charging too much – is painfully accurate. It is also a great device to make an important message stick in the mind.

Paul rightly warns of the tricks and shenanigans played by the financial services industry, but his most important warning is to mistrust our own behaviour. When it comes to managing our money, we are often our own worst enemy.

The good news is that with a little effort we can learn to overcome our poor financial instincts, to avoid the worst practices of the financial industry and to get more from our money. Forewarned is forearmed; with these books you can arm yourself for a more rewarding relationship with your money.

George Cooper
Author of *The Origin of Financial Crises and Money, Blood & Revolution*

What this book does and does not do

This book aims to help you make more informed decisions about your finances by helping you understand some fundamental concepts of human behaviour and personal finance.

The information contained here is generic guidance. I do NOT offer regulated financial advice – which means that I do NOT make specific recommendations for you to buy, sell or otherwise transact investments, or to engage in any investment strategies, or for you not to do any of these things.

The buck starts – and stops – with you

You are solely responsible for any decisions you make regarding your finances and investments. You are also solely responsible for any losses you incur from the actions you take (or do not take) having read this book.

Disclaimer

It's up to you to conduct your own due diligence before implementing investments, business plans, or other changes to your personal life – and you need to satisfy yourself as to the suitability of any particular investment.

Also, bear in mind that any figures in this book – such as potential returns from various assets held within different product wrappers – are only examples of possible outcomes. I offer no assurance that the returns from your investments will be similar to, or within the range of, example figures.

The value of shares and investments can go down as well as up. You may not get back the money that you invest. Past performance is not a guide to future performance.

If you require specific recommendations on investments, then I strongly recommend that you appoint an appropriately qualified and regulated professional adviser who will advise you in line with their own terms of business.

Contents

Introduction

It ain't what you don't know that gets you into trouble.
It's what you know for sure that just ain't so.

~ Mark Twain

In a nutshell – what's this book about?

This book will help you to **take more control** of your money – and **make much better decisions** about it.

It exposes the **'external enemies'** to your money and blows up the big myths.

There's a lot of nonsense written (and spoken) about money and thrown at us every day *by people trying to sell us their latest whiz bang product.* This book replaces that noise with the truth about money and gives you a solid foundation for planning your future.

Who is it for?

Wherever you live in the world – if you save or invest – this book will help you.

> Just keep in mind that some parts refer to UK laws on advice, tax and pensions.

In particular, this book will help you if:

- You're baffled or bored by personal finance
- You can't understand your adviser **or** you're not sure he/she is competent
- You suspect you may be paying too much for advice
- You want to spot the BIG financial tripwires **before** you fall over them.

That covers people of all ages – because good money management is a skill, like driving a car, which we all need to maintain throughout our lives. When we're young, we need to learn how to handle our money because we generally don't have very much of it – or, if we do, we need to learn to stop spending it! Then as we get older and build up some wealth, we need to learn where to invest it, for reasonable returns, without a risk of losing it all.

The ideas in this book will help you at any stage of your financial life – whether you're just starting out, saving regularly over the long term, or you have a capital sum ready to invest, or you already have monies invested. And, this book will fascinate anyone who's already an expert in this stuff!

Yes, but is it any fun?

Well, this book helps you **grasp the fundamentals of money** by demystifying all that boring and complicated stuff that surrounds it. And it's written in plain English; there's no gobbledygook here. Let's face it, most books about money are deadly dull but I think you'll have a laugh here as you start to discover just how very silly some 'experts'' ideas actually are.

I take on the overcharging salespeople – like the character on the front of this book (who 'charges' too much!) and other badly trained investment and pension advisers – and those unscrupulous scammers too.

You'll see how the great financial crisis was caused by the confused ideas of our politicians and economists. And you'll learn how these people (*and a few financial journalists*) are not quite as clever as they'd like you to believe!

What's inside each chapter?

- In Chapter 1 you'll learn how to save more for your future by seeing how the manipulative marketers get us to spend all our money today.

- Chapter 2 shows you how to deal with the truth that forecasts are wrong – and that our politicians can't really control our economy or the markets.

- In Chapter 3 you'll get some smart ideas for spotting overpriced markets – which could help you avoid some nasty future shocks.

- Chapter 4 is a must-read for investors and shows why your 'attitude to risk' is not the measure to focus on when making investment decisions. And you'll learn the right one, which is overlooked by too many advisers.

- Chapter 5 reveals the scary facts about 'balanced' investment funds that can turn out to be much riskier than you expect.

- And Chapter 6 offers powerful tips that could save you THOUSANDS of pounds in advice charges in the future.

- In Chapter 7 you'll learn what the government regulators can protect you from – and what they cannot.

- In Chapter 8 – you'll learn about the big tax traps to avoid and why you do NOT want to use 'aggressive' tax avoidance schemes.

- In Chapter 9 you'll learn how to cut the headline cost of a pension in half. If you only read one chapter, make it this one.

- In Chapter 10 you'll learn how a £4,000 'day trade' could lose you £8,000!

- Chapter 11 explains how to avoid all the big SCAMS, and...

- in Chapter 12 you'll learn how to get solid guidance about money – without paying through the nose.

There are some 'goodies' in the appendices too:

- In Appendix 1 you can learn what *really* caused the financial crisis of 2008-9 – and why it's probably not the last.

- In Appendix 2, discover how the confused economics profession has recently given **Nobel prizes to two experts . . . with opposing views!**

- Appendix 3 tells you what you must know about investment assets.

- Appendix 4 reveals **how state pensions** work, how they'll change in 2016 – for the better for many – and how **yours could be worth £200,000.**

- And in Appendix 5 there's a powerful chart to help you estimate the funds you could build up – simply by saving the price of a coffee each day.

Are there alternatives to reading this book?

Yes, of course. You could read the many *turgid textbooks* on investments, tax and pensions – and a pile of books on classical and behavioral economics.

But be warned – that's a very big job (I know, I've done it) – and you'll need at least twenty books to cover the ideas you'll find here. And some of those textbooks are over 800 pages long **and** they don't have cartoons . . . or jokes! That sort of reading would be tough enough, but then you'll discover how traditional investment theory is flawed. So after your first 20 books, you'll need another set to understand where the first set is wrong!

Do you really want to waste your time and money on all those books when all the key concepts and big ideas are right here, in your hands?

Am I having a laugh? Well, yes, but I'm not joking. If you really want to learn the fundamentals about long-term money management – you're in the right place – and you'll have a lot of fun learning it too.

Okay, but surely I could just talk to an expert?

Well, that's kind of the point. You need to know these basics about investing yourself – because there are so many problems with 'advice' in the world today. There are **some** very good financial advisers out there – you just have to know where to look – and be wealthy enough to cover their fees. If you're not very wealthy, then this book is essential for you because it can be so difficult to find good quality advice at a reasonable price. The problem is that most advice firms charge fees as a percentage of their 'funds under advice' (FUA) And too few offer discounts for larger funds – so they're keen to maximize the FUA!

It's quite simple really. The advisers that don't offer large case discounts earn ten times as much on a £250,000 portfolio as they do on just £25,000. So they focus their attention on the wealthiest people. Many advisers won't take on new clients with less than £250,000 to invest – and some set their thresholds at even higher levels.

If you **are** quite wealthy, and already have an adviser then this book will help you consider the quality of advice you're getting today – and whether the fees you're paying are reasonable for the work being done.

Get irate!

All the key learning points are listed at the end of each chapter under the *'Get irate!'* heading – to make it easy to go back to them later.

Just one final heads up:

All mention of UK tax and pensions rules refer to the 2015-16 tax year. I'll cover future regulatory changes at my website at www.paul-claireaux.com

So, who misleads YOU about money?

Let's get started and find out.

Chapter 1
The mood manipulators

How we're tricked into spending the money we need for our future

My problem lies in reconciling my gross habits with my net income.

~ Errol Flynn

© Copyright Paul Claireaux

Who's the real enemy?

In his book, *The Three Most Important Lessons You've Never Been Taught*, Martyn Lewis says that you should:

> *Know your enemy – a company is not your friend.*

He argues that companies are simply out to make money – which involves parting us from ours, stopping us from saving for our future. Now, I agree, that we do well to know our enemies. As Sun Tzu (Chinese general and philosopher from 2,500 years ago) advises in *The Art of War:*

> *If you **know your enemies** and you **know yourself** then you need not fear the results of a hundred battles.*

Indeed, that's exactly what this book is for – to uncover the enemies to your money – and in the next one we explore how we're often our own worst enemies and how it's our irrational behaviours that often lead to our biggest money mistakes.

I can see what Martyn is driving at – especially on the cheap tricks played by some supermarkets, like putting the sweets at child eye height at the checkouts. But I don't agree that all companies are our enemy. Personally, I love the computer I bought to write this book for you; I love the printer I use to print out each chapter (to scribble with red ink edits) and I love my mobile phone and tablet (for staying in touch with friends AND for clearing those emails so they're not stacked up when I get home) and I love my car for getting around but, most of all, I love my back massaging machine that relieves the pain of sitting all day and writing!

Yes, like many people I have a dodgy back but thanks to the high tech medical companies (and a great surgeon) I now have two titanium joints in my neck where two painful and collapsed discs used to live. So, I reckon there are plenty of good companies out there - including our chums at www.moneysavingexpert.com offering great products and services. They only survive by doing so.

Which of your gadgets (or other stuff) do you like best?

My point is that great technology can help us to work more efficiently – to get more done *and so earn more* in less time. And so, far from preventing us from saving, this stuff should help us to save more. Yes, I know, it's not that simple, when everyone has the same technology and we're all just working more efficiently for longer hours and we now have to compete with vast numbers of highly skilled people on low wages from developing countries who can do our administrative and creative tasks over the internet. Then again, the internet also allows us to sell our products and services worldwide too. So, it's not a one way street – but that's another story. But, let's be honest, we really can't expect to perform *more* effectively if we spend half the day on Facebook watching soppy videos of furry animals. What's that all about?

There is one point on which I think *we can all agree* – which is that one of the biggest enemies to wealth building is our tendency to **spend all our money** today on things we don't need. Or, worse still, on things we don't even want after we've bought them!

So why don't we resist this kind of spending and save for the future?

Well, there are many reasons for this and it's not just because we're weak willed or foolish. As you'll see, much of it is down to our natural emotions and hardwired behaviours which offer little defence against the army of marketers with multi million pound advertising budgets that suck us into buying stuff, regardless of our need for it. And if we're to stand a chance of winning the battle with these marketing folk we need to understand what they're doing and how they can control our minds.

Our fascination with emotion and personality

The weather and my mood have little connection. I have my foggy and my fine days within me; my prosperity or misfortune has little to do with the matter.

That was easy for Blaise Pascal to say. The early life of this great physicist, mathematician and inventor was dominated by the search for truths through scientific method and logic.

Of course, this is not how most of us ordinary mortals operate most of the time. Many of our actions – and for some people their whole lives – are dominated by emotional responses to external events. To varying degrees we're *fascinated* by the moods and personalities of ourselves, our friends, family, work colleagues and the characters in books and films.

But what are we fascinated about? What *are* these things we call emotions?

According to Robert Plutchik (Professor Emeritus at the Albert Einstein College of Medicine in New York), *"more than 90 definitions have been offered over the past century, and there are almost as many theories of emotion – not to mention a complex array of overlapping words in our languages to describe them."* In Plutchik's own model – which I've simplified in the table below – we have eight feelings (or advanced emotions), each of which is derived from a combination of two basic emotions. So, for example, we see that the feeling of optimism is derived from a combination of joy and anticipation. And love comes from having both joy and trust together.

Plutchik's model also suggests there are strong and mild forms of each basic emotion, as shown in the table below.

Feeling	Basic emotion	Strong form	Mild form
Optimism	Anticipation	Vigilance	Interest
	Joy	Ecstasy	Serenity
Love	Joy		
	Trust	Admiration	Acceptance
Submission	Trust		
	Fear	Terror	Apprehension
Awe	Fear		
	Surprise	Amazement	Distraction
Disapproval	Surprise		
	Sadness	Grief	Pensiveness
Remorse	Sadness		
	Disgust	Loathing	Boredom
Contempt	Disgust		
	Anger	Rage	Annoyance
Aggressiveness	Anger		
	Anticipation	Vigilance	Interest

That's a really neat table eh?

But it doesn't go anywhere near quenching our thirst for words to describe how we feel. Here are just a few of the thousands of words we use for that. At any given time we might be feeling:

alarmed, angry, anxious, apathetic, bashful, defeated, depressed, despairing, devastated, disappointed, disbelieving, disgruntled, distrustful, dreadful, dumb, embarrassed, envious, foolish, frustrated, grief-stricken, grumpy, guilty, horrified, hostile, hurt, lonely, mad, nervous, outraged, overwhelmed, pessimistic, pity, pitiful, remorseful, sad, scared, shamed, shocked, shy, sick, sorrowful, sour, startled, stupid, tearful, tired or weak.

Whilst at other times we may feel:

animated, attracted, attractive, bold, calm, cheerful, confident, content, courageous, eager, engrossed, enlightened, excited, festive, fortunate, free, gorgeous, happy, hopeful, intelligent, jolly, joyful, loved, loving, lucky, lustful, open, optimistic, passionate, playful, proud, relieved, relieved, satisfied, serene, smart, surprised, thrilled, understanding, or just wonderful!

Of course, life can be very frustrating for us – and for those around us – if we pay too much attention to how we're feeling rather than what we're doing all the time. That's especially true if we allow ourselves to flip back and forth between strongly positive and negative mood states for no good reason.

Our fascination with our emotions extends into personality too. The last time I counted, psychologists had developed about thirty different psychometric models to pigeon hole us by our behavioural traits. A good example is the widely accepted OCEAN model with its five dimensions which define us as being generally either:

1. **O**pen to new ideas or more closed-minded

2. **C**onscientious or less so

3. **E**xtraverted or introverted

4. **A**greeable/accommodating, or less so, and

5. **N**eurotic or not.

> Neurotics are less emotionally stable, more anxious, moody, worried and envious. And, in my experience, quite often more talented too!

Which is all very interesting and I'm sure that these tools can be helpful sometimes – but beware of reading too much into the results.

My personal view is that the industry of behavioural psychology has grown on the back of demand from big corporations keen to take some risk out of recruiting. The risk they're left with is ending up with a homogenous set of vanilla employees. A 'beige army' as Marianne Cantwell might call them, of less talented folk – recruited *because* they won't rock the boat – which is of course what most business boats need! So, I don't think we help ourselves or our businesses very much by labelling people as a certain 'type' – a type we *like or don't like,* as we might say on Facebook. Indeed, the risk of labelling people is that they spend their lives living up to (or down to) the label rather than stretching themselves to achieve what would help them and us more.

And we seem to have some strange ideas about which of these precious personality traits are the more useful.

Susan Cain, in *Quiet: The Power of Introverts in a World That Can't Stop Talking*, asserts that it's the extroverts who've taken over the western world. From personal experience of the banking and financial services sector, I'm inclined to agree. Shyness, sensitivity, seriousness and realism are often seen as weaknesses, and introverts may feel reproached for being the way they are. Blind optimism, on the other hand, seems to be a highly valued personality trait in some organisations!

Our labels about personality and mood mislead us. As Cain says, "*There's zero correlation between being the best talker and having the best ideas.*" I'd go further and suggest that the correlation might even be negative. In other words, that the best ideas tend to come from the quietest people *and* that the most stupid ideas come from the noisiest.

No, I have no data to prove this and I accept that most rules have exceptions but I do have a lot of experience of working in large teams of people in big companies and I'd guess there's a correlation there! Here's an example:

A particularly bright ex-colleague of mine seldom had much to say in our work meetings, and I once asked him (privately) why this was so. *"Oh that's easy"* he said, *"I see no reason to prolong the pain of those meetings any longer than necessary – and, unlike some others, I* **don't see the need to use ten words when none will do.***"*

He's a bright guy with a great sense of humour – two attributes that often go hand in hand. Perhaps the lesson here, for the noisy ones amongst us, is to shut up and listen occasionally! We might then benefit from the humour, the insights and the incisive questions of our quieter friends and colleagues.

Interestingly, Susan Cain, an introvert herself, runs a business called the Negotiation Company that trains people in negotiation and communication skills. The value of asking simple honest questions is a key part of her message, and her clients include investment banks and other firms in the financial sector – so perhaps the industry is learning. Let's hope so, because the quiet and thoughtful personality types are, in many contexts, more useful than the noisy and quick-acting types. We now know that we never really needed their machismo style of management in banking – and that style doesn't help us manage our own money either.

So, one thing is clear: if we allow ourselves to be dominated by our moods – whether they're low or high – we're asking for trouble.

Ideas for taking back control

You may think that we can't control our moods and this may be the case for some people with certain psychiatric illnesses. But, as Dr David Burns shows us in his widely acclaimed book, *Feeling Good: The New Mood Therapy*, many people can do something about their low mood and mild depression. He shows us how it's often simple errors in our perceptions that cause our low mood, and he outlines ten types of cognitive distortion (ways in which we distort the truth) that can trigger our upsets.

For example, we might overgeneralise a current challenge in our lives to be a repeating problem from our past, whilst in reality there is no comparison. Or we might have a tendency towards 'all or nothing thinking' in which we look at things in absolute black-and-white categories. So, we might decide that unless we're a total success in what we're doing, then we must be a complete failure. But reality is not black and white like this – it's full of shades of grey *(and no, that's not another book recommendation!)*

Burns' model of cognitive behavioural therapy (CBT) will sound tough to many as he rejects the idea that our lives have to be dominated by every emotion that hits us. But he is a highly experienced and quali-fied psychiatrist whose ideas are supported with scientific evidence. This is no voodoo self-help nonsense. *Feeling Good* is now thirty years old and has helped millions of people to deal with low mood. It's acclaimed by mental health practitioners around the world as one of the best books of its kind.

But overcoming low mood isn't enough to beat the marketers and curb our unnecessary spending. To do that, we need to get a handle on ALL our emotions – negative and positive – and, thankfully, help is at hand.

The Chimp Paradox is another wonderful book by Dr Steve Peters, the psychiatrist and mind coach to the incredibly successful British cycling team. It offers a powerful but simple model of how our mind works to help us make more of our lives by better management of our emotions.

The chimp is that part of your brain that interprets the outside world with feelings and impressions. The chimp determines your mood as either low or high, excitable, angry or anything else on the emotional spectrum. It uses emotions to decide how to react to external events, and when it's out of control, it can sabotage your successes and generally cause chaos. And Peters makes the point that your chimp is significantly stronger than the 'human' part of your brain – the part that deals with facts, truths and logical thinking. So it's no good trying to fight with your chimp – you won't win – better to learn some techniques for managing it. And Peters says it's okay to let it out for good rant sometimes, when it's upset about something. Don't bottle it all up is what I think that means – a very British thing to do, eh?

Obviously you need the 'human' (logical) part of your brain to manage more complex and longer-term issues in our lives – such as all that stuff we might generally call financial planning. A lot of that is best tackled with a calm and considered approach. I reckon we'd agree that running on emotions around investments, or even in day-to-day spending decisions, is not a good idea.

That said, there is one way you can use your emotions to your advan-tage in financial planning – and we'll come to that in a moment.

Did you know that you're being manipulated?

Unfortunately, that army of marketers out there (selling us all that stuff and stopping us making headway with our savings) understands your chimp only too well. And they're equipped with an arsenal of high-tech, high-emotion triggering messages to keep your chimp in a highly excited state. And did you know that those *mood marketers*, as I call them, have been refining their weapons for nearly 100 years now? It all started when a chap called Edward Bernays pioneered the field of peacetime, mass mind manipulation in 1920s America.

Bernays took the psychoanalytical ideas of his uncle (Sigmund Freud) and combined them with ideas on crowd psychology from Gustave Le Bon and Wilfred Trotter to develop ways to influence and control large sections of society. Bernays considered his work necessary as he regarded mankind as irrational and dangerous due to its herd instinct.

We may not like the idea that we're being manipulated, but we need to be aware that this activity is now widely accepted. The only difference is that nowadays we call it by the somewhat softer names of 'public relations and advertising'.

The history behind Bernays and his ideas is truly fascinating. In 'The Century of the Self', Adam Curtis' excellent, award-winning 2002 BBC documentary, Bernays is named one of the 100 most influential Americans of the 20th century.

According to Curtis, Bernays' greatest breakthrough came with his cigarette promotional campaign in 1929 in which he helped the tobacco industry to double its potential market overnight. At that time there was a strong social taboo (and law) against women smoking in public: women could smoke in designated areas, but it was preferred that they didn't smoke at all. To help the cigarette companies break down this market barrier, Bernays arranged an Easter parade in New York with a noisy brass band to attract attention. At an appointed time at the centre of the parade he directed a group of attractive female models to pull out their Lucky Strike cigarettes from their garters and light up. He rebranded the cigarettes as the girls' 'Torches of Freedom' and after that women everywhere started smoking. That's PR genius!

Bear in mind that women led a subservient existence to men before this time, only gaining the right to vote in 1920 in the USA. In the UK, women over the age of 30 (with certain minimum property qualifications) won the right to vote in 1918, but it was only in 1928 that they gained the same voting rights as men.

Bernays showed companies how to make us want things we don't need by simply connecting those things to our emotional – and sometimes unconscious – desires.

In the documentary, Curtis argues that the explosion in consumption and the associated stock market boom in the 'roaring twenties' was helped on its way by Bernays' ideas. The western world of the 1930s soon learned (as we appear to be learning again today) that you could only drive your population so far into debt-fuelled consumption. Then, when the limit is reached, we have a massive crash in spending (and risk to societal integrity) as everyone stops spending and the debt is paid down.

The mass hysteria and stock market selling panic of the 1929 crash was attended by a revulsion against consumerism, the Great Depression and the rise of the Nazis for which Goebbels adapted Bernays' new PR techniques to whip the German population into a frenzy of support for Hitler. And Curtis notes that more generally Bernays' ideas have now been developed into new political ideas on how to control the masses, saying *"that by satisfying people's inner selfish desires we make them happy, and thus docile. It may well have been Bernays who started the age of the all-consuming self which has come to dominate our world today."*

Very few modern-day marketers and PR people have heard of Bernays but most of them have learned his techniques. And now they can find all the emotional triggers to consumption in one easy manual.

Fascinate: Your 7 Triggers to Persuasion and Captivation by Sally Hogshead, shows marketers how to pack some super heavy emotional punches into promotions by being more fascinating, persuasive and captivating. Hogshead advises marketers to focus on just a few triggers of fascination as follows:

- **Alarm,** to threaten us with negative consequences if we fail to buy.

- **Mystique,** to lure us into buying with the intrigue of unanswered questions.

- **Prestige,** which promises us the respect of others and recognition from peers. For example, by surrounding ourselves with high quality and big brand name goods to demonstrate our achievements.

- **Power,** which promises us a position of command and control.

- **Lust,** which creates a craving for sensory pleasure.

- **Vice,** which tempts us with various 'forbidden fruits' – attractive to those who like to rebel against norms or authority.

- **Trust,** with its promise of certainty and reliability.

It's interesting to think about all our favourite consumer brands and their advertisements and ask which emotional fascinations they're playing to. Here are a couple of starters:

- Spicy chicken dinners can easily be cooked at home, but the adverts tell us that we need to go out for these because we don't know the mystical secret recipe for the real stuff – which only Colonel Sanders knows!

- The 'prestige' items offered at outrageous prices by designer clothes brands promise to enhance our image in the eyes of others. A designer logo meets our need to feel important and respected. Some brands stretch this fascination to absurd lengths, taking simple, non-prestigious products to a prestigious height through scarcity value. Hogshead offers the example of making a t-shirt so expensive that almost no one can afford it – like Chanel who sold a plain white t-shirt for US$500 and Prada whose version retailed at US$1,500!

We can make up our own minds about the value of emotional marketing when it results in these sorts of purchases! Clearly it's valuable to the product producer, but I'm not sure what it offers the consumer or society generally. And, in fairness to Sally Hogshead she presents her ideas in an ethical way, pointing out that they're about maximising business potential within a proper target market – not about tricking anyone into buying something they don't need.

But here's the thing – these powerful marketing ideas can actually help us in our personal lives too.

If we accept that we're drawn into consumption through fascination – we could ask ourselves what else we're fascinated by. And we might discover what's really important in our lives – like better personal relationships, helping others and looking after our health.

We'll develop this idea in a moment, but before that let me just warn you about another set of persuasive advertising techniques that are used on us every day. You can learn more about these in Robert Caldini's excellent book *Influence: The Psychology of Persuasion.* This is another must-have book for anyone involved in marketing or sales. Caldini describes how we're persuaded to spend more money through various techniques. Those he believes work best include:

- **Reciprocity** – makes us feel obliged to return gifts (such as giving tips after receiving free after dinner mints). Interestingly, if we receive more mints we pay higher tips *and* where the amount of mints is personalised with a note which says 'for you nice people here's some extras' then the value of our tips go through the roof.

- **Scarcity** – makes us where we want more of what we can't have, such as when Concorde announced it would no longer be flying – and bookings boomed!

- **Authority** – tends to make us pay more if we know up front that the seller is credible, knowledgeable and experienced – especially if that authority is stated by someone else.

- **Consistency** – compels us to be consistent with things we've previously said and done. We're activated into this consistency behaviour by the smallest (sometimes free) commitment to engage with the seller.

- **Liking** – draws us into doing business with people who are either similar to us, pay us compliments, or cooperate with us towards mutual goals.

- **Consensus** techniques draw our attention to the experiences of other buyers ('people like you') to persuade us to do likewise.

The bottom line here – for us as savers and wealth builders – is that our emotions are being targeted. Day in and day out.

So let's remember that it's our responsibility to decide what stuff is worth buying, whatever emotions get fired up by these techniques. In some cases we'll have a genuine need for that product or service but in many others we won't **and buying it will destroy the funds we'll need for something useful.**

Right, so now I want to turn this idea on its head.

Having argued that we need to be on our guard against emotional marketing attacks, I want to suggest that *we can benefit from more emotional thinking* in other aspects of our life.

What REALLY makes you happy?

Let's think for a moment about what's really important for our personal happiness. What seriously lifts our mood – without giving us a hangover afterwards? You might want to jot down your thoughts here or on a separate note so that you can come back and review them from time to time.

We'll all have our own, unique ideas about this. Here are some of mine, in no particular order of preference:

- Spending quality time with loved ones. Remembering great times: looking over old photographs and planning some more great times. Watching a great film. Having a good laugh.

- Working towards and delivering something worthwhile to others.

- Helping others to fulfil their potential, listening to their stories and supporting them in their efforts.

- A loving relationship, someone who listens and cares. Hugs and kisses too.

- Slowing down occasionally – taking time out to appreciate life, if only that we're free to choose what we do, which we all are over the longer term.

- Sitting, alone, very quietly – with no music or any other distractions – thinking through ideas, important issues, solving problems and writing.

- A session of seriously hard physical exercise.

- Trying out new and exhilarating activities: water skiing, snow skiing, skydiving, flying aeroplanes.

- Learning other new skills: in music, art, dancing, sports or anything else that stretches me.

- Literally stretching in a Yoga lesson or being stretched out with a massage.

- Resting and listening to great music – or better still, watching great musicians perform live.

- Reading a great book and discovering useful ideas.

- Getting outside in the fresh air, seeing and feeling nature all around.

It's no surprise that quality time with family and friends is on most people's 'real happiness' list and the 'back to nature' idea is apparently a universal mood improver too.

Oliver Burkeman spent some considerable time studying happiness philosophies – and the popular self-help industry. And his two books (*HELP! How to Become Slightly Happier and Get a Bit More Done* and *The Antidote: Happiness for People Who Can't Stand Positive Thinking*) offer valuable and often humorous insights into some truly useful (and some positively dangerous) ideas from around the world for achieving happiness. According to Burkeman we have a common attraction to the outdoors because it solves our control issues. He says:

> We spend our lives swinging back and forth between believing we have more control over the world than we do – and feeling, just as wrongly that we have none.... Nature seems to reset this wild pendulum and restores a realistic balance. Elemental landscapes drive home how tiny and powerless we are. And any encounter with nature, even a two mile stroll, requires self-reliance and demands that you take responsibility for what you can control. You have to not get lost and not fall off cliffs.

But perhaps the most interesting thing about anyone's happiness list is how very few items on it involve spending money. And yet, we continually spend vast sums, unnecessarily, in search of happiness! What's going on? We're clearly overwhelmed by the powers of 'fascination and persuasion' marketing.

So what can we do?

Well we could just let go of our attachment to pleasure seeking spending right now. Yes, I know that's easier said than done but as Burkeman points out in this second extract from *The Antidote*:

> **At the root of all suffering**, says the second of the Four Noble Truths that define Buddhism, **is attachment.** The fact that we desire some things and dislike or hate others is what motivates virtually every human activity.
>
> Rather than merely enjoying pleasurable things during the moments in which they occur, and experiencing the unpleasantness of painful things, **we develop the**

habits of clinging and aversion; we grasp at what we like, trying to hold onto it forever, and push away what we don't like, trying to avoid it at all costs.

Both constitute attachment. Pain is inevitable, from this perspective, but suffering is an optional extra, resulting from our attachments which represent our attempt to try to deny the unavoidable truth that everything is impermanent.

Develop an attachment to your good looks – as opposed to merely enjoying them while they last – and you will suffer when they fade, as they inevitably will; develop a strong attachment to your luxurious lifestyle, and your life may become an unhappy, fearful struggle to keep things that way.

So this attachment problem is something we'd do well to work on. And in the meantime, here's another idea that might give more tangible wealth benefits more quickly...

Turn the marketers' weapon against them.

You see, if we can make our savings goals emotionally fascinating (get more attached to them if you like) then we'll naturally bring our short term spending under control and achieve a lot more for our future.

Yes, I know I said a moment ago that we should keep emotions out of investment decisions. But this is about financial life planning – it's not a decision about which asset class (shares vs property etc.) to invest in. We're just looking to make a simple decision to save for the long term – and to provide insurance against things going wrong in the short term.

I also realise that these are not sexy subjects. How on earth can we form an emotional attachment to a pension plan? There's a ton of prestige in having a Rolls-Royce Phantom Drophead Coupe sat on your drive, but very little prestige in having a £300,000 pension plan in your filing cabinet.

We can be told the facts about our reality – that we're going to need an income to pay for our living expenses in our later years – and that a pension is one of the best ways of saving for that. We might even be able to prove it as we'll see later in this book. But a purely logical approach doesn't solve this problem for most of us. We really do need to engage our emotions. But how? Here's one way:

Project yourself forward in time, to the day when you're going to need those savings. Imagine you're having a conversation with yourself or your partner about the income you can now enjoy on top of the state pension for your later years. If you have children, imagine you're talking to your, now adult, child, who we want to help through higher education.

How will you – and your partner – feel when you've arrived at that time having done what you could and ended up in a position to provide some help, however modest, towards your financial goal? Thinking about this will likely stir feelings of calm, content and freedom.

Now, imagine reaching that point in your life knowing you could have achieved a lot more. That you could have saved a reasonable sum of money, without greatly affecting your lifestyle, but didn't. It hurts, doesn't it? But if we allow ourselves to feel these unpleasant emotions, we may be inspired to take action and do the right thing for our future. And it can be useful to see the stark choices that face us. Take this example for parents of young children who want to help their children with university costs.

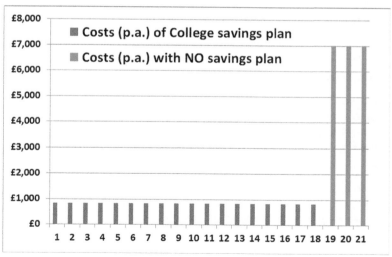

Here, a parent might only need to save about £3 per day to build up a fund of around £21,000 (in today's money terms) to provide

£7,000 p.a. for three years to support their child with maintenance costs whilst at university. It's really not much is it? Less than the price of a cappuccino each day.

The bottom line here is to understand that if we start saving early for our goals – then it's easy. If we don't – and we can't rely on help from others – then it's going to be tough.

See Appendix 5 for a powerful chart to help you estimate the funds you could build up – simply by saving the price of a coffee each day.

In a similar way, we might consider the real value of life assurance (or income protection) by thinking how our loved ones would fare in the event of our premature death, with and without any insurance in place. And let me be clear – this idea for raising our emotions about money is absolutely not about making anyone feel guilty for being short of money – we all have resources that are limited at some level. It's simply about using our emotions to fight the urge to spend everything today on stuff that we simply don't need.

Perhaps this sounds like a cheesy, old-fashioned pension or life insurance sales pitch? It's not – *I don't sell financial products.* This is simply an idea to help you make better decisions with **your money – so that it supports what you want in your life.**

The truth is that using our emotions to get serious about financial life planning works, just as it does every day for the mood marketers who sell us all that other stuff.

I urge you to try this exercise, preferably with the help of a competent financial planner or coach. A good conversation that connects our finances to the goals in our life – for ourselves and our family – can be a highly emotional experience but it can also be life-changing. Try it.

Gaining a clear and reasonable picture of what we need to save in order to achieve our goals can lift our mood immensely. It gives greater longer-term purpose to our efforts and removes some of life's uncertainty. And once we've sorted out our high level financial plan – *with the help of our emotional chimp* – we can apply more logical (human) thinking to finding the best (product and fund) solutions to our goals.

There are various ways to hit our financial goals: we can simply put more money into our savings, by cutting out wasteful spending; we can save tax and other unnecessary charges on our funds; we can seek out better investment returns (whilst being mindful of the risks); and we can access 'free' money from our employer's pension. If some of our goals turn out to be unaffordable after running the numbers on a reasonable set of assumptions, then we may have other options. For example with our pension planning we might just move our dream retirement date back a year or two –that's not so bad eh? And it's better than giving up on the dream altogether.

This is about checking the reality of our dreams and doing something about them. Research shows that many younger people dream that they'll be able to stop work when they're fifty years old. But the reality is that very few can afford to.

But if we want to slow down before we're too old to enjoy it, we could make a plan to top up our (later years) income with some work. And if we're smart about preparing for it that could mean an active retirement doing work that we really enjoy. Alternatively, we might go for that next promotion at work or develop that future business idea, to earn more now so that we can save more for that dream of a full stop retirement. Or we could simply cut back on our spending plans for later life.

Whatever your goals, I'd encourage you to check their viability with some guidance from a good financial planner. That might be the best investment you ever make.

Get irate!

- It's easy to let our lives become dominated by emotional responses but it's not helpful and most of us can overcome this tendency.

- Mood marketers use an increasingly smart set of tools to trigger our most powerful emotions and persuade us to spend all our money today. So we need to hone our defences to their emotional weapons or they'll take every spare pound of income we have – and more – pushing us into debt and leaving us with no savings at all for our more important, longer-term goals.

- However, *we can use emotional thinking to our advantage* in financial planning. Our emotions can help us determine what's really important for our own and our family's long-term finances.

- And having emotional attachments to our savings goals will make it much more likely that we'll stick to them once we've started.

In the next chapter...

Once we're on top of our spending, we'll be able to start thinking about saving and investing it for the future. And one of the first questions we should ask at this stage is how much attention we should pay to those 'forecasts' about stock markets, and housing markets. And how seriously we should take our politicians forecasts about the whole economy – or their claims that they can control it.

Let's explore these questions now...

Chapter 2
Parading politicians and
confused economists

Why forecasts are always wrong and politicians can't control our economy

Economics is the only subject in which the exam questions are the same every year... It's the answers that keep changing!

~ Anon

I found this little joke in the book *Money, Blood and Revolution* by Dr George Cooper. If, after reading this book, you decide that you want more detail on the fundamental ideas in economics (and how they're flawed) then that book and the author's previous book *The Origins of Financial crises* are excellent and accessible further reads.

But for now, let's just focus on our understanding of investments and the risks you might not know that you're taking with them by tackling three simple questions:

- Can our politicians (or central bankers) really control our economy?

- Can they save the world from deeply damaging recessions and 'put an end to boom and bust'?

- Can they provide a stable background for our investing?

The answers are obvious when we hit a nasty bump in our economic road, but we tend to forget these facts at calmer times. And it's worth remembering that before the 2008/09 crisis our economy – indeed the world economy – was very different.

We lived in what our central bankers called the 'nice' times (there was little or *no inflation* and we enjoyed *constant economic expansion*), and some politicians believed they had everything under control.

Look up 'no more boom and bust' on YouTube.

If you believe that our leaders can engineer a return to those 'nice' times in the future, that they can avoid the mistakes of the past and keep us on a steady road going forward, then there's no need to worry much about how you invest your money, or when. You can just shove it all in the stock market and leave it alone – everything will be fine. And, as it happens, this approach is actually quite a good one when starting out on your journey of long term savings for your future.

If you're saving regularly (as opposed to investing a lump sum) into a stock market based fund *and* **if** you won't need your money for a long time, then the big ups and downs in markets can work magic on your money. They lower your average cost of buying into those funds. This is called 'pound cost averaging', a concept we'll explore in detail in the next book time.

But if you've already accumulated most of the funds you're going to need for the future and need to start drawing down heavily on them relatively soon – to help a child through university or for your retirement, for example – then this approach is downright dangerous. A big fall in your asset values at the same time as you're making large withdrawals could wipe out your savings in double-quick time. This issue is sometimes called 'reverse pound cost averaging' and we'll also look at this in detail in the next book. For now, you just need to focus on getting an intelligent view about the riskiness of your investments. For that, you might want to know the future prospects for economic growth – and we turn, of course, to economists for that view.

However, the financial crisis of 2008-09 proved beyond doubt that economists could not predict economic shifts with any accuracy – which is worrying because these experts are the most important policy-shaping advisers behind our politicians. And not only have they struggled to be taken seriously since the crisis but there's now an abundance of jokes about their profession. Here are some classics you may have heard before:

- Economists have predicted seven out of the last three recessions, but failed to predict the current one.

- If you lined up all the world's economists head to toe, they still wouldn't reach a conclusion.

- Economists are like blind javelin throwers – not very accurate, but they hold the spectators' attention.

- Walking down the street with my economist friend I noticed a £50 note on the pavement and was about to bend down and pick it up when my friend grabbed my arm and insisted we walk on by. "It's not real" he said. "If it were, then it would have been picked up by now."

So, economists have had to put up with much ridicule in recent years – and even the Queen joined the chorus in 2008 when, on a visit to the London School of Economics and Political Science, she asked *"Why did no one see the crisis coming?"* (Which sounds funnier if you ask the question in your best queen's voice). And, according to the *Huffington Post*, when the Queen visited the Bank of England's gold vaults with the Duke of Edinburgh four years later in December 2012, she asked exactly the same question again. This time, the answer she was offered (by Sujit Kapadia, who sits on the Bank's Financial Services Committee) was extraordinarily revealing. He said:

People thought markets were efficient, people thought regulation wasn't necessary... because the economy was stable there was this growing complacency. People didn't realise just how interconnected the system had become.

The royals were also told that the people at the Bank of England were there **to prevent another such financial catastrophe** – to which the Duke apparently teased, "*So, is there another one coming?*"

Oh, how the Duke of Edinburgh loves to joke.

Prince Philip (the Duke) was 90 on 10 June 2011. His humour is from another era and is certainly not politically correct – as Ben Macintyre observed in his excellent article 'We are not amused and Prince Philip couldn't care less' (*The Times*, 31 May 2011). Of the Duke's many jokes (or gaffes) Macintyre reminds us of the best (or worst), including:

On a visit to China in 1986, when he described Beijing as "*ghastly*" and told a group of British exchange students: "*If you stay here much longer you'll all be slitty-eyed.*"

Again in 1986, with China still on his mind, he told the World Wildlife Fund: "If it has got four legs and it is not chair, if it has got two wings but is not an aeroplane, and if it swims and is not a submarine, the Cantonese will eat it."

Upon meeting the President of Nigeria, dressed in traditional robes he said, "*You look like you're ready for bed.*"

Looking at an ill-assembled electrical fuse box in a factory, he remarked that it "*looked as though it had been put in by an Indian.*"

But the 'natives' who've borne the brunt of the Duke's jokes are not all foreign. Talking to a Scottish driving instructor in Oban in 1995, the Prince wondered aloud: "*How do you keep the natives off the booze long enough to get them through the test?*"

Well, joke or no joke, the truth is that no one really knows whether another crisis is heading our way or when, and *it is essential to understand this point*:

Economists can't predict the future with any accuracy.

But here's the thing, economists know this perfectly well! Take Richard W. Fisher, President and CEO of the Federal Reserve Bank of Dallas, who in November 2009 quipped:

> *Mind you, you should take economic forecasts – even my own – with a big grain of salt. Jamie Galbraith's dad, John Kenneth Galbraith, may have been more right than econometricians like to think when he said that "the only function of economic forecasting is to make astrology look respectable."*

Another highly amusing perspective on the challenges faced by all forecasters of complex systems comes from Nobel Prize-winning economist Kenneth Arrow who, during the Second World War, served as a weather officer in the US Army Air Corps. He worked with those charged with the particularly difficult task of producing month-ahead weather forecasts. And as Arrow and his team reviewed these predictions, they confirmed statistically what you and I might just as easily have guessed: that weather forecasts were no more accurate than random rolls of a die.

Understandably, the forecasters asked to be relieved of this seemingly futile duty but Arrow's recollection of his superiors' response was priceless:

> *The commanding general is well aware that the forecasts are no good. However, he needs them for planning purposes.*

And finally, Robin Harding (*Financial Times*, 28 July 2009) makes the following points:

> *... Economists got plenty of things wrong – such as the dismal assumption that securitisation and credit default swaps were making the financial system safer – but it is compounding the error to say that they should have predicted how all this would add up to "the crisis".*

An aeronautical engineer may tell you that there is a one-in-ten million chance of being killed on a given flight, but we don't expect him to predict that the crash will happen on the 1515 from Narita to London Heathrow. A doctor will warn that smoking increases the risk of cancer, but we don't expect her to foretell who will fall victim and when.

What we expect is that the doctor will tell us to quit cigarettes and the engineer will try to turn one-in-ten million to one-in-100 million. That is the point of economists. They should try to identify policies that reduce the risk of big fluctuations in output, they should warn when the danger of such fluctuations is great and they should do so in a way the world can understand.

If economists try to predict crises, they will get it wrong, and that will reduce their credibility when they try to warn of risks. And it was in their warnings that economists failed: plenty talked of "global imbalances" or "excessive credit growth"; few followed that through to the proximate sources of danger in the financial system, and then forcibly argued for something to be done about it.

So what can we make of this?

Yes, economists **might** (just might) be able to identify how certain trends and policies (atmospheric changes, if you like) **could** cause big shifts in our economy. And yes, it would be useful if they gave louder warnings of such potential shifts **and** in a language we can all understand. But I don't think you should hold your breath for those warnings. Given the uncertainty of any predicted shifts actually happening, the economists risk yet more ridicule by giving loud warnings.

Anyway, given what I've said, why on earth are we given all those forecasts that fill the newspapers day in and day out? Because, like the commanding general, we ask for them! We (or rather our politicians and business leaders) have an appetite for simple story predictions to impossibly complex questions. And our newscasters demand the forecasting sound bite on their news shows. TV news editors realise very well how we're all bored stiff by finance, so they restrict their interview invitations to those experts who are willing to offer ten-second views on these complex economic questions.

As a result, very few good economists talk to the media these days.

The thing is we love nice simple stories. It's how we've evolved to communicate over tens of thousands of years. So we're not going to lose our love of stories in less than one hundred years of new technology. The media know this, so without the airtime to look at the issues in depth, they just make stories up.

Am I joking? No, I'm deadly serious. **Listen carefully to the news** when they talk about boring financial stuff and you'll notice something odd. One day you'll be told that new data – for example, showing *increased* unemployment – has wiped billions of pounds from the stock market. And that sounds logical enough, right? Right. Except that one month later, when the market rebounds strongly, you'll be assured that the cause is ... the same thing – *increased* unemployment.

How curious! How on earth can that be?

Well, we crave a good story, you see, and the story this time is that the bad employment data means that interest rates will be lowered in the future. And because we all love lower interest rates (unless we're savers, of course) we'll start spending and investing more (all other things being equal) which is good for the profits of the companies selling their stuff which means their profits rise and so – eventually – will their share prices.

Simples!

Similarly, one day we might be told to prepare for higher **inflation** due to rising oil prices, only to be told a few days later that the big risk is of **deflation** – falling prices! How could this be? Well, that story would be around the idea that prices of goods fall if demand for them falls. And rising oil prices might mean we have less to spend on other stuff – so our demand for it falls.

You see, all these contradictory stories are quite plausible. And whilst we're on the subject, this 'outlook for inflation' question really gets economists excited.

By the way do you know how you can tell 'extrovert' economists from all the rest? They're the ones who look at your shoes when they talk to you.

A couple of years back I counted forty pages of comments under just one *Financial Times* article on this question of inflation. The comments must surely have contained every possible argument – about the nature of the problem and possible solutions – from every economic school of thought. And there are many schools! *As George Cooper says (in Money, Blood and Revolution: How Darwin and the doctor of King Charles I could turn economics into a science):*

> *The very fact that there are so many disparate schools of economics both on and off our economic plane is a symptom that all is not well in the field of economics. A further aspect of the problem is inconsistency over time. Up to this point I have described the neoclassical school as the consensus opinion. This is true today, but it was not always the case. We could imagine the economic plane as a real plane populated with all of the economists in the world. Over the last century or so there would have been some considerable migrations around the plane – I have in my mind's eye something that looks like the herds of wildebeest on the East African Serengeti.*
>
> *In the 1930s through to the 60s, the bulk of the herd would have been clustered around the Keynesian school, with substantial populations in the Marxist, Austrian and neoclassical quarters. In the 1970s, there would have been a migration away from the Marxist and towards the monetarist areas. From the 1980s onwards, the drift would have been increasingly toward the entire herd moving into the neoclassical quadrant.*
>
> *In 2008, as Lehman Brothers was failing, there would have been a stampede away from the neoclassical quarter towards the Minsky zone as everyone suddenly rejected the silly notion of an inherently stable economy and embraced Minsky's idea of an inherently unstable economy. It was around this time that the term "Minsky moment" became briefly fashionable.*
>
> *Then in the years since 2008, Minsky has been forgotten and the herd has quickly drifted back to recolonize the neoclassical zone, conveniently forgetting that it ever left.*

So, what we have here are the world's experts disagreeing on the fundamental ideas about which system is best for running economies. And constantly shifting their ideas too. Not helpful, eh? So let's move away from these broader issues and try to get an answer from the economists on one of the most important questions facing us all right now. This question influences how people vote and it sits at the very heart of the Scottish National Party's idea that they need to break up the UK – so we ought to have some thoughts on it right? The question is:

Does 'austerity' actually work?

Let's assume that you had just two choices at a general election – a party that wants to attempt to pay down our debts now versus one that wants to borrow more for jobs and growth now, and pay down the debt later on, when we've secured that growth. Who are you going to vote for?

Now you may ask why any party would want to borrow more if we were already up to our eyeballs in debt – and that's a good question. Obviously, if we borrowed more but wasted it on silly (unsustainable) projects, then we'd just end up with more debt and a bigger problem. And who's best placed and skilled to borrow and invest for the most sustainable jobs – government or private industry? There are good arguments on both sides of that question!

Clearly the government lacks the hard profit motive to seek out the really best ideas for growth in new technologies. The Millennium Dome is one example of government spending that delivered less than a great return! But on the other hand, the government can borrow vast quantities of cash at very low interest rates which are simply not available to the private sector. The government is also more likely to direct spending into projects that *do* produce jobs in the UK, rather than simply profits in the UK but jobs abroad.

So, you see, this is yet another economic question with no right answer. But if we believe in *any* benefits of capitalism at all, then we might lean towards allowing private capital to take the big risks in the long term. If things go wrong, surely it's investors who should pay the price, not the rest of us, through bailouts and higher taxes?

That, by the way, is why our banks need significant reform: so that the next time one of them lends badly and goes belly up, we, the taxpayers, are not left holding the bad debts.

Anyway, whilst politicians and economists disagree about the ideal mix between private and government-run industries, they have agreed on the (intuitively obvious) point that there has to be some kind of limit on government borrowing. The trickier challenge has been getting agreement – even on a ballpark figure – on what that limit should be. Tricky that is until two respected economists, Carmen Reinhart and Kenneth Rogoff (R&R), produced research a while back that many (and allegedly themselves, from time to time) interpreted as pointing to the danger point for government debt, at 90% of GDP.

> GDP (gross domestic product) describes the total of everything we produce each year. So that's both things and services sold. And it includes what we sell as exports too – less the value of imports.

Go beyond this 90% level – the argument goes – and we risk getting caught in a spiral of decline where our rising debt interest becomes too much to support alongside providing other services. This causes cutbacks that reduce economic activity that then reduces tax revenues/push up welfare costs further and so on, into oblivion. You might say that this is where Greece found itself in 2015 – and where the UK found itself in the 1970s!

Unfortunately for R&R, some errors were found in their work – leaving some politicians to conclude that their conclusions were also wrong and that the **90% critical limit** might not be critical after all. If this is true, it could mean that there's not so much rush to pay down the debt after all. That said, I think most reasonable politicians on both sides of the political divide now agree that running up debt in the 'good times' is not a good idea. If you do that, you'll have little room for manoeuvre for borrowing money when you really need it in the bad times.

The truth is that all governments have based some very big decisions on flawed economic ideas. For example, allowing a huge house price bubble to blow up is never a smart idea as it pushes prices away from those saving for a deposit. But this is exactly what UK governments have done with monotonous regularity for decades. And on any reasonable measure, our house prices here in the UK remain grossly overpriced as of mid-2015. And yet we continue with schemes to help people buy houses and push prices further up.

Does that make any sense to you?

Of course, it was the same confidence in house prices – that they could never fall more than a few percentage points – that sat behind the collapse in the worldwide financial system in 2008. The 40%+ drop in US house prices left many banks around the world (that held mortgage securities secured on those houses) effectively bust and in need of rescue from taxpayers.

> There's more background to the 2008-09 financial crisis in Appendix 1.

But let's get back to debt limits and just think about this on a basic level. Surely this is a simple question? Surely there must be a point at which too much government borrowing causes a recession because there's just too much debt interest to pay?

This question was argued vigorously between leading economists in all the top journals in the Spring of 2013. And at one point it even looked like they might reach some agreement. Unfortunately they didn't quite get there on that occasion – and attention has since moved from **our** debt problems to those of Greece and others.

Now, it would add 400 pages to this book to cover every economist's argument on the question of 'how much debt is too much?' So, I won't do that! What I *will* do, however is to show you just how confused our economists and politicians are on this key question. When you fully understand that these 'bigwigs' are not in control of your money, I think you'll want to take more control of it yourself.

So, let me give you the economists' thinking on this austerity issue. And, just for fun, I'll do that by paraphrasing what they've said using an imaginary conversation. But be in no doubt, these answers are based upon much longer versions given in **real** debates.

Here's that key question again and my spoof version of their answers:

Surely there is a point at which too much government borrowing causes a recession because there's too much debt interest to pay?

> *Um, well, we think that too much debt might be a problem and cause recessionary spirals but it could also work the other way round – with a recession causing the debt to rise.*

This is a reasonable explanation. After all, when we have recessions there is a greater need for government welfare whilst tax revenues are falling.

But wait, the economist hasn't finished speaking:

> *On the other hand, perhaps it is high government debt that causes the recession after all. This could be the case where confidence of business leaders and individuals is dented when they see the government debt mountain. They realise that government spending will then have to be cut and so reduce their own spending and investments in anticipation.*

> *The truth is we're not really sure. It's a kind of "chicken and egg" question. Indeed, both of these answers might be right at different times and in different places.*

So, there you have it. Any hope we may have had – that the world's greatest economic minds would reach agreement on the biggest challenge facing the world in living memory – has been dashed. They don't have the faintest idea of the answer and are happy to admit it.

Economics truly is the most dismal of sciences.

But hang on, what's this?

Despite this evidence that supports the earlier joke that economists can never agree on anything, the incredible thing is that they do!

The one thing economists DO agree on...

Grab yourself a set of any end of year forecasts and you'll see that most of them (for interest rates, stock market levels, economic growth etc.) all huddle around the same numbers. And what are those numbers? Well, they're whatever they actually were in the 'real world' at the time of the forecast – perhaps plus or minus a tiny bit.

This isn't surprising when you consider that, for the forecaster, a forecast that is close to today's number has a good chance of being close to the pack of other forecasts. And being in the pack is a good place to be. Being wrong is one thing, but being wrong and being very different to everyone else is as career-threatening to an economist as it is to a fund manager, as you'll see later.

John Maynard Keynes, who many regard as the greatest economist of all time, summed up this problem of forecasting for investment managers way back in 1936. And he said:

> ... *professional investment may be likened to those newspaper competitions in which the competitors have to pick out the six prettiest faces from 100 photographs, the prize being awarded to the competitor whose choice most nearly corresponds to the average preferences of the competitors as a whole: so that each competitor has to pick, not those faces which he himself finds prettiest but those which he thinks likeliest to catch the fancy of the other competitors, all of whom are looking at the problem from the same point of view. It is not a case of choosing those which, to the best of one's judgement, are really the prettiest, nor even those which average opinion genuinely thinks the prettiest. We have reached the third degree, where we devote our intelligences to anticipating what average opinion expects the average opinion to be! And there are some, I believe, who practise the fourth, fifth, and higher degrees.*

A flawed theory of markets

If economic forecasts are generally just an adjustment from today's situation and if, as economists themselves admit, they're completely unreliable, what are you left with? Can you have any hope that today's prices – for stock markets or our houses – are reasonable and might remain stable in the future?

Well, at many times, no, I don't think so.

The evidence shows that asset prices move quite rapidly (faster than any long-term trend) away from their recent values. They head off to levels either much higher or much lower than today and, over the long term (decades, not days!), they generally zoom in one direction like this before reaching a turning point and reversing. You seldom see an asset price bobbling gently along a nice trend line for any reasonable period of time. Just look at the charts!

Does this mean you should throw your hands up in despair and just ignore asset prices altogether? Well, yes... and no.

Yes, you should ignore prices on their own, because they tell you nothing. Take house prices as an example. The average house price in the UK was about £1,900(!) on the Nationwide index when our present Queen was crowned in 1953. But were they cheap or expensive back then? And what about now (2015) at an average price **100 times higher** at c. £190,000. **Is that expensive or cheap?**

You see, we just can't tell just by looking at prices alone.

What we do know is that the prices of 'real' assets (like houses and shares in successful companies) tend to keep pace with inflation over the very long term. But when we adjust for the effects of inflation there isn't much growth in the price alone – and right now there isn't much inflation either. And if you think about it, there's no reason why house prices *should* rise above earnings inflation over the long term. As Phillip Coggan says (in his Buttonwood column, *The Economist*, June 2014) *"in the end houses can only be worth what citizens can afford"*.

So if earnings don't go up, why should house prices? Assuming that they start at fair value, that is.

But here's the problem. UK housing is *not* at fair value right now – and, as Coggan noted last year, *"British housing is 36% overvalued against rents"*.

It's important to understand this: UK house prices have been propped up by ultra low interest rates, and these have allowed British home-owners (who tend to use variable or short-term fixed mortgages) to service debt that would otherwise be unaffordable. This in turn makes prices extremely vulnerable to increases in interest rates.

As Roger Bootle, one of this country's most respected economists said in a recent interview (*Money Week*, 13 May 2015):

> *Once we start getting bank rates at 2% or 3%, which of course is very low by historical standards, there's going to be mayhem in the mortgage market. And if ever we get back to 5% or 6%, which I think we will, it doesn't look good. What I say to my children is that just because housing has been a fantastic investment in the last 20, 25 years, don't assume that it's going to be that over the next twenty (or even ten) years. Yes, we've all got to live somewhere, and living in your own home is nicer*

in all sorts of ways than living somewhere owned by someone else. But don't do it because you think you're going to make a lot of money, because I think housing is a pretty lousy investment starting from where we are now.

Regardless of whether today's prices (for houses or shares) are cheap or expensive, understand this: the largest part of the total returns (over the long term) you make by owning these assets does not come from capital growth but from the income they generate. Or for your own home, from the rental payments you avoid.

If you invest in shares and reinvest the income those shares produce, then your total returns will be a lot (and I mean a LOT) higher over time – than if you take out the income along the way. See the chart below for proof of that.

The power - of reinvested income

— FTSE All share index rebased to 31st Dec 1985

— FTSE All share index (total return- with income reinvested)

Chart by Paul Claireaux. Data from FTSE the index company

But, as you can also see, these stock markets can bounce up and down a lot – and that's what puts people off investing. So I think it's useful to have some kind of measure to warn us when they might be particularly over or under priced. What can we use as that measure if it's not prices?

How to work out if property and share prices are too high (or low)...

Let's look at houses first. We know that they cost a lot less (in £ terms) back in 1953. But then people also earned a great deal less than they do today –and that's the **key to valuation – we need to look at prices relative to earnings.**

For houses you can look at the rental yield – the income produced by the house if you rent it out – **as a proportion** of the house value. Or you can look at the price to (buyer) earnings ratios. Both of these measures offer great clues to value. For company shares you can also look at the **share price to earnings** (PE) ratio, but as company earnings tend to bounce around a great deal from year to year, it's a good idea to smooth out that number over a period of years.

Don't worry, I'm not going into all the grisly detail of asset valuation models here. That's a huge subject on its own requiring years of study! The key points you need to know are simply that:

- There are some simple measures of value for the popular asset types (houses and shares), and

- **Some** financial advisers take the idea of perfect markets too far and ignore valuations altogether when giving investment advice.

We'll explore this some more in the next chapter but for now let's keep things ultra simple by describing two broad types of investment assets:

1. Short-term safe/boring stuff (like bank or building society deposits) that tend to produce low returns, and

2. Longer-term real assets (like shares and property) which offer better return prospects but whose prices can zoom into outer space one year and crash to earth the next. To understand why the prices of these assets are so volatile, **we need to question the very fundamentals of economic theory**.

   And don't worry – this next bit is simple – and worth it.

What the economists have got right
– and so horribly wrong

Economics is not a science like mechanics – you can't use the theory to accurately predict the motion of inanimate objects (like the planets around the sun or the revs of a car engine).Economies have many unpredictable **inputs** – and a vast number of unpredictable outcomes.

The biggest **inputs** to an economy are the choices we make – as individuals, companies, governments or other groups – about what to buy or where to invest or whether to buy or invest in anything at all.

It's impossible to predict how we'll make these choices because our moods (our 'animal spirits', as Keynes called them) are changing all the time. At one moment the mood of a group (of consumers, for example) might be very optimistic. But then that mood can turn in an instant and we can become despondent and pessimistic. When that happens we may start saving more for the predicted rainy days and spending less in the shops. And if we all decide to start saving at the same time, we can easily blow up an entire economy. Economists call this the 'paradox of thrift' – because, whilst it's a great idea (for us individually) to save for the future, – it's a really bad idea for us *all* to do it at the same time.

There may be no discernible reason for a collective change of mood or we may be influenced by a large and unexpected event – like a terrorist attack, or a natural disaster, or the failure of a big bank and stock market collapse. And, of course, our moods can also change the other way – turning positive after being negative – although it seems that these upswings are normally slower than the downturns, which can be quite violent and catch us off guard.

Now, economic forecasters obviously cannot predict these mood swings or the random events that might cause them. So, in the past they've tended to ignore them, assuming that over time they'll probably just balance out. And economists generally assume that we humans act rationally to optimise our well-being.

So, when stuff gets cheaper, we tend to buy more of it, and vice versa. Which all sounds perfectly reasonable – right? Yes, and the knock-on effect is that although prices may wobble around a bit over time, they will, all other things being equal, tend to revert back to their long-term trend after each wobble.

You may have heard about this idea (that market prices are *always right* – at least, roughly so) and if we're trying to predict the prices of goods we buy in our day-to-day lives, this may be a reasonable assumption. After all, if the price of butter goes up, then we'd expect sales of it to fall a bit, especially if there's a substitute like margarine we can buy instead. **But** we hit a big problem when economists take this idea about our day-to-day shopping behaviour and assert that it also applies to how we buy and sell investment assets. These are very different things to milk and butter.

According to George Cooper, in *The Origin of Financial Crises*, that's exactly what happened. He traces this jump in academic thinking to an economist called Paul A. Samuelson who, in his work, *Economics: An Introductory Analysis*, said:

> *What is true of markets for consumer goods is also true of markets for factors of production such as labour, land and capital inputs.*

Cooper says Samuelson gave no evidence or reason why this should be so, just an assertion that it is.

In fact, plenty of economists believed that markets were generally stable systems (albeit that prices bounce around a bit, each side of an equilibrium), and this has been the central idea behind orthodox economics from the time of Adam Smith and his *Inquiry into the Nature and Causes of the Wealth of Nations* (1776) right up to Eugene Fama's efficient markets hypothesis in 1970.

Indeed, according to Mark Buchanan, in his book *Forecast: What Physics, Meteorology, and the Natural Sciences Can Teach Us About Economics*, it was Fama who took a purely mathematical theorem about unpredictable markets from Samuelson and asserted that something like this was true in the real world. Buchanan explains that Samuelson's paper ('Proof That Properly Anticipated Prices Fluctuate Randomly') had only shown that market predictability would be wiped out (if any existed to begin with) if we assumed that investors used all information *available and acted rationally.*

And this is easy to understand. For example, if it were possible to predict that the price of shares in the computing giant Apple would rise by 5% tomorrow, then all *rational investors* would pay extra for them today and wipe out the potential gain tomorrow. Similarly, if we knew a share was going to fall tomorrow, then it would actually fall right now as we all sold to avoid the fall.

But regardless of who made the mental leap of supposing that investors would – even on average – **act rationally when dealing with investments . . . it's quite clear that as investors we don't.**

Why some advisers give out misleading advice

This is an incredibly important point to understand – because this simple idea (that asset prices are reasonably stable) sits behind the advice many financial advisers will give you as an investor. And in the past, it also sat behind government and central bank actions to manage the UK and world economies!

Now, quite clearly, given their answer to the Queen's big question (see earlier), the officials at the Bank of England know that these old theories are flawed. And, it appears that the thinking in the USA has also have moved on, as evidenced by the admission from former Federal Reserve chair, Alan Greenspan, of 'the flaw' in their models.

See here www.theflawmovie.com

But I guess you're less concerned with the challenges of managing the Bank of England (or the US Federal Reserve) than you are with managing your own funds. And so you need to ask yourself whether you *really believe that investment asset prices are reasonably stable and behave like the prices of consumer goods.*

Many advisers do believe this (indeed, their training tells them to believe it), and it's a compelling idea. After all, if investment assets were ever incorrectly priced – either too cheap or too expensive – then surely investors would realise this and start buying or selling them to bring the price back into balance. This can be likened to a situation at the supermarket, when a short queue opens up. Provided that there are some active shoppers (active fund managers) around to spot the opportunities, then the short queues don't stay short for long!

The other compelling thing about this 'price is always right' theory (for governments and central bankers of recent times) was that by following it, they felt little need to interfere with markets to dampen down the overpricing. They believed that the *invisible hand* of the market would sort it all out and therefore that asset price bubbles were unlikely to blow up.

But this 'self-correcting' markets theory does not reflect reality and to show why it doesn't – let's look at an example of real life.

Suppose that you own your own home and decide to buy a second house as an investment. You take out a mortgage to help with the purchase and the property goes up in value by 25% in the first year. Now, logically, if the property was at a fair price when you bought it then it might be 'rational' to look again at the price (relative to the general level of earnings) and consider whether it is now overpriced and sell out. But you're only human and you're now quite excited about your returns, so you go back to the bank to borrow some more money to buy a third property. You're keen to repeat your good fortune.

And what will the bank say? Well, the chances are that they'll say 'Yes' and give you the money to roll the dice again. They can see that prices are rising and that you've now got more equity in that first property. Equity in this instance, is the value of your property over and above the amount owed on your mortgage.

So the bank is thinking that they'd be mad not to let you borrow some more. In fact, during a steady rise in house prices, the banks might decide, en masse, that their risks of further lending are small – and they might even be willing to lend to people on very low incomes too.

Is this starting to sound familiar?

It's obvious, in this scenario, that rising house prices have caused *more* buying, *not less*, as the orthodox theory would suggest. And the increased buying of houses causes further increases to prices, which encourages more borrowing and buying, and so on. We've just started to inflate a house price bubble.

Let's complete this story. After some considerable time, when most ordinary investors and banks have become so accustomed to rising house prices that they begin to think the party can go on forever, the banks start to run out of borrowers with good credit records. And at around the same time, the early investors have spotted the price bubble and start to sell out for profit.

So, with few new buyers available and a rush of sellers, the whole system shifts into reverse gear and prices crash. And at this point, of course, when prices are collapsing back to fair value, you'll be lucky to find a bank to lend you any money at all!

So, we have a problem here as investors. The idea that market prices are *not* always fair value goes completely against the orthodox market theory that's been developed and embedded into economics textbooks for 200 years. What's more, that basic theory is still taught to financial advisers today – which means that there are relatively few of them who can help you to spot an overvalued market – or who'd be prepared to risk their reputation by doing so.

Let's just remember that our world leaders, supported by experts in this flawed economic theory, failed to recognise when our economic ship was getting close to the rocks. They assumed that assets were always broadly priced at the correct level by the market. They couldn't see the rocks (the house price bubbles) because they didn't believe such things existed at all!

I know, this is scary stuff, and to be clear, it doesn't make all economists or politicians bad people. Many are now acutely aware of these flawed theories, including, as we've seen, the Bank of England. And there were a lot of wise people – economists, investment managers, philosophers and even some politicians – who gave warnings of the impending house price and banking tsunami back in 2005 or earlier. They included Roger Bootle, John Calverley, Robert J. Shiller, Nouriel Roubini, Nassim N. Taleb, George Cooper, Vince Cable and many others (some of their books are listed in the Bibliography, and it is well worth reading more from them).

The tragedy is that these great thinkers were all ignored. No one in power was prepared to bring the party to a stop. It doesn't win you friends (or votes) if you end a good party!

But the 2008 crisis was a long time ago, and you might have expected that we'd learned our lessons from it. You might have hoped that we'd put our economies, banks and asset markets back onto a stable footing by now, right?

Well, no, I don't think we have – not yet anyway. The western world has dug itself into an extraordinarily deep hole of debt, and we're a very long way from coming out of that hole. We still operate in a period of abnormally low interest rates which are propping up house and other asset prices (or at least they were, at the time of writing – markets move quite fast sometimes), and according to the acclaimed experts on this matter, we still have various problems with our banking system in that various parts of it remain 'too big to fail' yet still under-capitalised. So, they could go bust again if we see some big falls in asset prices – and the taxpayer might have to step in again!

And the experts keep shifting their view on what needs to be done to make our banking system safe again. The *Financial Times* reported (8 September 2013), that Sir John Vickers, the chief architect of Britain's post-crisis regulatory reforms, said *bank capital should be at least twice as high* as the level that his Independent Commission on Banking had recommended two years previously.

We clearly need to get to a position where any future bank collapses are paid for by their investors and not by the taxpayer. What happens next is anyone's guess. Some experts believe the next financial crisis is imminent.

Look up 'Overdose: The Next Financial Crisis' on YouTube

It's possible that the Duke of Edinburgh's little joke might not turn out to be so funny after all.

Get irate!

- Our 'big ideas' people (the politicians, bankers, central bankers and economists) might not seem like dangerous animals, but their orthodox free market pricing ideas have caused a lot of trouble for the world.

- These experts are *unable* (despite their claims) to deliver stability to economies or investment asset prices so we must remember to protect ourselves from events they cannot predict – and from those events that they're too afraid to predict.

- Do not expect to find headline forecasts that whole economies are out of control or that asset prices (stock markets, housing markets) are sitting at highly unstable valuation levels (either high or low).

- You can find intelligent and independent views on longer-term market valuations, but you have to dig them out. And whilst it's true to say that no one can predict the direction of asset prices (especially in the short term), we can see when valuations are reaching extreme levels (expensive or cheap) by long-term historical averages. And by taking note of valuations, we might make more purchases at cheaper values and avoid the 'herds' buying at the top of the market.

For more on the issues that persist in the banking sector, read *The Bankers' New Clothes: What's Wrong with Banking and What to Do About It* by Anat Admati and Martin Hellwig.

You can find more on the causes of the financial crisis in Appendix 1.

Postscript: the nutty Nobels

In 2013 the Royal Swedish Academy of Sciences awarded the Nobel Memorial Prize in Economics to two economists, Eugene Fama and Robert Shiller, whose separate studies were central to the debate on the behaviour of asset markets.

The astonishing thing about those awards, as John Kay pointed out in the *Financial Times* (15 October 2013), was that *"Prof Fama made his name by developing the efficient market hypothesis (EMH), long the cornerstone of finance theory – whilst Prof Shiller is the most prominent critic of that same hypothesis."*

"It was", as Kay put it, *"like awarding the physics prize jointly to Ptolemy for his theory that the Earth is the centre of the universe and to Copernicus for showing that it is not."*

See Appendix 2 for more on this topic.

Coming up in the next chapter...

We've seen here that the old orthodox economic/markets theory ('the price is always right') was a dangerous one for the world but sadly that same idea is still used quite widely by financial advisers today (both here and in the USA).

These advisers take the view that it's okay to help you put large proportions of your wealth into stock markets even when they're screaming out red danger signals of overvaluation, as they were in late 1999. Sales of the riskiest types of equity funds (technology start-ups) were booming at that time, and plenty of financial advisers were promoting them.

So it's essential to be aware of these risks during every boom – and to be aware of other flawed thinking that's used in sales pitches to persuade you to buy into the markets and stay there at all times.

This next chapter could save you a fortune and help you sleep better at night.

Chapter 3
Dangerously trained
investment advisers

How the mad ideas that contributed to the crisis
are still being used to advise us today

*I can calculate the motion of heavenly bodies,
but not the madness of people.*

~ Isaac Newton

© copyright Paul Claireaux and Noel Ford

I'm not a fiction writer but I wonder if you'll bear with me as I attempt a short story to illustrate a massive problem with investment advice today.

I'd like you to imagine that you're going on the holiday of a lifetime, to a remote island in the Caribbean.

That's exciting, eh?

The only trouble is that you're a very nervous flyer.

If you really are a nervous flyer, then I'm really sorry about this story but it's essential to understand this idea – and this is the best way I can think of to explain it.

Now, you've done your nervous flyer homework and discovered that this is the stormy season in the Caribbean, which is also one of the stormiest parts of the world. So now you're doubly nervous. But friends and family reassure you that flying is incredibly safe these days and that your aircraft will be extremely well equipped with storm detection radar and various other safety gizmos. You've paid extra to book onto a major airline in the hope that their pilots might be trained to a higher standard (although I'm not aware of any truth in that idea).

The day of the holiday arrives and you head off to the airport, leaving plenty of time to spare. You're still very nervous and there's some additional agony of a two-hour wait in Departures, but finally you're called to board your 'bird to paradise'.

Once under way, you can't believe you made all that fuss beforehand. All is calm on the flight – some turbulence about two hours in does set you on edge for a while but then things settle down again and you're able to relax.

After a few more hours of an uneventful flight – let's ignore that argument with the guy in the seat behind who got stroppy when you reclined your seat to take a nap – you catch your first glimpse of some beautiful islands dotted around the intense turquoise of the Caribbean Sea.

Staring out of the window, you also notice a line of towering black storm clouds up ahead – and as you focus on them you can see their tops bulging higher and higher. But then you remind yourself that pilots are well trained about thunderstorms and that they'll have a good view of these clouds from their window. They'll *obviously* take the necessary action to get around them – so you can relax, sit back in your seat and dream of being down there, on those beaches in the sun.

But then, *bang*, a thunderclap explodes as if right outside your window, accompanied by a flash of lightning that lights up the whole cabin. You know that means it must have been very close to hitting the plane.

There's a loud roar of hail smashing onto the plane and all around is just black cloud and flashes of lightning. The 'fasten seatbelt' sign is on now and you pull yours tight as the turbulence starts throwing the plane about in all directions. You're pitched up and down and rolled from side to side with gut-wrenching violence. Overhead lockers ping open with every jolt and the hand baggage is falling out, hitting and hurting the passengers.

The crew cannot help – they're strapped tightly into their seats – but what's more upsetting is that they look completely terrified.

At one moment the front of the plane drops down and it feels as if you're screaming towards the ground. Your seatbelt tightens across your lap as you're lifted off your seat. Then you're pushed hard back into your seat as the nose pitches up. You're in what feels like a vertical climb! How long can this possibly last?

Then the noise gets louder as hailstones the size of golf balls crash onto the plane – and when you dare to look out of your window, you can see dents in the wing as the hail smashes into it. But then, quite suddenly, and as quickly as the chaos struck, it stops. You're out of the storm and engulfed by brilliant sunshine and blue skies. The ride is perfectly calm again, although a lot of passengers are still panicking and screaming for help.

The emergency is over and you've survived – *this time at least.*

The crew get up and tidy the loose luggage away, attend to the passengers with minor cuts and bruises and generally calm things down. And a little while later the pilot pulls off the smoothest landing ever. Everyone cheers and applauds the landing of course – but much more loudly than usual. And even the crew join in with the cheering this time! Everyone is so very grateful to be alive and safely back on the ground.

As you're getting off the plane the crew are at the door as normal, looking immaculate and calm. They offer reassuring words about the safety of flight and the rarity of that event. But you decide you're having none of it; you can see the pilot and co-pilot standing just behind the crew, and you want to know why they'd taken you into that thunderstorm. So you call out, "How did you manage to hit that storm?"

The pilot looks around and stares at you like a teacher would stare down a naughty child, but you stare right back waiting for a reply. "Well?" you demand.

There's a further pause. The pilot really does *not* wish to discuss this in front of the other passengers, most of whom seem quite happy just to get off the plane and get on with their holiday. But you stand your ground and eventually the pilot caves in to offer an explanation.

"Well, it's like this" he says. "Our weather models tell us that the chances of hitting a thunderstorm of that force are next to zero. So our policy is to ignore them and plough straight on through. It's too costly to make detours every time we think it might get a bit bumpy. You wouldn't want us to double your ticket price would you? But look, don't worry, there's no chance of facing another storm like that in your lifetime – even if you lived to be a thousand years old and you flew here twice a day."

You have to admit, that's a pretty clear explanation – or so you think. So, slightly calmer now, you join the other passengers and head off on your holiday. At least that won't happen again – right?

You'll be glad to hear that my poor attempt at fiction writing is over – although I might tell you another story or two later on!

But let me assure you (as an ex-private pilot) that the story I've told you here is total fiction. This is *not* how things work in the real world of aviation. Pilots absolutely do know very well about the instability and destructive forces in thunderclouds. They call these monsters **CBs** – which is short for Cumulonimbus – and they avoid them like the plague. So it's genuinely unthinkable that you'd encounter a situation like that with a responsible pilot – not because the pilots fly *through* these storms, but because they're trained to *ruddy well avoid them!*

How this applies to stock market investing

You may be wondering what this has to do with investing or financial advice. And whilst I accept that this analogy isn't perfect (none are), I do think it's useful to compare the seriousness with which pilots treat thunderstorms with the way in which some advisers treat market thunderstorms, aka, 'crashes'.

So let's explore the more dangerous ideas about investing – about stock markets – that have unfortunately become a belief system for some advisers in the UK, the USA and other parts of the world. And let's see how well it equips them to advise us on the very real risks of crashes (or thunderstorms) in stock markets.

It's worth noting that these are deeply rooted beliefs amongst some financial adviser groups – as I found out when I joined a leading discussion group of American financial planners last year. Hoping for an open and serious debate about investment risk, my challenges were met with anger and agitation amongst the group and in no time at all, I was invited to leave the group! Of course, I was more than happy to leave that so-called discussion group. I really don't care for organisations based on random beliefs rather than objective and useful facts. Such groups are only self-serving and they reinforce the dogma of their belief system.

Now, there's a lot of (allegedly) complicated mathematics around the measurement of risk in stock markets, and it's easy to become overwhelmed by the apparent science behind it all. The easiest thing to do is to simply give up and accept that *if there's maths behind it, then it must be okay.* Right?

Wrong.

Yes, it's true that maths is a pure and perfect subject on its own. It's simply logic, so it cannot be wrong. However, **you can be wrong – big time – if you use the wrong maths model to describe the real world.** And that's the problem with the way in which investment risk is measured by some advisers. So, I hope that you'll stick with me a while – I promise that we won't head into the dark world of calculus or partial differential equations as we explore this subject in plain English.

We'll only explore the core beliefs about 'perfect markets' that can get us into trouble. And we'll look at these ideas one step at a time.

First, let's outline the beliefs and then explore what's wrong with them.

The followers of the 'perfect markets' belief system will tell you something like this:

1. Prices in the stock market are always right (or at least, roughly so).

2. The best guess we can make for future, real (inflation-adjusted) long-term investment returns is the same as the long-term past performance, regardless of when we invest.

3. There's no point in trying to time our entry into the markets.

   - If you're silly enough to try to do this, you risk missing the very small number of days when the biggest market gains occur.

4. There's no point trying to pick the best stocks (or the best sectors, or the best geographical regions for investment).

   - You (or any active fund manager for that matter) simply cannot know better than everyone else in the market as to which stocks will do better than others. So it makes no sense to invest in anything other than all the shares in the market.

   - For the same reason, you should invest in stocks in the same proportion to that which they represent in the market. This is based on the 'market is always right' idea and translates into using index-tracking funds (passive funds) to track the performance of all the companies in that index.

   - Similarly, if you want a spread of funds across all markets in the world (which might be seen as sensible diversification), then you should buy index-tracking funds from each country in the same proportions to that which each represents of the world market. So, for example, if the US stock market represents 40% of world capitalisation, then we should match that proportion by holding about 40% of our shares in the US.

5. You should, however, expect wobbles in market prices along the way.

   - This is simply part of the deal with investment. You accept the wobbliness of asset prices because it is their very wobbliness that ensures a better return. Prices are always at or around a level that offers higher prospective returns than a risk-free investment.

   - If prices ever get too expensive (or cheap), then **rational** investors – which we are all assumed to be – will sell (or buy more of) the asset until they return to a reasonable level.

6. But you don't need to worry about these wobbles.

   - The wobbles are merely random price moves that are just as likely to be above or below the line of our expected return.

   - The chances of prices crashing really badly are infinitesimally small. So small in fact that we can ignore them – just like the pilots did in our story.

   - We know this because we can predict the chances of various sized market wobbles with a clever mathematical tool (a stochastic model) based on a *normal* distribution of prices. The normal distribution is a perfectly valid model for representing many types of randomly distributed data – so we're happy to use it for share price movements too.

   - What we mean when we say don't worry about stock market price wobbles is that most of the time, markets will chug along at our *expected rate of return. And that's about* 5% p.a. above inflation.

   - Yes, there will be some wobbles, but most of these will be small. Indeed, we predict that roughly 70% of the wobbles will be less than one **'average-sized wobble'** – above or below our *expected return* line.

   - We call an average-sized wobble a 'standard deviation'. This is simply the average size of all wobbles – both up and down – away from the average return line over some agreed time period.

   - And nearly all wobbles (over 95% in fact) will be smaller than two average-sized wobbles.

- And, as we've said, very large wobbles are very rare indeed. Using our model, we can predict that a major stock market (like our own FTSE 100 or the S&P 500 in the USA) will move by 6% or more in one day only once every two million years! So it really is okay to ignore these risks – just like the pilots in the story.

- Now, the equation behind this 'normal distribution' is a bit ugly and complicated, but it's actually quite easy to see how the shape (the distribution) builds up over time. In fact, you might say it's child's play because you can see this shape building up if you pretend prices (randomly bouncing up or down) are like balls falling through a maze of nails (or pennies dropping through those machines at the amusement arcade, if they still have them!).

- Just take a look at this Quincunx model on the wonderful 'Math is fun' site at www.mathsisfun.com/data/quincunx.html

- Click on the button to speed up the flow of balls to make the picture emerge faster. You'll soon see how this normal distribution shape (see below) emerges naturally over time.

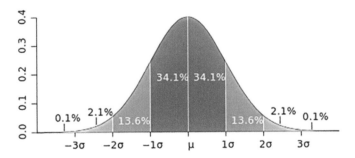

So there you have it. That, in a nutshell, is the 'perfect stock market' behaviour belief system. You may have even have heard something along these lines from your investment adviser. And I think we'd all have to agree that this belief system *sounds* reasonable. In fact, it feels far more robust than some random belief system. It clearly has maths and science behind it, and – as noted in the previous chapter – a lot of this thinking is based broadly on serious academic work known as the *efficient markets hypothesis* (EMH) – although the perfect market belief system undoubtedly stretches and twists the EMH – and a lot of academics disagree with the EMH in the first place.

Okay, fine, but just for fun (yes I call this fun!) let's look at these ideas again – just to see if there's any evidence against them.

Point 1: The price is right

You may recall from Chapter 2 how the man at the Bank of England told the Queen that *efficient market ideas were now considered out of date*. That's a serious group of thinkers who are not running with this theory any more. And we also learned that the former chair of the Federal Reserve in the USA (Alan Greenspan) has now admitted to there being a 'flaw' in their economic models. So it appears that they don't run with these theories any more either.

Oh dear – this is not looking good for the belief system is it?

But there's more. In the most respected of economic journals (*The Economist*, Buttonwood on investing, 28 January 2013), we're told that there *is* an inverse relationship between starting valuations and likely future investment returns. In other words, when valuations are high, future returns are low, and vice versa. And that article also cited projections from Standard Life (a leading UK investment house) that the returns from a diversified portfolio would be quite low relative to those we've enjoyed in the past. Why did they say this? Because their view is that markets have become overvalued.

Regularly updated and intelligent views on market prospects (looking forward seven years) can be found from GMO, another leading investment house www.gmo.com At the time of writing they're forecasting negative real returns from US equities, for example.

The Economist also quoted from a highly regarded book, *Expected Returns*, by Antti Ilmanen, who sums up the question of what returns we might expect from our investments like this:

> ***Forward-looking indicators, such as valuation ratios, have a better track record in forecasting asset class returns than do rear-view-mirror measures.*** *The practice of using the historical average return as the best estimate of future return – as is often done with the 85-year history of the equity premium – relies on the idea of constant expected returns. The boom-bust*

*cycles of the 2000s have helped to cause both aca-
demic and practitioner views to shift toward accepting
the idea of time-varying expected returns. And as a
result, institutional investors no longer embrace static
asset class weights, nor do they reject market timing
out of hand. (Emphasis added)*

So in short, we should *not* expect the returns we've seen in the past.

> You might think this is all very obvious – and I'd agree
> with you. However, it's not obvious to the believers in
> perfect markets – and there are a lot of these people
> (wearing financial adviser hats) around the world. So
> read on – this is important!

Points 2 and 3: Future returns are likely to be similar to past returns (in real terms), and we cannot time the market

Oh, dear. Well, we've just seen that this idea is in trouble – but let's be clear on this point.

We most certainly *cannot* perfectly 'time' our entry to markets at any time and especially so over very short periods of time. It's impossible to accurately predict market movements so as to perfectly time a stock market purchase on a daily or even hourly basis.

> And this should beg the question as to why this form of
> gambling is so popular – but we'll come back to that
> when we look at spread betting (aka, day trading) in the
> next chapter.

However, it is not fair to say that we have no measures at all for identifying when the market is trading at *extreme* levels – either very high or very low – compared to its long-term historic range. Whilst there are no *perfect* measures of fair value, there are some measures, and we'll look at a particularly useful one in a moment. But before we do, **let's try to understand** why many advisers are reluctant to use such measures.

First, it could genuinely make their work very complicated. They would need to constantly adjust their standard investment portfolios over time to take account of market valuation. And such changes would be in addition to the adjustments they're already making to our personal holdings across their portfolios as our risk appetite changes. For many advisers, this is too difficult. The reporting and communications necessary to manage our money against two moving parts like this would be extraordinarily challenging. It would be like trying to bake a cake whilst someone's constantly changing the recipe. So I understand their difficulty here – but I don't think it excuses a process which ignores market valuations.

A second – and unjustified – reason why **some** advisers don't like to take market valuation on board is because it would mean that when markets are overpriced, they would have to tell you not to invest at all – and that's not good for their business. You see, advisers who sell *expensive* investment products need you to make high investment returns just to cover the product costs. So they won't want to put you into bank deposits or low risk/low return funds even if that might be a good idea given the market outlook at some points in time.

Of course, good advisers are perfectly happy to recommend we leave our money in bank deposits at certain times – or hold it in very low cost investment products where lower risk/lower return investing can work.

But it's not just certain advisers who hate us going on strike with our investing from time to time, when markets are overpriced! The marketers at some of the big fund management companies are especially wary of this threat, and, like their cousins in the high street shops, they have some powerful marketing messages to keep us investing at all times – and prevent us from being over-cautious.

Lies, damned lies and financial product marketing

You need to be aware of this particularly misleading piece of investment marketing spin you'll hear positioned as a 'golden rule' of investing. I call it the 'time in the market' mantra and it goes like this:

*It's the **time in the market** – **not timing the market** – that delivers the best investment returns.*

This classic mantra has been repeated more times than anyone has had hot dinners. Have you heard it yet? If not, then you will soon, because this catchy little phrase is dusted down and trotted out every time the markets hit a bad patch. You'll be given tables of data (or perhaps nowadays, some kind of 'whizzy' online moving image) to 'prove' just how much you'd be missing out if you were ever stupid enough to be out of the markets. And the data clearly shows that just by missing out on the 'best days' – when the markets make their biggest gains – we effectively wipe out **any** chance of making good returns over the long term.

Is this starting to sound familiar now?

And yes, it's quite true, that the biggest market gains do indeed occur on a small number of days. So it must be reasonable to say that we should be in the markets on those days, right?

Hmm, I think we need to slow down a bit here. Let's think this through more carefully.

How could we possibly engineer our transactions with such precision as to be out of the market on precisely these best days but only on those days? Wouldn't that be the most incredible feat of bad timing?

Yes, it would – and that's precisely what Greg Cooper of Schroders (a leading investment house) said when he **debunked this idea** in a marketing communication to advisers in May 2009.

And anyway, when do you think the very 'best days' in the market occur?

Yes, that's right, they tend to happen right on the heels of the very 'worst days'! So, the chances are that if you're missing out on the best days, you're also missing out on the worst days too. So, on average, it's really no big deal to be out of the markets for a while – and if it helps you sleep better then that's a good reason.

But let's tackle this misleading marketing with some facts and I'll take the data from a useful paper on this very subject, called 'The Fallacy of Missing the Best Days in the Market' by Daniel Hughes (a US certified financial planner).

Mr Hughes looked at the S&P 500 USA stock market index (but the principles apply to the UK or any other stock market) over a 25-year period from 1 January 1985 to 30 December 2009. Here's what he found...

Over this 25-year period:

- The average *annual* return of the S&P 500 index was 7.88%.

> This would be our investment return (before charges) if we'd invested in that index and stayed invested for the whole period.

- This rate of return would convert US$10,000 into nearly US$67,000.

- By missing the best 20 days on the stock market over this period our returns would have been significantly reduced – to just 2.75% p.a. This would turn our US$10,000 into less than US$20,000. *Ouch!*

- However, if, instead of being so unlucky as to miss the best 20 days we were lucky enough to miss the *worst* 20 days, then our returns would have increased to 14.62% p.a. That would have turned our US$10,000 into over US$300,000!

Remarkable numbers, eh?

Yes, but the point here is that it's *stupid* (yes, I mean stupid) to say that by choosing to be out of the market at certain times you'll only miss out on the best days and still be exposed to all the worst days. It would of course be equally stupid to say that you could somehow avoid all the worst days and catch all the good days.

The simple truth is that when you're out of the market you miss both good and bad days. So it's perhaps more interesting to look at the returns we'd make if we missed out on both the best 20 *and* the worst 20 days over 25 years. And here are the results for this scenario:

- Our annual returns would have increased to 9.17% p.a.

- This would turn our US$10,000 into about US$90,000.

Now, that's better than simply staying invested throughout. But it's still not an outcome that we could possibly engineer!

What's more interesting is to look at when the best and worst days in the US stock market occurred. And, of the 80 extreme days listed (40 best and 40 worst), it turns out that more than half of them occurred during just two years – 2008 and 2009. In short, our markets shook violently as the banks fell apart. What we know for sure is that a lot of the best days in the stock market occur during very volatile times *and* when we're in a bear (downward-tracking) market.

For example, had you invested heavily (as a great many people did) into the UK stock market at the turn of the millennium, then you'd have suffered price falls of over 50% in the following three years, despite enjoying plenty of those good 'up-days' along the way!

Remind an investment salesperson of those times, and you'll be told that simply by *sitting tight* at that time you'd have seen your investments recover by the summer of 2007. And that's true – as is the fact that the market then proceeded to crash *again* by another 50% in 2008-09. The index was down about 50% some nine years after the start of 2000.

That's a viciously rough rollercoaster, even for those with steel stomachs – which I don't have.

But this is far from the steepest rollercoaster in UK stock market history. For that we need to go back to the time when the Jackson Five topped the music charts and Barbara Streisand was number one with the wonderful title song to the film *The Way We Were* (that's a song worth looking up).

What we can learn from the UK in the 1970s

The way we were back then – in 1973 in the UK – can best be described as **grim**. Government finances were in tatters and we were the poor man of Europe, taking our begging bowl to the International Monetary Fund (IMF) for a loan to get us through the worst. Yes, we were in a desperate condition, like Greece today. And our stock market reflected our troubles – it fell by around 70% in just two-and-a-half years to November 1974.

Again, those who could afford to hold on to their vanishing investments did see a bounce-back when confidence returned. But a great many investors were simply thrown off the roller coaster ride and lost most of their money. That's the nature of a real crash: the price falls frighten people so much that they sell out. And their forced selling then steepens the market fall.

Towards the end of a crash, the lucky ones (and a few smart ones) start buying up the assets at knock-down prices and a great new bull run begins. After that great crash in 1973-74 the UK stock market took off like never before, and in the next 25 years it posted average returns (on top of inflation, which ran above 20% in some years) of about 14% p.a.. These were astonishingly good returns that just kept coming, year after year, after year (with only a minor hiccough in 1987), and many people started to believe that you really couldn't go wrong by having most of your money invested in the stock market.

But then the Japanese showed us something different.

How the Japanese dream became a nightmare

The Japanese were enjoying their own economic miracle in 1989: their stock market had grown a staggering 15% p.a. on average over the previous 25 years, from the early 1960s. (And this figure ignores the further, albeit very modest, growth investors received from reinvested income.)

The Japanese market was also the hot favourite amongst the 'experts' to keep growing in the years ahead. What could possibly go wrong? Their manufacturing was the envy of the world and was putting the UK motor industry out of business. We could buy nearly everything we needed from Japan – from cars to TV sets to some new-fangled Sony Walkman music player. Their products were great quality *and* were available at better prices than anything we could get at home. With such a long record of economic growth and a steadily rising stock market, it was considered conservative to predict anything less than 10% p.a. growth for Japanese-based investment funds going forward from that time.

What happened next shocked every investor with money in Japan – and that included most people with any investments at all. Japanese stocks were in everyone's pension or other investment products in abundance. But their market had been bid up to stratospheric valuations and the 'smart money' investors could see that there was little prospect of further growth – so they started to sell out.

At the end of 1989 the Japanese stock market (as measured by the Nikkei 225 index) was around 39,000. By the end of 2012 (23 years later), it stood close to 10,000, a fall of nearly 75%. That's one hell of a long and painful decline in stock market values, and surely proves the point better than any other example that *the past performance of markets is no guide at all to future performance.* A warning using words along those lines is printed on all regulated investment product sales literature in the UK. It's just incredible that so few people bother to take any notice of it.

But the Japanese stock market bubble is not unique – far from it.

Time and again we rush into the latest hot investment idea. In the run-up to the end of the millennium it was technology funds that were taking in most of the money. Then, when they crashed, it was property funds that everyone wanted and then it was bond funds and latterly it's stock market funds that are back in vogue once more.

At the time of writing, the bond funds have started to creak and crack – so if you're holding a lot of these in your portfolio (and especially if they're the long-term variety) I'd suggest that you get some good quality investment advice very quickly. It clearly makes sense to avoid too much exposure to overvalued markets if we want to protect any wealth we've accumulated from being destroyed in a nasty market crash. Sure, we may miss a few of those big up-days – with that part of our money we hold in safer assets – but we'll also avoid the downs too, and we'll sleep a whole lot better at night.

Funnily enough, that Schroder's paper I mentioned earlier suggests exactly this approach. We can always increase our exposure to risky assets when markets have returned into a more reasonable valuation range.

The Japanese stock market had quite clearly flown off the top of any reasonable valuation chart by 1989. The Nikkei index stood on a price to earnings ratio (PE) of 80 (that's silly – a more reasonable figure is somewhere between 10 and 20) and their market had swollen to become by far the largest in the world, accounting for about 60% of the total value of all stock markets worldwide! (And that's very silly.)

At the start of 2015 the capitalisation of the Japanese stock market was about 7% of the world total (that's less than the UK's 10%) and around one fifth of US markets. The Nikkei index fell back to a PE of about 10 by March 2009. And for anyone who bothered to look, the UK and US markets were also quite clearly flashing red warning valuation signals in the run-up to the end of the millennium. So let's look at a valuation signal we might use to avoid the destruction of our wealth when a future stock market bubble bursts.

The warning sign that could help protect your wealth from future slides

At the time of writing (summer 2015) the view held by well-informed commentators is that the US stock market – which heavily influences most others – is overpriced. The ultra-low interest rate environment has propped up markets in stocks and housing and a similar story applies here in the UK and elsewhere.

It also appears that the US may have another house price boom on their hands – which, right on the back of the last one, is probably not a great idea. That said, their housing market did at least deflate properly before prices started rising again.

In the UK our property prices remain overinflated and are now being propped up not just by low interest rates but also by new taxpayer-backed loan guarantees in the form of the various 'Help to Buy' schemes. A couple of years back even Lloyds Banking Group – which across its range of banks was the UK's biggest mortgage lender – warned about this risk. It's been quieter of late – perhaps because it doesn't want to disturb the rise in its share price as the Government tries to offload its shares.

The US Federal Reserve (under Ben Bernanke) also acknowledged in 2013 that their bond buying programme (quantitative easing, which kept interest rates low in the short and medium terms) may have inflated asset prices. Yes, well, we'd agree with that!

The Fed also warned investors against speculation that relies on these continued low rates. That warning was seen as a signal that the very long period (since 2008) of very low interest rates was finally drawing to a close. But two years on and interest rates are still on the floor. Of course, no one knows when rates will make a significant move back up again, but when they do it seems reasonable to expect that the move will spook investors and cause some major market tremors.

But this is all about the short term and the short term is almost certainly out of date as you read this book. So what about a longer-term valuation picture? How can we get our hands on one of those?

Very simply – it's just a mouse click away.

I mentioned in Chapter 1 that for shares we can look at the share price to earnings (PE) ratio for valuation clues. ('Earnings' is just another word for profits). I also said that company profits bounce around quite violently, and so the 'E' bit of PE ratio is not a reasonable reflection of the longer-term earnings history – or future potential – on a given company. For this reason, some clever people (Benjamin Graham and David Dodd) came up with the idea (in their 1934 book, *Security Analysis*) of averaging out earnings over a period of time – say, ten years or more – to take account of earnings fluctuations over a business cycle. This is called a Cyclically Adjusted PE, or CAPE.

> Don't worry, we're not about to delve into the detail of valuing individual company shares. We'll leave that to professional fund managers and other experts in accounting and in the 'going rates' for earnings in various company sectors. Finding a bargain company on the stock market presents plenty of tripwires for the unwary. For example, just because a company has a high PE (or CAPE) does not necessarily mean that it's expensive. It may just mean that its earnings have high growth potential. Some such companies will live up to this hope, whilst others will fall short. It's the share prices of the second group that get hammered as the reality doesn't live up to the expectation. However, we can look at a measure for valuing the world's largest stock market in the US (see below). And we can use this without any expertise in accountancy or any industry sector.

The benefit of Graham and Dodd's idea (to average out the earnings of a company over a period of time) is that it takes out the time-based spikes in any earnings data. Similarly, if we look at a whole market rather than a single company, we *average out* the anomalies between individual companies. One company may stand on an unjustifiably high PE, but will typically be balanced out by another one which stands at an unfairly low price. So it's reasonable to say that the PE (and better still, the CAPE) on a whole market is more likely to reflect the value in that market than a PE on the shares of a single company.

And lucky for us, a certain Professor Robert Shiller of Yale University has taken this idea from Graham and Dodd and done all the CAPE data crunching for us across the whole US stock market. You can obtain his data for free online at www.econ.yale.edu/~shiller/data. htm

Robert Shiller's bestselling book, *Irrational Exuberance*, was first published in 2000 and predicted the tech stock market crash that followed the end of the millennium. Shiller used Alan Greenspan's infamous 1996 phrase 'irrational exuberance' to explain the alternately soaring and declining stock market. Then, in his second edition (2005), Shiller added property into his analysis of markets, and gave evidence that house prices were also dangerously inflated, and that a bubble could soon burst, leading to a string of bankruptcies and a worldwide recession.

I guess he got that right too, eh?

Shiller's data gives us an excellent long run chart (like the one on the following page), which you'll see in many articles on stock market value.

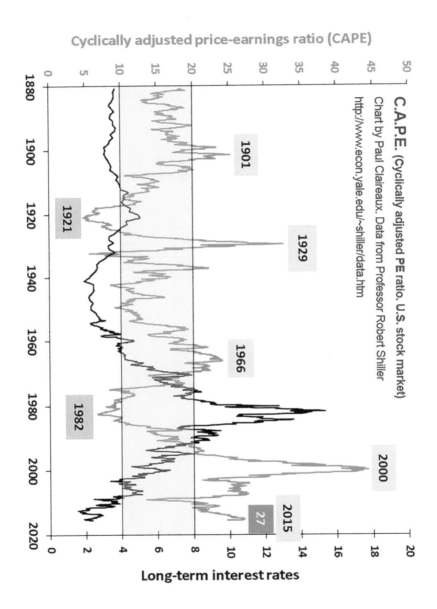

Cyclically adjusted price-earnings ratio (CAPE)

C.A.P.E. (Cyclically adjusted **PE** ratio. **U.S.** stock market)

Chart by Paul Claireaux. Data from Professor Robert Shiller

http://www.econ.yale.edu/~shiller/data.htm

Long-term interest rates

And what might this CAPE picture be able to tell us?

Well, yes, it's bounced up and down (a lot) over the last 100 years! But take a closer look. For much of the time it's been in a range between around 10 and 20.

Right, so is this a reasonable range?

Good question. Now, remember that earnings are profits – so a PE of 10 means that profits are around 10% of the total share prices in the index. Equally a PE of 20 means profits are 5% of prices (1 divided by 20). And profits of 5% to 10% p.a., whether paid out in dividends or reinvested for growth back into the companies themselves, should deliver investment returns of the same sort of order (plus a bit for inflation and growth) over the long term.

These sorts of prospective return are clearly above what you'd expect from cash deposits or other risk-free investments. And that's reasonable for an investment that carries risk – which investing in shares most certainly does. However, when this CAPE ratio peaked at 45 at the end of the millennium – suggesting a 2.2% prospective return (1 divided by 45) – that did not seem reasonable to me. Nor did it to everyone else when they woke up at the end of 1999 and starting selling out!

Note that these are very long-term waves in the chart – we're talking decades here, not months, days or even minutes, as allegedly used for intelligent trading by spread betters! What we're seeing here are long-term shifts in people's appetite for investing in risky assets.

In 2000, with the CAPE in outer space at the astonishing level of 45, investors around the world must clearly have thought that the high tech stocks of the new millennium would create wealth and corporate profits beyond any previous dreams. You may recall that a vast number of new tech companies went bust around then – though it's also true that a very small number did survive (like Amazon and Google), and have done extraordinarily well.

Note how that peak of 45 on the US CAPE was far higher than the previous all-time high of around 33, which was reached at the end of the roaring 1920s. Note also how the CAPE metric crashed to around 6 in the 1930s depression, and see how it fell to around 14 in the 2008-09 crash. Recently it's climbed back up to nearly 27 and that's well above a level that many consider to be its long-term safe range.

So is the CAPE a perfect predictor of future returns, at least on the US stock market? Well, no, it's not perfect – there is no such thing as the perfect market predictor. And, as we can see, the ratio moves across very long ranges – so a good deal of the time it offers no clues at all. However, it is helpful for identifying the times when we've reached extreme valuation levels – both high and low. These are the times of greatest danger and opportunity.

What I find funny (or rather sad) is how the CAPE indicator loses its friends in the investment industry when it starts issuing warning signals that might slow down sales of investment funds – as now.

In a *Financial Times* article ('The CAPE of Less Hope', 13 August 2013) John Authers reported that Merrill Lynch was pointing to CAPE being the only one of 15 popular measures of equity valuation that was currently making stocks look expensive, the implication being that CAPE must be a flawed measure. The trouble with their argument is that their other 'popular' measures either don't smooth out company earnings – so they're simply a snapshot in time – or they're based on the, invariably optimistic, forward projections of earnings from analysts.

Yes, any price to earnings ratio – including those that 'smooth out' earnings over a period – is imperfect. By choosing the length of the period over which to smooth – which happens to be ten years in the case of the Shiller CAPE – the numbers are still affected by the history of earnings fluctuations during that period. And yes, in the last ten years we've seen the very worst of crashes in profits. Merrill Lynch might therefore justifiably question whether this most recent ten-year period is a representative sample.

But as John Authers points out: *"It is true that real earnings, as measured by Prof Shiller, fell sharply – according to his own measure, they fell in the 21 months from June 2007 by 86 per cent. This was the greatest fall over such a short period in all his data back to 1871. But that precipitous fall in profits only tells half the story."* And the fact is that the incredible bounce-back in company profits over the last few years is much bigger than the profits crash in 2008-09.

So, yes, there have been some incredibly big shifts in company earnings over the last ten years, *but they've been both up and down.* That's the point – and is why using 'average' company earnings over a decent period makes much more sense than taking a snapshot of a single year.

I'm in line with the folk at the *Financial Times* and *Money Week* on this, when I say that the CAPE measure remains a useful one. And at the time of writing, it suggests stocks (in the USA at least) are overvalued. To quote Shiller himself from that *Financial Times* article:

> ... *I'm a behavioural finance type, and I understand that people make all kinds of investing errors. In a purely public spirit I want to make it simple and easy. Ten years is very simple. I would have preferred to make it an exponentially weighted moving average but we tried that and it didn't seem to make any difference. You also have something that's easy to explain.*

Other critics of CAPE argue that we shouldn't use a measure that, because of differing tax rates over the years, has delivered different after-tax returns to investors. What matters, they say, are the after-tax returns.

This is a reasonable challenge. And thanks to that guy John Authers again (*Financial Times*, February 2010), we learn that Alain Bokobza (an analyst from investment bank Société Générale) undertook the grisly task of 'normalising' the data for varying corporate tax rates over the period. Those tax rates rose from 12% before 1932 to 35% in 2010, with a peak of 50% in the 1960s. And to normalise the earnings across the period he increased the tax rate in the low tax/early years and reduced it in the high years.

Those adjustments apparently give slightly less deep troughs in the CAPE, at about 6.5 for 1932, 9.9 in 1982 and 13.3 (close to the actual low) in 2009. Anyway, we're currently much higher than average, however we tweak it for long term consistency.

> Valuations change quickly and will be out of date before this book is available. Look up the latest numbers.

Yet more critics of CAPE say there's no point in using historic earnings data – it's the future that matters for where stock prices will settle. That's quite true, but no one knows the future, do they? Analyst forecasts are very often wrong (by a lot) and over-optimistic, which makes them quite useless at a danger point. At least we can see the past, it's real and in this case, we've got the data over a very long period.

The final criticism of using CAPE is around what to use as a reasonable average. In other words, where do we say the normal range should be (my green zone in the chart)?

That's tricky, because the average is simply a function of the period over which you measure it. Take the average over the 1990s and it would be a lot higher than the longer-term average.

I'm comfortable living with this minor problem in this valuation model –and I'm happy to put my green zone roughly where it is in my chart, perhaps raising the lower level to around 12 to take account of that tax normalisation issue. Look, we know that the CAPE is not a perfect indicator – and we should not expect it to be so – but it's certainly a useful one for those prepared to take the *long view* on investing. It can help us see when stock markets might have gone haywire, when valuations are at wackily cheap or expensive levels, relative to long-term history. Yes, it's rough and ready and doesn't promise any precision, unlike that truly stupid normal distribution model which is so widely used to mislead investors about risk.

CAPE, or some other similar (some prefer a dividend-based) value model, is more useful than simply saying that markets are fairly priced at all times. 'The Price is Right' was a fun family TV game with Bruce Forsyth. It should not be used as an excuse for *heavily exposing people to stock markets* regardless of the climate.

We've already looked at why some advisers (those wedded to constructing their own investment portfolios) find it difficult to develop an investment advice process that takes account of bubbles and crashes. In short, to do so could be very difficult to manage and to communicate. So they tend to stick with broadly 'static' asset allocations for a given client's risk profile, regardless of market valuations.

But who really cares about market valuations anyway?

Well, for regular savers with very long-term timescales for their money – for example, younger people saving for retirement – it's fair to say that market valuation levels don't matter very much *provided* that the market has some realistic prospect of trending upwards over the long term. And often such long-term prospects are reasonable – although, let's not forget the Japanese market experience from 1989 onwards. Their market overvaluation was so extreme and it was so slow in correcting that the returns from that market were poor, even for very long-term regular savers.

More typically, where overvaluations are corrected more quickly, then any **big falls in market prices are good news for longer-term savers.** Why? Because at those times we buy more units at a cheaper price. Indeed, such savers over the period from January 2000 to January 2015 would have made very good returns by saving into a pure UK stock market-based investment. Their returns would be well above those from ordinary cash deposits, despite the market being broadly flat overall in that time. How could this be? It's simply because the average price at which they bought into the market will have been a lot lower than the market price at the end point because the market bounced around, with two falls of around 50% in that time.

However, these big market gyrations are a much bigger worry when we're older and if we've finished putting money into our savings pots. If we're drawing quite heavily on our savings pots for income, then 'price bumpiness' of markets turns from being a friend into an enemy. Big falls in markets at this time can completely wipe out our wealth.

> The different implications of bumpy markets – for younger, regular savers versus older income seekers – are critically important to understand and are explained in Chapter 14.

Most of us (savers and investors) will sit somewhere in between these two extremes. During much of our life we'll want to: (a) protect what we've accumulated to date, perhaps with some value-based investment risk management on that part of our money whilst (b) being happy to expose our future regular savings to more of the ups and downs for reasons given above.

Point 4: There's no point trying to pick stocks or sectors; just buy the whole worldwide market with an index tracker

Let's be clear on this point. There **can be benefits** from using ultra low-cost index trackers as part of our investment. Index tracking is often called passive investing because the fund provider is not paying

a fund manager for moving our funds around. They're simply pas-
sively following the index – by buying shares in the same proportions
as they're held in the index. That said, it's not the answer to all our
investing challenges. We still need a way to balance the risks in a
stock market-based fund (whether it's passive or active) with other
lower risk investments (like cash deposits) elsewhere.

A big risk with passive investment is timing. Anyone buying into a
stock market tracking fund in December 1999 would have realised
that saving a *couple of tenths of one per cent* on the management
charge was actually a lot less important than preventing the drop of
50% in the fund value over the following few years.

But the risk is not just about whether the market as a whole is
overpriced – it's equally about whether certain sectors or shares are
overpriced. So, anyone buying an allegedly well-diversified worldwide
index-tracking fund in 1989 would have picked up a *belly full* of Japanese shares – and that would have been very painful over the next
few years, as we've already seen. And anyone who bought a FTSE
100 or S&P 500 index tracking fund in early 2000 was, as Merryn
Somerset Webb in the *Financial Times* put it, "*effectively forced to
buy big stakes in obscenely overvalued companies, with no history
of profits or even sales, as their prices rose*", and worse still, they
"*ended up under-exposed to stocks with long and proud histories
of earnings and dividend growth.*" That was the dotcom bubble in
technology stocks.

The Japanese stock market and the worldwide technology bubbles
are just two examples of what the textbooks call a 'capitalisation
weighting' problem with traditional tracker funds. Once the price of
a share has risen significantly, it makes up more of the index – and
because tracker funds must track the index they're obliged to hold
more of the stuff that's already gone up a lot in price.

Conversely, the trackers are also forced to let their holdings shrink
in those shares that have fallen out of favour and become under-
valued. And when a share falls in value so far that it falls out of the
index altogether, an index-tracking fund will have to sell it in order to
continue replicating the index. So, these tracking funds are not very
clever. They're run by computers that just copy the index.

Okay, so what about actively managed, intelligently managed, funds?

Well, there is a group – quite a large group in fact – of active fund
managers who like to hold broadly the same types of shares as are

in the index. This is because they're measured against the index and don't want to risk being too far away from it (more on that anon). Some people – less kind commentators – call these types of active fund managers 'closet index trackers' because that's all they're really doing. The trouble is that they charge more than a computer to do it!

So closet trackers generally follow the index but then they underperform it due to their costs. And, like the trackers, they get exposed to the same capitalisation weighting risks. They buy pretty much everything regardless of how ridiculously overpriced it is.

Devoted followers of passive (tracking) investing will point to studies showing that 70-80% of all active fund managers fail to beat a simple index over a reasonable time frame. And yes, these claims are true. Indeed they're not really surprising when you consider that all the closet trackers are classed as actively managed funds. However, it's also true that around 98% of footballers across Europe are not good enough to play in the premier league. But that does not mean that there are no great footballers. You just have to be careful about picking your fund manager. Pick one who does something different to everyone else (the trackers) and yes, pick several in case the one you pick breaks a leg at a critical time!

The fact is that the vast majority of funds – including 100% of index trackers – fail to beat the index over the long term because they're only aiming to match it. They copy (or closet copy) everything in the index so cannot beat it once they've taken charges for fund administration and trading. They might get close to it, and many good index funds do so, but they should certainly not beat it. Indeed, it's not their objective to beat the index, and any tracker fund that does so is not being managed properly!

When it comes to the stock market bit of our investments then we might want to look for funds that have a chance of achieving what we need them to, given current market conditions. So that might mean, for example, at a time like the late 1990s when markets were roaring up in price, that we would look for funds with a good defensive track record – that tend not to fall as fast as the overall market when it falls back. At other times (and if we have the appetite and capacity to take the risk) we might look for more aggressive funds that will bounce back after a big market fall.

Good active fund managers need a strong team behind them to investigate a whole range of factors about the companies whose shares they might hold in their funds, including the quality of the management team of those companies, their current and past profits, cash flow, debt levels and dividend payments. But critically, they'll consider the prospects on these measures for the future. Index-tracking funds do none of this – they just buy everything in the index – and yes, that can be perfectly okay as a core holding at non-extreme times, when the market is broadly fairly valued. But let's not be fooled into thinking that they're some kind of wonder investment fund in all market conditions just because they're 'cheap'. At times these trackers can be very risky funds indeed.

Also, the cost difference (between active and tracking funds) is not that significant. The difference in cost – as we can now see in the UK – is not that great once you compare them on a like-for-like basis. That means stripping out all the trail commission and front-end costs and other broker 'kick backs'. These days good quality actively managed funds are available at around 0.6% annual costs.

What bewilders me about the tracker/passive fund fanatics – many of whom are intelligent people – is the inconsistency of their actions. They clearly see the need for rebalancing our overall mix of assets (between shares, bonds, cash, property etc.) in order to control risk, yet they *don't see the need for rebalancing* the contents of the largest part of it – the equity (shares) part.

I guess this all comes back to their belief in the 'price is right' idea of efficient markets. Why would they ease us out of certain stocks or sectors if they believe that they're all correctly valued at all times?

But let's be under no illusion here. By *not* reducing our exposure to those companies or sectors with inflated values – like dotcom companies in the late 1990s – we end up with a riskier fund than holding a good, actively managed fund that does.

Point 5: We should expect some bumpiness in stock market prices

I reckon we can all agree on that point!

Point 6: We don't need to worry about market wobbles – and can predict that the chances of a really big wobble are negligible.

I think we've largely dealt with this claim, but let's just make sure.

The idea that we can ignore the possibility of very big moves in major stock markets is simply nonsense. The model used by some advisers for measuring risk may say that the chance of a 6% or more price move in a single day is only *'one day in two million years'*, but this is not the reality. There were around 15 such market moves in the S&P 500 within the space of **not two million years**, but just **two years** – and those years were right next to each other, in 2008 and 2009.

In 1987 there were shifts in market prices of more than 20 standard deviations. On 19 October that year, the S&P 500 fell by over 20% in a single day. This is completely impossible, according to the model that is used to predict market risks.

What's incredible is not that these models don't work for predicting risk – that much is obvious – but that our most highly paid and senior investment bankers ever believed that they did.

During the financial crisis that started in August 2007, David Viniar, Chief Financial Officer of Goldman Sachs, famously commented that 25 standard deviation (aka, sigma) events had occurred on several successive days. Sometime later an academic paper, 'How Unlucky is 25-Sigma?' was produced by Kevin Dowd, John Cotter, Chris Humphrey and Margaret Woods from Nottingham University Business School. They addressed the question of just how likely a single 25 standard deviation event would be – and their highly amusing paper can be found here:

www.nottingham.ac.uk/business/businesscentres/crbfs/documents/cris-reports/cris-paper-2008-3.pdf

The chances of this event – as described by Mr Viniar at Goldman Sachs, presumably based on a normal distribution model of returns – is truly breathtaking. The Nottingham University team describe it as follows:

- A 5-sigma event is equal to an expected occurrence of less than just one day in the entire period since the end of the last Ice Age,

- an 8-sigma event is equal to an expected occurrence of just once in a period, which is considerably longer than that which has elapsed since Big Bang, and

- a 20-sigma event is equal to an expected occurrence of one day in the number of years equal to ten times the likely number of particles in the universe.

These are impossibly small chances!

But wait, we're not yet at Mr Viniar's 25-sigma assessment of what happened in 2008. According to the academics, we would need to take that 20-sigma event chance and divide it by 10 – not once but … 50 times in succession.

As you can see, these chances are *unimaginably small*. So just think **how unlucky** you'd need to be for a 25 sigma event to happen **several days in a row!**

And what can we conclude from all this? Well, surely it's this: that the world's highest paid investment bankers had no idea what risks they were taking with our money.

That's a scary thought, eh? So you might want to check in with your advisers on this question of risk measurement, just to make sure that they're not working to the same risk model as Mr Viniar!

Now, I just want to finish with a thought on that bell-shaped curve, the Gaussian (aka 'normal') distribution that sits at the centre of this risk measurement problem.

The Gaussian can be very useful if it's used to predict systems that follow this sort of distribution. For example in looking at the height of humans – we know that there are no twelve foot tall giants and no one foot tall people either – at least I don't think so. The heights of most people are gathered around the average – so this sort of model works well. And we can use it in a host of ways – for example to predict the most popular shoe size of men in the UK. That's useful data for shoemakers when planning production runs.

But this is NOT a good model for predicting the behaviour of markets.

Nassim Taleb in his one of his early books *Fooled by Randomness* (Penguin 2004) tells a wonderful story about the Gaussian as follows:

I was transiting through Frankfurt airport in December 2001, on my way between Olso and Zurich. I had time to kill at the airport and it was a great occasion for me to buy dark European chocolate, especially as I have managed to successfully convince myself that airport calories don't count. The cashier handed me, among other things, a ten Deutschemark bill. The Deutsche-mark banknotes were going to be put out of circulation in a matter of days, as Europe was switching to the Euro. I kept it as a valedictory. Before the coming of the Euro, Europe had plenty of national currencies, which was good for printers, money changers, and, of course, currency traders like this (more or less) humble author. As I was eating my dark European chocolate and wistfully looking at the bill, I almost choked. I suddenly noticed, for the first time, that there was something curious. The bill bore the portrait of Karl Friedrich Gauss and the Gaussian "bell curve" smack on it.

The striking irony is that the last possible object that can be linked to the German currency is precisely such a curve: the Reichsmark (as the currency was then called) went from four per dollar to four trillion per dollar in the space of a few years during the 1920s – an outcome that tells you that the bell curve is meaningless as a description of the randomness in currency fluctuations. All you need to reject the bell curve is for such a

movement to occur once and only once – just consider the consequences. Yet there was the bell curve, and to its right Herr Professor Doktor Gauss, unprepossessing, a little stern, certainly not someone I'd want to spend time with lounging on a terrace drinking pastis and holding a conversation without a subject.

Taleb has made an excellent contribution to the debunking of traditional risk modelling theories and his books *Black Swan* and *Antifragile* are must-reads for anyone wishing to delve deeper into questions of investment risk.

Get irate!

- There is a massive elephant in the economics and finance rooms around risk definitions.

- We must accept the world as it is and stop pretending that those models give us any idea about the level of risks we're taking. Market prices do *not* follow those models. In the real world there are gigantic moves over short timescales. Bubbles and *crashes do happen,* and with far greater frequency than the bankers believed possible.

- If you invest heavily into stock markets at the peaks of bubbles you can easily have your wealth wiped out, especially if you're relying on it for regular or ad hoc fund withdrawals. Many people lose their nerve and bail out at the bottom of a crash – losing most of their wealth.

- At these times it's not only the investors who get wiped out. Many advisers are wiped out of business too. Then we all brush ourselves down, blame it all on nasty 'Mr Market' and start all over again with a new set of customers but the same old games.

- It's therefore essential to get intelligent help around investment risk and the possible outcomes.

- Precise or short-term market timing is not possible, but broad risk reduction during manias is possible and advisable. Similarly, an acceptance of increased market exposure during full-blown panics can significantly enhance subsequent returns.

- Market valuations matter, measures are available and a good investment adviser will know this.

- A purely index-tracking approach to stock market investment lacks active risk management so it may not be suitable where preservation of capital is a primary goal. However, very low cost index-tracking funds are perfectly okay in the early savings/ wealth building phase of our financial lives.

- Tracker funds cost money too so they underperform the market index they follow, albeit only by a little.

- There are no guarantees of wonderful returns with actively managed funds but, for example, a good quality UK equity income fund might outperform an index *and* reduce exposure to crash risk in the short term. These sorts of fund operate under a forced discipline of selling overbought shares, as the yield on those shares sinks below the fund's target. This is the reverse of what can happen with index-tracking funds that are forced to hold more of the more expensive shares, as we saw in the run-up to the year 2000.

- Just sticking to a fixed percentage of shares versus bonds (or adding bonds to lower risk) can be dangerous, especially at times like now, when central bank interventions are skewing the free market. Good risk management is what M&G (a leading UK investment house) calls 'episode' investing, and means taking account of valuations.

- If your adviser offers investment management services (and some charge 1% p.a. or more of your funds) ask them to compare their services to those of using simple managed funds from leading investment houses.

- Active management from a good fund manager (with vast research and analysis resources) can add real value to the risk reward profile of your funds compared to many home-grown adviser portfolios.

- Some financial advisers will tell you – like Mr Viniar – that the risks of huge short-term losses in stock markets are minimal. You may be told that it's okay to invest heavily in the stock market *regardless* of market valuations, that the 'water's lovely' at all times and you should jump right in. Others put more thought into their work.

- There's only one certainty about stock markets. **Nothing is certain.**

Final thought on tracking funds

The problems we've explored here with index-tracking funds assume that the tracking is based upon a capitalisation weighting. If you want to explore other (non-capitalisation weighted) methods of index tracking there's some research at www.cassknowledge.com/research/article/evaluation-alternative-equity-indices-cass-knowledge but *be warned – this is heavy going.*

In the next chapter...

We've seen in this chapter that some advisers are confused about the nature of risk in investments. This isn't entirely surprising given that their training has emphasised these 'normal' models in the past. But there is another, even bigger issue about investment advice – which, at the time of writing is a 'hot potato' for the UK's financial regulator (the FCA) so you really need to know about this. This is around how some advisers are failing to distinguish between your general attitude to investment risk and your 'capacity' to take that risk.

Let's explore the issue now...

Chapter 4
The temperament
temperature takers

How our attitude to investment risk is very different to our capacity to take it

We will not have any more crashes in our time.

~ John Maynard Keynes in 1927!

We saw in chapter one how our emotions, whilst making us vulnerable to the trickery of mood manipulating marketers, are also immensely useful for alerting us to the things that **really matter** in our lives. But let's be clear up front here: we should *not* rely on emotional decision-making for choosing investment assets. Sadly, though, that's exactly what we very often do.

We tend to feel happier when our investments rise in value. And this happiness 'wealth effect' has been deliberately engineered by our central banks ever since our collective spending habits ground to a halt in the financial crisis of 2008-09. Part of their plan, by providing support for asset prices, is to make those of us with assets, feel a bit richer in the hope that we'll re-start our spending and stop the economy from collapsing again.

Now, I think we should leave the economists to work out what positive impact, if any, this will have on our whole economy over the longer term – and there's certainly an argument that in giving life support to weak businesses, we're weakening our economy – but that's another story. What we can say is that rising asset prices tempt us to buy more of them. Indeed, we're generally much happier to invest in risky assets *after* they've risen in price. And we positively pile in to buying them after they've risen by a *significant* amount.

Of course, this makes no sense at all. It's like going mad with our shopping in the sales – but rather than waiting for discounts, we wait until the prices have gone up!

© Copyright Paul Claireaux

As crazy as this sounds, it's what most people do with stock market investing – as we can see in the chart below. ***This is the scariest picture I know about our investment behaviours.*** This chart shows you the net sales of stock market-based retail investment funds against the year-end level of the UK stock market. Retail funds are those we buy as individual investors, as opposed to the lower-cost institutional funds bought by the big pension funds and insurance companies.

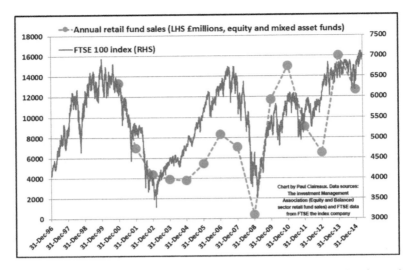

What this shows you is that our appetite for stock market-based investing goes up and down almost exactly in line with the level of the market itself. And this trend goes back a very long way – the chart only shows the last 14 years' worth of sales data, but it proves quite conclusively that we repeatedly make the most fundamental mistake of all when it comes to investing.

We buy high and we sell low.

Take a close look at the numbers on the left-hand scale of the chart. We're talking about tens of billions of pounds' worth of badly timed investments here. Not once, but twice (and possibly three times) in just the past 14 years. This is what happens when people are hyped up on 'happiness' emotions whilst having their temperature taken for new investments.

You might hope that your adviser – if you have one – would prevent you from doing silly things like this, piling into the markets with all those 'daft' investors at the top. After all, why would an adviser let you sink your life's savings into the stock market just before it drops by 50%? (In fact, the fall in the value of technology funds, which were all the rage in 1999, was closer to 80% between 2000 and 2003). And _good advisers_ will warn you against over-exposure to stock markets and certain sectors at times of obvious high valuations, like 1998-99 and 2007 – but as we saw in the previous chapter, quite a few advisers won't do this. They refuse to offer an opinion on the question of market value. Their 'perfect market' theory says that markets are always priced correctly, and their message is that if you want the best returns, you just have to 'get in there and stay there for the long haul'.

The debate will rage on as to whether there's any point in adjusting our market exposure – not daily, but over longer periods of time – according to broad market value measures. But there can be little doubt that we need to learn how to control our passion for risk at those times when markets have already risen significantly above any reasonable level of value.

Dan Ariely is Professor of Psychology & Behavioural Economics at Duke University in Durham, North Carolina, and author of the *New York Times* bestseller *Predictably Irrational*. He has a lot to say about making decisions in a heightened emotional state. Ariely worked with George Loewenstein to produce research called 'The Heat of the Moment: The Effect of Sexual Arousal on Sexual Decision Making', which shows just how crazy our ideas become when we're excited and aroused. I'll leave you to look that one up!

More generally, Ariely points out that the heat of the moment is an awful time for decision making, and our emotions can often drive us to bad decisions, such as shooting off annoyed emails to our boss, fighting with spouses and selling everything in the stock market at the bottom of a crash. He has also described the methods used to determine our attitude to investment risk (ATR) as "absurd". He points out, quite correctly, that most people tend to put themselves somewhere close to the middle of the risk scale, presumably because we believe that the middle is somehow normal.

This may have something to do with the weakness of particular ATR questionnaires – a tool used by advisers to measure our general investment risk appetite (some are better than others). But perhaps Ariely's criticism doesn't go far enough. Over recent years, the methods used by some advisers for assessing a suitable level of investment risk have not just been absurd – they've been positively dangerous.

So let's look at this issue in a bit more detail.

The ATR questionnaire is, unfortunately, used by some advisers as the sole basis for deciding which investments to recommend. The result from the questionnaire may, for example, show that our investment risk profile is 'cautious' (shown as say, a level 3 on a risk scale of 1 to 10). Another person may be categorised as having a 'balanced' (level

5 or 6) risk profile whilst another may be classed as 'adventurous' (level 8 or 9).

If you take advice on investments it's likely that you'll undergo some kind of ATR assessment. In any event you should be told, in a language that you can understand, what this means in terms of the investment assets your adviser would then recommend. The feedback you receive on your ATR assessment may be something like this example – for an investor with a balanced risk profile:

You would be likely to accept moderate risk with your longer-term investments for growth or income if this gives the potential for higher returns.

You would probably feel comfortable with an investment that includes a high level of stock market-linked investments, including some over-seas shares.

You understand and accept that the value of your investment may go up and down and that on final encashment you might get back less than you invested.

And this is all fine as far as it goes, but it's really not much use if you're planning for a specific financial goal (such as building a fund for retirement or to help a child through university). These ATR questionnaires do not, typically, take account of some critically important factors for determining an **appropriate** level of investment risk.

Let's look at how these factors should affect how you invest. We'll take a fictional investor, Chris, who has a 'balanced' attitude to risk according to his ATR questionnaire results. A 'balanced' ATR on some scales would mean that it's okay for Chris' money to be in funds that invest up to 85% in the stock market.

> In the next chapter, we'll question whether an 85% expo-sure to risky stock market based assets is reasonable for someone with a 'balanced' attitude to investment risk!

Investment 1

Chris is investing most of his non-pension money for six years, after which he'll need the funds to help his child through university. Chris would like to achieve a return above what he'd get from a bank or building society account, but it's important to protect these funds from severe losses because he has no other funds to draw on for this goal.

Despite the ATR questionnaire result, a typical balanced fund with about 85% exposure to risky assets would clearly **not be appropriate** for this situation: Chris does not have the 'capacity' to take this level of risk with this investment. He really cannot afford for these funds to fall far short of what he needs to help his child.

Investment 2

Chris is making a regular monthly payment into a personal pension, which he plans to keep in force for the next 20 years, to age 60. He will pay increasing amounts into it over time and accepts that he cannot access these funds for *around 17* years (at age 57).

Clearly it's **no big deal if investment fund prices (in Chris' pension) fall in the short term.** In fact, in many ways, this would be a good thing, as his ongoing payments would then buy units at reduced cost which could deliver a better overall investment return. An adventurous fund (100% exposed to stock markets and thus higher risk but with higher potential returns) might be perfectly suitable for this situation.

So, we can see that the result of the ATR questionnaire gives the wrong answer for *both* of Chris' investments!

That's not to say that the ATR is a waste of time – it's not. It's a perfectly good starting point for understanding your risk appetite. But that's all it is – a starting point from which you should take other factors into account to arrive at the most suitable risk profile for each of your investment goals.

It may sound incredible, but our financial regulator (the Financial Services Authority, FSA – now renamed the Financial Conduct Authority, FCA) only picked up on this fundamental problem with how investment advice was delivered in 2011. Before that there was no clear guidance to advisers that a single ATR measure was not good enough when considering suitable investments for various life goals.

The FSA has since issued a special update, stating the importance of considering the investors' **'capacity for risk' (CFR)** as well as their general attitude to it. And whilst some advisers were on top of this issue long before 2011, they were not in the majority and the FCA is still (four years on!) finding lots of errors in this aspect of advice.

So it's essential to understand this issue and to make sure that your adviser, if you use one, is up to speed on it. You really don't want them to blindly slot your money into the wrong risk category based upon a general attitude to risk (ATR) assessment.

Determining your own capacity for risk is not a precise science because some factors increase it, while others reduce it. However, it's simple enough to understand the general direction of risk – higher or lower – you could move towards, depending on each factor. And it's certainly worth the minimal effort to improve your investment decision making.

Let's look at those factors now.

Let's assume that your generalised ATR – using one of those questionnaires – has been measured as 'balanced' (most are!) and then consider whether to adjust your risk profile (up or down) for any **specific** investment goal you have in mind.

Term to the selected goal

If you're investing over the long term (say 15 years+), then you can consider increasing your risk profile (assuming the ATR is not already a high one) because any short-term market falls will have time to recover.

> I assume here that markets are trading at fair value. See Chapter 3 for more on this.

Conversely, if your investment horizon is shorter than, say, ten years, this might suggest you have a lower capacity for risk. If you've a lump sum investment that you'll encash fully within five years, I would question whether it makes sense to hold any risky assets at all.

Access required

If there's a good chance that you'll need access to your capital earlier than your intended investment term, or if you're planning to take a high percentage of regular withdrawals from the investment, then this suggests a lower capacity for risk.

Besides 'investment' risk issues, you also need to take account of product wrapper legislative restrictions to accessing your capital. So, for example, with a UK pension plan it's not normally possible to access your funds before you turn 55 (a limit that's planned to be raised in line with ten years before state pension age in the future). You would normally decide which 'box' (e.g. pension or ISA) is most suitable for each savings goal, at the start of your financial planning process. But this is an iterative process. So you may start by assuming that you'll use one type of box for your money to reach a particular savings goal, only to find a better solution (using a different type of box) once you're into the detailed planning.

Proportion of total investment pot

You might have a higher capacity for risk if you're only investing a small proportion of your investable funds, **and** you plan to keep the rest in low-risk assets such as bank deposits. Conversely, if you're investing a large proportion of your total funds, then you might consider lowering your risk compared to your generalised ATR.

Lump sum versus regular (and/or phased) investment

Some investment product providers provide a feature that allows you to 'phase' your money into a risk-based investment over a few weeks or months. This can be a helpful technique to reduce any very short-term worries about market wobbles, but it should **not** affect your capacity for risk because you're not spreading your timing risk over much of the intended term.

However, if you phase your money into the market (for example by regular payments) over several years, then this would suggest a higher capacity for risk. Conversely if you invest a lump sum on a single day, it might tend to push you towards a lower capacity for risk.

When deciding how much investment risk is appropriate – for any given savings or investment goal – you might need to consider any or all of these factors.

Get irate!

It's dangerous to be led by your emotions when making decisions on investment risk. The markets don't care how you feel and can brutally punish over-optimism.

Attitude to risk (ATR) questionnaires only tell you about your broad attitude to investment risk on one particular day. An overly optimistic mood about markets might change quickly (as might those of your adviser!) when markets fall suddenly, by say 20% or more.

You need to understand your 'capacity for risk' (CFR) for **each** of your various financial goals. It may be completely different for each goal, as it was for Chris in our example.

Make sure that your adviser is on top of this 'capacity for risk' issue. Not enough of them are.

In the next chapter, we'll see how 'balanced' funds that have been sold over many years were not always, exactly what you might have expected.

Chapter 5
Fully invested fund managers

Why some of your investments may be 'hotter' than you expected

October is one of the peculiarly dangerous months to speculate in stocks. The others are July, January, September, April, November, May, March, June, December, August and February.

~ Mark Twain

© Copyright Paul Claireaux

Now we'll explore an important issue about investment risk – and this relates to whoever manages your investments – be it a fund manager, stockbroker or financial adviser.

If you'd like to read a basic outline of the main types of investment asset before you get started here, read Appendix 3 first.

The easiest way to explain this crucial issue is by using an example – so I'd like you to imagine that it's the summer of 2009. You're enjoying your holidays, but you're slightly troubled by the need to do something with some money you've recently inherited. You'd like to invest it for growth for the next ten years to top up the funds you expect you'll need in retirement. The money is currently sitting on deposit at the bank and, frustratingly, is earning virtually no interest at all. And whilst you don't want to take on too much risk, you're keen to obtain a better return. But you're nervous about investments generally – this is **2009**, remember – and whilst you don't know it yet, you've just been through one of the worst financial crises in living memory. (And as of summer 2015 – I'm not sure it's over yet!)

Thankfully, you've had no exposure to stock market risks recently. Your main investment, other than that money on deposit and your home, is your defined benefit (DB) pension, which, as we'll see later, promises you a specific level of pension income (for each year you're in the scheme) when you retire. So you have no worries about nasty investment and interest rate risks there. Your employer deals with all that and you feel that you have everything under control on the pension front.

Now, you've spoken to a financial adviser about ideas for investing the money sitting idly in your bank account, and he's suggested you consider putting it into some kind of collective fund. This would give you a spread of investments – to avoid having *all your eggs in one basket* – and would also give you lower-cost access to the markets than buying your own small selection of securities. What's more, it will avoid the headache of having to choose which securities to buy – you wouldn't know where to start with that. Your adviser can help you find a suitable collective fund and he suggests that you hold this inside an Individual Savings Account (ISA) wrapper to **save tax** on both the income and any capital growth.

Whilst the amount you have to invest is several times the amount of the annual ISA allowance, your adviser shows you a clever wheeze to get the growth you want on all your investment now, and over time, making it all tax efficient too.

The plan is to put all your investment money into a 'suitable' fund now, with part being placed under the ISA wrapper (to use up this year's allowance) and the rest into the same fund but outside the ISA wrapper. The non-ISA funds are then moved into the ISA wrapper in stages as your ISA allowance is renewed each year.

Okay, so this is now shaping up to be a reasonable plan but you're still nervous about stock market investment and decide to think on this a while longer. You don't follow the stock market that closely but you do know that it plunged by around 50% over the last 18 months (from the summer of 2007), and that the price falls in the winter of 2008-09 were quite horrific. One of your friends was so worried about her investments at that time that she sold out of them completely and suffered some very heavy losses. So you have another conversation with the adviser, this time about investment risk, and you take one of those 'attitude to risk' (ATR) tests – which shows that your ATR is mid-range or 'balanced'. The adviser says that this is reassuringly similar to most people (now there's a surprise).

The good news is that your adviser is well aware of the need to determine your capacity for risk (CFR) for this specific investment, not just your general attitude to risk. He points out that, given the likely ten-year duration of your investment, the balanced investment approach is probably right.

You agree that you certainly do *not* want to go all in on the stock market – given your concerns and your friend's experience – so a balanced approach sounds about right to you too.

The adviser recommends the ABC balanced managed fund for your money and shows you how it performed during the recent stock market crash in 2008-09 to demonstrate its defensive qualities. You see that the fund did suffer a modest fall in value at that time, but only by about 16% compared to the 50% fall in the wider stock market over the same period. Your adviser says this means you're exposed to less than one third of the risk in the stock market. The adviser also points out how the ABC fund price has since recovered its losses and is now up 12% in the two years since the summer of 2007. The wider market, by comparison, is still down by 25%.

So, this looks like a very attractive investment – the ABC fund is clearly lower risk than those racier pure stock market funds that your friend had complained about. And it's also delivering good performance relative to the miserly rates on offer in bank deposits. All in all it sounds ideal and means that the hassles of deciding which assets to buy and sell, when to do so *and* in what proportions are all dealt with by an expert – a fund manager.

But before you jump in, you want to understand a bit more about how a fund manager can possibly deliver that sort of performance, in bad times as well as good. Frankly, it sounds a bit too good to be true!

Now I'm going to show your adviser's explanation about the ABC fund in italics below. I'll put my own observations indented in square brackets beneath each comment.

Your adviser's explanation of why this fund performs so well...

The total returns on the ABC balanced fund – like any fund – are driven by the types of asset it holds. This fund contains a mix of around 50% growth assets (company shares) and 50% 'safer' assets (fixed interest bonds).

[This sounds okay up to a point, but the safety of the safer (bond) element of a fund depends on various factors including: the quality of the bonds inside the fund, the expectations for future interest rates and inflation and currently, the extent to which the market for bonds has been distorted by central bank money printing – aka quantitative easing.]

The growth (riskier) part of the fund is invested in the shares of a range of blue chip companies, such as Vodafone, Rolls-Royce or M&S, whilst the fixed interest (safer) part is invested in a mix of bonds issued (a) by similarly large and secure companies and (b) by our own and other stable country governments.

And government-issued bonds (called Gilts in the UK) are the safest asset money can buy because governments in the UK or USA, for example, do not default on their debt.

[Oh dear, this adviser is confusing a direct holding of gilts with buying a fund – see Appendix 3 for more details. The thing is that bond funds do not typically have maturity dates like individual gilts, and are **not** guaranteed. They can and do fall in value – especially when longer-term interest rates are starting to rise.]

The shares provide most of the growth when markets are rising – together with some additional return from the income on those shares (the dividends) and income from the bonds. The safer part of the fund alone will produce a higher return than bank deposits.

[This is wrong. The safer part of your fund is not completely safe and will not **necessarily** produce higher returns than bank deposits. Indeed, at the time of writing (summer 2015) long-term bond funds are generally seen as quite risky due to the market distortion mentioned above.]

If stock markets fall, then only half the fund – the 50% in shares – is exposed to the fall. However, the fall is cushioned by the additional income from the shares (the dividends) and the income from the bonds, and is further cushioned from the price of the bonds rising, which is what they tend to do when share prices fall. This diversification – with uncorrelated assets – reduces your risk as the prices of shares and bonds move in opposite directions.

[Now the adviser is getting far too excited. It's wrong to suggest that bonds always go up as share prices fall. This certainly happens some of the time, but not all of the time, as investors have found out during past major market crises, and as we've started to find out again in 2015. When a bond market bull run finishes, then bond prices and share prices can both fall together – and by a lot.]

So, this all explains why the ABC fund only fell by one third of the fall in the stock market during the worst of times and has recovered strongly since.

[Clearly it doesn't!]

I pay close attention to what the manager reports about this ABC fund – and it's clear that he intends to hold this defensive (50-50) positioning of this fund between

*bonds and shares quite steadily over time. This means
that if the growth part of the fund surges ahead, he'll
sell off the profits on that part and allocate the proceeds
to the safer portion. This will prevent the fund becoming
any riskier as markets rise.*

[I guess we'll see about that!]

Right, so that's the end of the sales pitch from your financial adviser
on the wonderful ABC fund. Please try to imagine you only got to hear
his comments – which I guess might be quite convincing to many
people – and that you couldn't hear me whispering in your ear.

Fast-forward to spring 2010 and stock markets have taken a nasty
tumble, falling back by about 17% at one point. Central bank leaders
in the UK and the USA make some reassuring comments about continuing their policy of very low interest rates and the markets start to
recover.

But you're feeling very shaken. You notice that your fund fell in value
by about 12% during this market pull back – that's far more than half
the amount that the market fell. You were expecting no more than a
third of any falls. So you call your adviser to find out what's going on.
He reassures you that this is simply a one-off blip and that the fund
manager has everything under control. He suggests that you look
back at the track record of the fund he gave you when you invested
and that you should stop worrying, saying *"Just forget about these
minor wobbles, sit back and relax."*

Then in summer 2011, stock markets fall hard again – this time by
nearly 20% – and your fund falls by 17%, almost as much as the
market. Now you're really worried and you demand a proper explanation from your adviser. He says he'll investigate and a few days later
he comes back with a report of the current assets held in your fund.

It turns out that your fund is now 85% invested in higher risk assets
(shares), not the 50% you were expecting. And this means you're now
exposed to most of any downturns in the stock market.

You ask how this could possibly have been allowed to happen. You're
told that the fund is in the 'balanced' sector, which means that the
manager is allowed to invest up to 85% of it in shares. And that's
exactly what he's done as the market has risen. Apparently the fund
manager felt that this was the right thing to do because the safer

portion (the bonds) had become overvalued and seemed to be presenting too high a risk.

Right, so now you're utterly confused and really struggling to understand what on earth is going on with your money. How can a *rising* stock market result in the fund manager taking *more* risk? And how can the *safer* portion of the fund become *high risk?* The adviser clearly told you that in a rising market, your fund manager would take the profits on the growth assets and allocate the proceeds to safer assets. But this is exactly the opposite of what's happened. So you talk to your adviser again and remind him of his assurance that the fund would not go over 50% in risky assets.

He denies having said anything of the kind, and emails you a copy of the 'key investor information' document. This clearly states that the fund manager can indeed raise the proportion in equities up to 85%, if he so wishes. You agree to disagree with your adviser on what was said at your original meeting, and seriously consider making a formal complaint and, if necessary, taking this to the financial ombudsman.

But you don't bother – you know you don't have a leg to stand on. After all, you signed all the paperwork for this investment which said you'd read the key information document before investing, despite the fact that you hadn't read a word of it – you'd just taken everything on trust. You feel severely let down – partly by your adviser but mostly by yourself – and decide to encash your investment a few weeks later. Unfortunately there was quite a high initial charge on your investment and the value you get back is no more than what you put in two years ago.

You vow never to leave the safety of bank deposits again.

The madness of 'balanced' funds

This story is sadly quite common, with several unfortunate elements including some misleading statements from the adviser about the safety of balanced funds and in particular about the safer (bond) element.

As it turned out, over this period of time bond funds have done okay, so the misleading statements had no consequences on this element of the investment. But the risks in these 'safer' funds will be revealed as market interest rates rise again – as they are starting to do now, summer 2015.

The key point here is that it's just plain mad – given that stock markets can and do fall by 50% occasionally – for a fund described as 'balanced' to be allowed to invest up to 85% in shares. This is too high a risk level for someone with a moderate or balanced capacity for investment risk. Since when was an 85% holding in risky assets considered to be a balanced proportion? Well, I'm afraid that's been the limit for a great many years.

The good news is that the fund management industry now agrees with us. In 2011 it abandoned the term 'balanced' and replaced it with the rather bland – but more descriptive – term, *mixed investment 40-85% shares.* Yes, I know that's not a very inspiring name for a fund – and it certainly wouldn't pass Sally Hogshead's test for emotionally attractive marketing labels! But at least it describes on the tin what the fund might do.

The Investment Management Association (IMA) and Association of British Insurers (ABI) have now both relabelled all their mixed/managed fund sectors to make them easier to understand.

The ABI governs the description of funds within insurance-based product wrappers whilst the IMA governs things within the pure fund industry.

Here are the four new mixed-asset fund sectors with their previous names in brackets:

1. Flexible investment (active managed)

2. Mixed investment 40-85% shares (balanced managed)

3. Mixed investment 20-60% shares (cautious managed)

4. Mixed investment 0-35% shares (no previous sector)

Interestingly, the ABI had originally proposed naming the first of these sectors 'mixed investment 60-100% shares' – that is, they'd planned to use the same approach as the other sectors. This might have made it clearer as to how risky some of the 'flexible' funds can be. However, this category of funds can also include much lower risk funds that may sometimes reduce their equity holdings to near zero. Giving the sector the name 'mixed investment 0-100% shares' wouldn't have offered any insights into the riskiness of these funds, so they've opted for the 'flexible' name instead.

The key thing with all these sectors is to *understand the fund manager's investment objective* – as described in the key information document.

Now, that figure of 85% in shares for the old balanced funds was just a maximum – so you might assume that at most times the fund manager would hold a much lower proportion in risky assets. And you might reasonably hope that he would lower the risk exposure as markets rose to higher valuations, as promised earlier by your adviser. But as we've seen, you simply cannot rely on all fund managers to do this, and there's every chance that your balanced fund will hold something near the maximum 85% in shares at the very worst of times, when markets crash from an all-time high.

The reason for this apparently absurd behaviour (of taking on more risk with our funds at times of market euphoria) is really quite simple: the fund manager is incentivised to do precisely this. Let's see why that is.

Why fund manager take big risks with our money

Towards the end of a bull market a good many leading fund managers in the mixed-asset fund sector will necessarily hold a high proportion of high risk/high return assets in their funds. It's only by holding a lot of these assets that they can (ordinarily) have outperformed their competitors during the bull run. Fund managers who reduced their holdings in risky assets during the early part of the bull run will have underperformed their competitors. And most fund managers do not like to risk underperformance for fear of the consequences (see below).

This means – just like our economists – that a lot of fund managers of mixed asset funds converge towards a single view. They end up with very similar (maximum) holdings in risky assets, right at the riskiest of times. And whilst this is not what most of us might expect from a balanced fund, you'll recall from earlier chapters how the 'perfect markets' theory will tell the fund manager that asset prices are always generally about right. So, he/she doesn't need to worry about these risky times or that bubbles might have blown up and be about to burst. In the land of perfect markets, bubbles don't exist!

But what about the odd occasion when, as we all know, reality gets in the way of this theory? In other words, when Mr Market decides to misbehave, a bubble does inflate **and** bursts and blows our funds away in the process. What then?

Well, by sticking to the theory, the fund manager can simply blame **market failure.** And that's certainly a lot less painful (for them at least) than taking any responsibility for misjudging market values. You see, most of these fully invested mixed funds will fall at a similar rate to each other during a market crash. So their position, **relative to the other funds in the same sector,** isn't much affected by it. They all go down together. And that means that there's very little incentive to ease out of risky assets whilst markets are booming.

This was the exactly the logic offered by Chuck Prince (former CEO of the Citi Group) when he made his infamous remark to the *Financial Times* in July 2007 that, *"when the music stops (in liquidity terms), things will be complicated – but as long as the music is playing, you've got to get up and dance. We're still dancing."*

Mr Prince was answering questions about potential problems in the US subprime mortgage market. The subprime loans were those made by irresponsible banks to very low-income borrowers who never stood a chance of making the repayments. When those loans – which by clever packaging into securities had been spread around the world's banking system – started going bad, there was a worldwide collapse in those banks and the whole world economy was brought to its knees.

Not knowing that we're taking too much risk with a mixed-asset fund in our investments may be less serious for the world economy, but it's still a big issue for our personal finances.

Okay, so we've just seen how mixed-asset fund managers have an incentive to increase risk levels on their funds during market booms. Indeed such behaviour is generally accepted (by industry insiders) as the market rule. You may find that hard to believe but it's perfectly true. Let me tell you what happened to one of the UK's most respected fund managers when he went against that rule.

The sad but true story of 'Dr Doom'

Tony Dye was the Chief Investment Officer of Phillips & Drew, one of the largest UK pension fund managers, between 1985 and 2000. He was a well-known figure in the investment industry and held strong and controversial opinions about the outlook for global stock markets. In the mid-1990s those markets were soaring, but Dye was convinced that they'd become overinflated and that the bubble was going to burst.

His views, not surprisingly, put him at odds with much of the rest of the investment management community, earning him the nickname 'Dr Doom'. In 1995, as the FTSE 100 approached 4,000, Dye started making the case that markets were becoming too expensive. Then in 1996 he began to move large sums (tens of billions of pounds in today's money) of his pension fund clients' money out of equities and into safer assets – cash deposits and bonds.

In the three years after 1996, stock markets continued soaring higher, driven by optimism about the new millennium and the potential for enhanced company earnings from the latest new technologies. But Dye stuck to his guns and shunned the high-growth, high-risk internet stocks, keeping large positions in those safer assets. Because of this, his funds started to underperform their more fully invested rivals; by 1999, this previously leading fund manager was ranked 66th out of 67 institutions in the performance tables.

Phillips & Drew were losing some very big clients who were tired of the underperformance of their pension funds and bored by Tony Dye's doom-laden predictions.

In February 2000, just weeks after the FTSE 100 index had broken through an all-time high of 6,900 points, Dye was sacked. Days later, his prophesy came true: stock markets started a three-year slump, which took more than 50% off global values.

The Phillips & Drew funds were well protected at this time of course, as they held a lot of those safer assets. And as many other funds saw their values cut in half by market falls, the Phillips & Drew funds climbed straight back to the top of the performance tables. More impressive still was the fact that the Phillips & Drew pension funds had risen steadily between 1996 and 2006. They grew more slowly than other funds in the final burst of the stock market bull run up to 2000, but then they didn't crash when the others did.

Tony Dye's predictions of a market crash were right – and whilst he was about three years too early in calling it, he might well have been proved right much earlier.

A crisis in Asian economies in 1997 and then a collapse of a multi-billion dollar hedge fund – Long-Term Capital Management (LTCM) – in 1998, hit the world's stock markets so hard that central banks decided to rescue the situation by slashing interest rates to record lows and arranging a rescue of the LTCM fund. This saved stock markets from immediate collapse and delayed the inevitable correction to their wildly overvalued prices.

So Dye had to wait until after his sacking in 2000 to be vindicated.

After leaving Phillips & Drew, Dye continued offering apparently controversial views on market valuations. At the end of 2002, he wrote to the *Financial Times* predicting a house price crash in the UK, on a similar scale to the house price slump of the early 1990s, saying that at least 30% would be wiped off the value of the average residential property. Falls of more than this figure did occur in the USA and other countries, but only after that asset bubble had inflated for several more years up to 2007.

His prophecy for correction in house prices has yet to come true in the UK, but it might just do so, when our interest rates return to more normal levels.

Tony Dye was right about bubbles blowing up and their subsequent bursting, but because he called these events too early, he lost his job. Fund managers know this story and very few are about to vote for their own dismissal by being out of risky assets in a raging bull market. And in fairness to fund managers, it's difficult to operate any other way. Think what would have happened to Tony Dye's remaining clients if he'd been wrong: if markets had, like the theory says, been correctly priced throughout those boom years and hadn't crashed in the early 2000s.

Phillips & Drew clients would have been stuck with poor performance relative to the herd and would probably have all gone to other, more aggressive, fund managers. This, after all, is what was already happening in the run-up to Dye's sacking. Phillips & Drew *were* losing clients in the late 1990s due to his cautious approach.

So I'm not sure we can expect many fund management groups to behave the way we'd like them to, and to take some risk off the table on their mixed-asset funds when markets are booming. Some good fund managers are brave enough to do so, but many are not. Fund managers are caught between a rock and a hard place – and to mix my metaphors, it's because we want our cake and to eat it too. We demand strong performance at all times when the stock market is racing up. We are not interested in modestly good performance at these times.

If this is how we operate, then we must be ready to accept only cake crumbs on our table if markets collapse whilst we're fully invested.

Get irate!

- Most managers of mixed-asset funds will maximise their holdings of higher risk assets (subject to any limits) to maximise their returns during bull runs.

- A fund that before 2011 carried a 'balanced' label is allowed to hold up to 85% in shares. If you hold such funds you need to review them to see if they're still suitable for your needs. Most providers have alternative, lower-risk fund options you can switch into if it's appropriate to your circumstances.

- Alternatively, you can control the mix between risky and safer assets yourself and/or with an adviser. You can buy discrete funds for each asset type (shares, property, bonds and cash deposits) to create the asset mix you want for your own risk/return profile. But if you follow this approach, make sure that there's robust ongoing management and rebalancing of your portfolio. Without that, your exposure to risk could change significantly over time.

- It's easy to let our emotions get the best of us during strong bull or bear markets – and to become overexposed to risk at high market points or to sell out at the bottom of a crash.

- Three of the four new mixed-asset fund sector definitions are clear about the amounts that can be held in shares. But remember - the fourth sector ('flexible' investment) can hold up to 100% in shares.

- Try to understand how your fund manager manages your funds, the benchmarks they try to beat and the maximum and minimum levels of 'risky type' assets they can use.

- Shares are generally higher risk assets – but so are bonds sometimes!

- Lower-risk mixed-asset funds are likely to be of more interest to you if you have a lower **'capacity for investment risk'** (CFR) – perhaps because you're nearing your investment goal horizon and/or plan to take regular withdrawals from your funds.

- Using higher yielding investments can also reduce the risk of loss if you're taking a regular income from your funds – provided you don't want to access a large proportion of your capital.

- Higher risk, pure stock market-based funds may be more suitable than lower risk funds when you're younger **and** you have a long time horizon for investing ahead of you **and** when you're paying into your investment plan on a regular basis – rather than in one lump sum. However, this assumes that you're not starting out on your savings journey at some extremely high point of market valuation (like Japan in 1989).

- That said, many first-time investors and savers prefer to see their savings making positive progress each year – and in this case a more cautiously managed fund may be a good first step into risk-based investing.

Coming up in the next chapter

You'll learn how some advisers seriously overcharge for financial advice – and what you can do about it – to save yourself thousands of pounds in the future.

Chapter 6
Hard-nosed, overcharging sales people

How to save yourself thousands in unnecessary advice charges

Nothing is as irritating as the fellow who chats pleasantly while he's overcharging you.

~ Kin Hubbard

© Copyright Paul Claireaux

In this chapter we're going to talk about overcharging and poor quality advice – so let's be clear about the scale of the problem up front.

These issues do not apply to all financial advisers. There are plenty of good (and some very good) advisers offering valuable advice – and some offer it at a reasonable price. However, some 'rogue' advisers will rip you off if you're not careful – so it's important to understand this stuff. Let's get started.

You might compare a rogue adviser's service to a teapot. Not the traditionally useless 'chocolate teapot' – although that analogy also applies – but rather one of those stainless steel types.

If you've ever stopped for a cup of tea in a motorway service station then you'll understand perfectly how this relates to excessive charging for financial advice. With those teapots it is possible to pour *some* of your tea into your cup *some* of the time, but a large proportion of it ends up on the table, and invariably some of it runs off to burn your legs. Those teapots are badly designed yet somehow they survive. Perhaps this is because we don't complain enough when we get hurt! Either way, this is exactly how the bad parts of the financial services industry work – they rely upon our inertia and we end up losing a lot of our tea (I mean money) in charges.

Continuing the fun with analogies we could also describe the advisers who push these expensive teapots as the 'rhinos' of the financial services industry. They are very thick-skinned – so they don't genuinely care for our well-being – and they charge a lot!

Indeed, it's not just the rhino's skin that's thick either. There remains a small (and thankfully dwindling) population of financial salespeople out there with only a basic understanding of the core subjects (pensions, protection, investments, risk, tax and trusts), so the scope of their advice is very limited.

Or rather, it should be.

And, the truth is that some financial advice firms are only superficially about providing advice. Their core objective is to **increase product sales** and maximise the value of their Funds Under Advice – or FUA as they call it. Of course, there's nothing *necessarily* wrong with paying advice charges as a percentage of your funds – unless those charges are unreasonably high given the advice you receive. And that's where you need to look out, because a small increase in that % charge can make a massive difference to the amount you'll pay over the years.

Financial product sales-focused firms compete with each other to recruit the best salespeople – the people that can bring in the FUA – and this has bid up the earnings/bonus levels of their 'high fliers' to eye-watering levels. Some of these salespeople earn several thousand pounds for half a day's work.

Now that would *not* be a massive problem if their work delivered very high added value, or if it required extremely advanced skills and knowledge to complete some complex analysis. We might then liken their work to that of a surgeon – and I talk from experience – where we accept their high fees because we need their expertise. But this is not the case with much of what goes on in these 'rhino' advice firms. A lot of their analysis is very straightforward – and in many cases it is easy enough for you to do yourself using basic calculation tools.

Overcharging has not been the only problem at some of these investment product sales firms in recent years. Some of them, including some *leading high street banks,* have been busy pushing variously described guaranteed or secure products. Billions of pounds worth of these products have been sold by promoting juicy headline interest rates, whilst playing down the risks.

Unfortunately, many of these products are very risky indeed. For example, did you know that your entire investment is at risk if the underlying asset provider (normally an investment bank) goes bust?

> Lehman Brothers was an investment bank that provided assets for such investment products – before it went belly up in 2008.

So we need to be sceptical about promises of guaranteed returns. A guarantee is only as good as the institution providing the underlying assets – and no one guarantees their survival, as we saw with Lehman Brothers.

Now, the UK's financial regulator – previously named the Financial Services Authority (FSA) and now called the Financial Conduct Authority (FCA) – has done a lot to clean up the financial advice industry in recent years. It has raised the threshold for technical qualifications – which has pushed some of the least competent advisers out of the industry – and made advice charges more transparent, as we'll see in the next chapter. It has also aggressively seeking out the more serious financial advice failures, and is now imposing severe multi-million pound fines on organisations that fail to give suitable advice to their customers.

We really need to understand that advice failings have been widespread for many years and some of the largest firms in the UK (those selling tens of thousands of investment products) have been identified as failing on some very basic issues, such as:

- Failing to explain clearly why recommended investments were considered to be suitable.

- Failing to gather sufficient information from customers before making investment recommendations, including failure to confirm how much investment risk its customers were prepared to take.

- Failing to match their customers' stated investment objectives (and attitude to risk) to the product sold.

- Failing to explain the level of risk the customer would be taking.

- Failing to check that their customers could manage financially if their investment fell in value. (That's the 'capacity for risk' issue again.)

- Telling customers that their income or capital growth on their investments was guaranteed – when it was not.

- Failing to advise customers how product charges would affect the returns they could expect from their investment.

The FCA is particularly concerned about the advice and sales activities in the wealth management and private banking sectors – and it has set up a new division to monitor it and clamp down where necessary. Specifically, the FCA is concerned about conflicts of interest, with many of these advisers selling mainly in-house products rather than researching and selecting suitable products from the whole market.

The FCA is clearly on the warpath with wealth managers, after its predecessor (the FSA) noted serious concerns about this adviser group as long ago as 2011. In its thematic review at that time, it looked into Centralised Investment Propositions' (CIPs), where advice is typically combined with a Discretionary Fund Management Service (DFM), and found "widespread failings" across the 17 wealth management firms reviewed. Indeed, of the 181 investment files analysed, the FSA found that the advice was "unsuitable" in 33 cases, "unclear" in 103 cases and the quality of disclosure (about charges) was "unacceptable" in 108 cases.

The FSA was concerned that customers were being *"inappropriately 'shoe-horned' into a one size fits all investment, without proper consideration of whether a switch (from their existing investments) was suitable."*

The regulator's concerns about wealth managers in recent years have included:

- Failure to properly consider all product and service charges when recommending a switch into their investment proposition.

- Failure to justify why their investment proposition is likely to outperform the client's existing investments, where 'performance prospects' is the reason given for the switch.

- Poor alignment of the investment portfolio to client objectives.

- Poor client record keeping from the outset and poor review processes to stay up to date with their client's situation – resulting in uncertainty that their individual investment portfolios continue to be suitable.

- Lack of clarity around the menu of services that their customers have signed up for – and the price of those services and the method of payment.

For an up to date picture of which firms are getting fined – and for what – see: www.fca.org.uk/firms/being-regulated/enforcement/fines

So is there any good news?

Well, yes, it's fair to say that there are far fewer 'rhinos' roaming the **regulated** part of the financial advice industry than a few years ago. They haven't all gone, however, and that's because **we allow them to overcharge us for very little (or even bad) advice.**

It seems that we humans (and perhaps especially we Brits) are naturally trusting of each other – and that's okay in some situations. But we shouldn't trust all financial advisers to charge fairly – they don't! The rhinos don't deserve our trust so we need to learn to spot them *before they hit us.*

By learning the basics about investments and pensions, you'll understand what advice work you may need to pay for – and how to avoid paying for work you don't need. So keep reading these books to be well equipped!

How to avoid being overcharged

Nowadays there *should* be less confusion between the costs of your **financial products** and the cost for **financial advice.** A new regulatory regime was introduced at the start of 2013 to clear this up (more on that in the next chapter) but I'm not convinced that the new rules are working as well as they should – and neither is the FCA.

It's fair to say that most investment and pension products from leading providers are generally quite keenly priced (as we'll see) although the best priced supplier for your circumstances may be different to that for someone else investing a different amount. So, it's worth shopping around and a **good** adviser will help you with this. However, the products can't give you great value unless they're still priced competitively after advice charges are added in. So it's **essential to check that you're not overcharged for advice.**

You might ask if it's worth paying for financial advice or coaching at all? And I'd say, yes, absolutely. I'm a huge advocate of high quality/fair value financial planners. They can help you to understand your personal financial situation; they can also show you how various investment, pension and protection products can help you achieve your important life goals – at significantly less personal cost than by simply saving in bank deposits. They can also show you how to use these products *alongside* your other assets, such as your home and bank accounts. You simply need to avoid the bad advisers who ignore stock market risk or put you into the wrong products, or load up your investments with so many charges that there's no point investing at all.

Let me show you what I mean by that.

How seemingly 'small' charges could cost you thousands

Let's say you make a reasonable sized investment of £50,000 into a straightforward investment product with a leading investment or insurance house. This might be into a collective investment fund, an investment bond or a personal pension, for example. You might be using new money – that's to say, money that is currently sitting on deposit at the bank. Or you might be transferring your funds out of existing investments or pensions into new ones – perhaps in search of lower costs or improved investment returns.

You may be surprised to learn that the **'factory gate' price** (that's the price before advice charges are added on) on such a product is likely to be around 0.5% p.a. or possibly even less, depending on the product provider. And that charge covers everything – other than advice – on the product. So it will include the product provider's charges for:

- all the pre-sales material and any projections of benefits you request

- administration of the application – applying your money to the product on their systems

- connecting that product to a range of investment funds

- the administration, safe custody and expert fund management of those funds, and

- all basic administration services on an ongoing basis, enabling you to obtain valuations, make fund switches and take withdrawals etc.

Yes, you can have all that for about 0.5% p.a. total cost – with no upfront charge either. However, by the time you've taken advice and invested in this product, there will likely be some additional charges applied (either on this product or another one if you're buying several at the same time) as follows:

- an initial charge for the initial advice

- an ongoing charge for any ongoing advice

- possible further charges where you're using more expensive investment funds, and

- further charges that may apply for holding records of your investments on an adviser's administration platform (sometimes called a 'wrap' – this helps your adviser keep track and to manage everything you have).

The additional *initial charges* will likely be somewhere between 1%

and 5% of the investment value, depending upon how much you invest. The additional *ongoing charges* could easily add another 2% each year. So, if we then add these two sets of charges together then we end up with an *effective, additional charge drag* on your investments of around 2.5% *each year* (I've simply added 0.5% p.a. (the effect of a heavy initial charge, of 5%, over say 10 years) to the 2% p.a. ongoing charge).

Now, 2.5% p.a. may not sound like a high charge – and certainly not a number worth getting excited about, right? But when you consider that it'll reduce your fund value by over 20% over 10 years – versus a basic (non-advised) investment product – then you might see it as a bigger problem. Indeed, over 20 years, that additional charge will reduce your funds by about 35%.

To put that another way (and assuming that you earn average total investment returns on these funds of, say, 7% p.a.), then your £50,000 investment might grow to about £193,000 over 20 years in a 'non-advised' and low-cost product, but only about £126,000 in the highly charged version. ***That's a £67,000 shortfall.***

The shortfall is about £21,000 over 10 years and nearly £10,000 over just five.

Ouch!

If you're going to incur these sorts of costs, then you should demand some seriously added value services, right? Sadly, the fact is that thousands of investors are hit by these sorts of charges (and higher) on their investment and pension products whilst receiving very little valuable advice in return. What's more, it's easy to argue that, outside of pension arrangements – which enjoy additional boosts from tax relief – an investor suffering such high charges might as well not bother investing at all.

You see, an additional annual charge of 2.5% means that a typical investor in a 'balanced' or 'moderate' risk fund will ***lose all*** the investment returns they might reasonably hope to make above cash deposits. So, in effect, all you'd achieve – by investing in products carrying these sorts of charges – would be exposure to unnecessary risk.

At the time of writing many investors are being tempted to put their funds into riskier assets because bank deposit rates have been crushed by central bank interventions. But we should avoid running too far up the investment risk scale with too much of our money in search of higher returns. Current bank rates are exceptionally low. Normally, and over the long term, we'd expect deposits to offer interest rate returns at around the rate of inflation.

A large number of private investors choose to avoid financial advice in order to avoid these high charges. This is the wrong solution in my view – at least for most people – because the benefits from good quality advice are enormous. A better idea is to challenge your advisers to keep their charges at fair value and to show you how they're doing so. You could ask them to explain their services in detail, so that you can see where they're adding value. And a good adviser **will** add value to your finances in return for their fees – but don't just assume that they all do.

Now, the regulator is concerned about the amount of annual (aka 'trail') commission being paid to adviser firms who don't offer ongoing services. You can see the FCA's warning to consumers at the link here:

www.fca.org.uk/consumers/financial-services-products/investments/financial-advice/trail-commission

The warning says:

> If you received financial advice or used an intermediary to buy an investment product before 31 December 2012, you may be paying trail commission. See three ways to stop paying it.

And later, it goes on to say:

> The trail commission may be intended to cover an ongoing service but it is often paid to advisers each year without them reviewing their customers' investments or providing further advice.

The FCA also outlines three ways to 'tackle trail commission' as:

1. Selling your investments

2. Asking for a better service – in return for the payments

3. Claiming the trail commission for yourself.

This is all good headline-grabbing stuff, but you need to tread carefully before following this simplistic guidance from the regulator. It only briefly mentions that there may be product penalties attached to selling your investment, but you should be aware that these could be significant. By selling up, you may lose a valuable product feature, such as a guaranteed growth rate on your funds. So **check the potential impact on your investment or pension product before deciding to sell up.**

The FCA's warning about the possible tax penalties of selling your existing investment is also very thin and I'd recommend that you check this very carefully – especially on pension plan encashments under the new rules that came into being in April 2015; a lot of people are tripping over some unnecessary taxes there. But also look out for any investments that are 'pregnant' with significant gains. The timing of selling such an investment could make a big difference to your tax bill.

The FCA's guidance also misses a key point about ongoing fees – it says:

> You could then buy the same or a similar product which,
> because you are buying it after our changes came in,
> will not include trail commission.

Whilst that's technically correct, you should be aware that most good advisers who undertake ongoing work to look after your finances will want some kind of ongoing fee for their work. So, if you're not careful you could sell your investment product (to cancel the trail commission) only to end up with a new product on which you suffer an equal or higher ongoing charge.

You might even incur an additional 'initial charge' to set up the replacement product too!

The FCA also got confused about fund rebates – this is a slice of the annual fund charge that's paid back to our account in some situations. Where these fund rebates are provided by a 'direct discount' broker, it's because they don't offer any advice – either up front or on an ongoing basis.

In summary, be careful how you tackle your adviser on this issue. If you want to cut out their ongoing fees, be prepared to be cut out of their ongoing advice services too!

> It was common, some years ago, for advisers to take an ongoing (trail) commission payment in lieu of a reduced 'upfront' payment for selling investment products. This 'spread initial' commission was not conditional upon an ongoing service being provided, so it's hardly fair to demand that these advisers start providing one now, after receiving a reduced upfront payment. That said, if your original arrangement with your adviser was for an ongoing service, then you should get one. And if you don't – or you're not happy with it – then explore how to remove the charge.

The key word around all of this is 'transparency'. Your adviser – or your direct/non-advising broker – should inform you about:

- The total effect of charges on your investments – before advice costs.

- The additional fees – up front and ongoing – for advice.

Okay, but what is a 'reasonable' fee for financial advice?

I'm afraid I can't answer that here – at least not with any precision. The right answer depends upon your situation, the complexity of your needs, what investments or pension plans you're looking to place and the competency of your adviser on a range of issues. In an ideal world the fees you'd pay for advice would relate to the amount of (necessary) work done by the adviser (and their support staff), and that work would be priced according to the expertise of the person doing the work.

If you need a lot of time to get help from a highly qualified, senior (expensive) adviser just to understand the basics about investment, then your fees could be very high. The good news is that this book

– and future books in this series – will help you to significantly reduce those educational costs from your adviser.

> However, each investment or pension arrangement you place is likely to be either a 'one-off' or an occasional transaction, so I wouldn't expect you to become so expert as to be able to eliminate this cost altogether. Most of us will need some time with our advisers to understand and challenge their advice and to explore alternatives.

You'll certainly incur fees if you need a detailed analysis of your existing investment or pension arrangements and/or several meetings to explore your options for the future. And many financial advisers do charge on the basis of a percentage of funds under advice (% of FUA), but that doesn't necessarily make them a 'rhino'. You need to ask them to convert those percentages into hard cash hourly rates to see if they're reasonable.

If you're in need of specialist advice, be prepared for some high fees. An hourly charging fee-based adviser specialising in, say, the complex financial needs of business owners and high net worth individuals, might charge somewhere between £200 and £400 per hour for their advice. It's expensive, but then good advice in any industry costs good money. On the other hand, if your finances are relatively straightforward, you should be able to arrange a review and implement some basic savings products for much less than this with a more 'generalist' financial adviser. Better still, if you do your own homework – perhaps with the help of a financial life coach – you might save even more on adviser fees. If you can draw up a plan clearly setting out your financial situation and your financial life goals, this might enable you to negotiate better rates for the final piece of work – the implementation of your savings products. After all, you'll have done a lot of the leg work already.

Most advisers I've spoken to are very happy to work with people on this 'better prepared' basis – it makes their life easier too.

Whatever you do, don't select an adviser solely on price. We often get what we pay for in life, and if an adviser is very cheap and desperate for business, that should tell you something about the quality of their offering! Equally, there's no guarantee of great quality service just because you accept a high fee structure – especially in this business. The fact is that **some advisers do overcharge,** so shop around if you suspect your adviser of doing so.

The easiest way to see the impact of advice charges on a prospective investment is to study the 'illustration of benefits' document. And if you struggle with tables of numbers, just ask a friend or a coach who's good with numbers, to help you understand them.

It really is worth paying for competent and trustworthy fee-based advice or coaching, whether you have:

- funds to invest
- spare income that you need to save for the future
- a potential need for life or health insurance
- a need for help with pension planning, or
- a need for help with estate/inheritance tax planning.

A good planner or coach will help you understand your investments and pensions and help you explore your options for connecting this stuff to your goals in life. You may be surprised at how much you can save in unnecessary product charges or tax (quite legitimately!) with some simple re-arrangement of your plans.

Just don't get hit by a rhino – it usually hurts!

Get irate!

- The numbers of overcharging and incompetent financial adviser 'rhinos' are dwindling, but if we're careless, we may still get hit by one. It's essential to avoid them because *their charges can destroy all the benefits of investing.*

- Financial products can add real value to your life but only if you buy the right products to support your personal financial plans *and* if you buy them at a reasonable price.

- Find a competent and trustworthy adviser or coach to help with this planning, and make sure to negotiate *reasonable* fees for their work up front. That alone could save you thousands of pounds over the coming years.

In the next chapter, we'll see which of these problems the regulator can (and cannot) protect us from.

Chapter 7
Slow reacting regulators

What they can (and cannot) protect us from

*Good people do not need laws to tell them to act responsibly,
while bad people will find a way around the laws.*

~ Plato

© Copyright Paul Claireaux

You might wonder why the overcharging rhino has survived for so long in an advanced economy such as the UK. After all, the UK has had regulated financial services (FS) since 1985, when the Financial Services Authority (FSA) was established. Originally called the Securities and Investments Board (SIB) until 1997, the FSA regulated banks, insurance companies and financial advisers. It also covered mortgage advisers from 2004 and general insurance intermediaries from 2005.

Since April 2013 the conduct of advisers has been regulated by the newly and appropriately named Financial Conduct Authority (FCA), which aims to ensure that:

- financial markets work well so that consumers get a fair deal

- the financial industry is run with integrity

- firms provide consumers with appropriate products and services

- consumers can trust that firms have their best interests at heart.

The FCA also plays key roles in overseeing:

- the *Money Advice Service* (MAS) www.moneyadviceservice.org. uk which provides useful and free basic information and tools to help us understand and plan our money

- the *Financial Ombudsman Service* (FOS) www.financial-ombuds-man.org.uk the official body for settling complaints between consumers and FS providers

- the *Financial Services Compensation Scheme* (FSCS) www.fscs. org.uk This is the 'compensation fund of last resort' for customers of authorised FS firms. The FSCS may pay out compensation, up to certain limits, if a firm is unable to pay claims against it, usually because it has stopped trading or has been declared in default.

The FCA, like the FSA before it, aims *"to secure an appropriate degree of protection for consumers"*, and in its approach to regulation it states that its aim is to *"make financial markets work well so that consumers get a fair deal."*

So, is the FCA delivering on its promises? Can you, as a consumer, be sure of **getting a fair deal**? I'm not convinced. I'm not aware that the FCA sets limits on advice charges, so we'll have to see what this means in practice. Certainly, one of the hoped-for benefits of a new regulator (and their new rules – see below) was for advice charges to come down – but unfortunately, some advisers reacted to the burdens of the new regulatory regime by actually *increasing* their charges. Note also the FCA's careful use of the words 'appropriate degree' of protection. It does *not* protect you from investments that simply fall in value.

You would, however, have cause to complain if your losses were due to an unfair contract, such as one based on misleading advice. And you would have a case to claim for losses if your adviser failed to undertake certain promised activities that might have prevented those losses, such as rebalancing funds to prevent the higher risk assets from becoming too large a proportion of your funds during a strong period of market growth. But if you've been through a robust advice process (including an assessment of your capacity for risk (CFR), rather than a test to simply measure your attitude to it) and you've signed your agreement to invest in a certain type of fund, then any investment losses you incur due to a market crash are not the responsibility of your adviser. You cannot expect any compensation for market crashes alone.

Interestingly, the name originally proposed for the FCA was the Consumer Protection and Markets Authority (CPMA). This was changed after the Treasury Select Committee pointed out that it might mislead consumers into thinking they enjoyed protection from a whole range of losses that are *not* covered by the regulator.

That said, the FCA is 'expected' to deliver more protection for consumers than its predecessor by intervening earlier when new products are launched to address the root causes of problems. At the outset it pledged to differentiate between *useful* product innovation that meets genuine consumer needs, and other innovations that are simply designed to exploit us.

From one mis-selling scandal to another...

The FCA is certainly coming down hard on individual advisers who break the rules. In one case, an arranger of 'sale and rent back' schemes was fined nearly £1 million and banned from the financial services (FS) industry for life for a catalogue of misleading statements made to customers.

A 'sale and rent back' scheme is where a home owner sells their home and immediately rents it back from the new owner. The idea is that the original owner reduces their outgoings (swapping an unaffordable mortgage for an affordable rent) and continues to live in their house. People selling their homes this way are often desperate to avoid imminent repossession and are vulnerable to misleading and very expensive advice.

And there is plenty of evidence over many years to show the need for tighter regulation of the FS industry. It was described by the FSA some time ago, as having persistent problems and insufficient consumer trust and confidence.

There were wholesale mis-selling scandals around mortgage repayment endowment policies and personal pensions during the 1980s and 1990s. In both cases the estimates of potential investment returns given to investors vastly exceeded any reasonable projection. Endowment plan holders were left deeply disappointed at shortfalls in their accumulated funds for mortgage repayment. And personal pensions were used to persuade people to opt out of good company (and public service) pension schemes.

Another mis-selling debacle surrounded the marketing of allegedly low-risk split capital investment trusts (splits). Many of these trusts collapsed in value, due to high levels of borrowing and large cross-holdings in other splits during the big stock market falls of 2001 and 2002. And let's not forget the mis-selling disaster of supposedly low-risk 'structured products' or, as they're now called by the regulator, 'structured capital at risk products' (SCARPs). Some of the income-yielding versions of these 'precipice bonds', as they were affectionately renamed by their unfortunate owners, returned *less than half* of the original capital at maturity – during the same period of market turmoil after 2000.

These and other mis-selling reviews have resulted in many billions of pounds of compensation being awarded and paid to consumers, and in many cases, though not all, the full amount of financial loss was made good. So a regulated industry can provide a significant safety net.

The FSA has also expressed concerns about:

- the promotion of 'absolute return funds' that aim to deliver positive (absolute) returns in any market conditions, but from which the returns have, generally, not been as 'absolute' as we'd like

- the growth in the self-invested personal pensions (SIPP) market, because the charges in these products are generally higher than for simple personal pensions – especially at lower levels of investment

- the 'rhino' salesperson's tendency to overcharge.

In September 2006 the chair of the FSA, Callum McCarthy, gave a talk to the leaders of the savings and pensions industry at their leaders' summit in Gleneagles. His now celebrated speech made a monumental attack on the industry for what he saw as the root cause of mis-selling – namely, high commission payments. His talk about incentives was **extremely** powerful. Here's an extract from it.

> Let me start with a little history: one distant example, one recent. Both relate to incentives.
>
> In the 18th century, we exported our criminals to Australia, and paid on the basis of every convict shipped aboard at the quayside at Bristol or London. On average, 12 per cent of those who were shipped aboard in Britain died en route; on some voyages more than one in three of those shipped died before reaching Australia. In 1792, the system was changed (according to some reports, on the suggestion of Jeremy Bentham). Shippers were paid for every convict delivered alive in Australia, rather than shipped aboard in Britain. In 1793, three convict ships sailed to Australia transporting 422 convicts, of whom 421 were delivered alive – a mortality rate about 1/50th of what had previously occurred. The new reward structure produced immediate and dramatic change.
>
> My second example is much more recent and relates to the opening of the retail market for gas and electricity in the UK to competition in the late 1990s. In practice this was done by door-to-door salesmen and women, on commission. Originally, all the energy companies paid their sales forces against signed contracts to buy gas and electricity, with the result that there were numerous

abuses: forged signatures, signatures from children, incorrect claims of the savings from benefits, disputed contracts. Eventually (and with some regulatory encouragement), all the energy companies changed to paying commission against signed contracts only after they had been subsequently confirmed by the customer, and abuses essentially stopped – not because door-to-door salesmen and women had become more ethical, but because it was not profitable to cheat.

This was a clear warning of tougher regulatory action ahead, but note that this speech was made in September 2006. It took until January 2013 for the regulator to implement their 'big bazooka' – the Retail Distribution Review (RDR) – in an attempt to solve the industry's worst problems.

What took the FCA so long to do its job?

I can't help wondering how we'd react if, say, doctors or airline pilots took this long – seven years – to clean up significant elements of bad conduct or poor training in their professions? It's surely unthinkable. There's obviously more incentive to deal seriously with risks when real lives are at risk – and less urgency when it's only people's 'financial' lives at risk **and** when we have the option of resuscitation by compensation later on. That said, the long-awaited RDR did introduce useful changes to the financial advice business landscape. It has:

- *Improved the clarity with which firms describe their services*: this is about defining advice services as either 'independent' or 'restricted', the latter being restricted to a limited range of products.

- *Widened the range of regulated investment products*: the range of regulated investment products now extends beyond traditional packaged products (pensions, collective investment funds such as unit trusts, OEICS and open-ended investment companies, ISAs and insurance company bonds etc.) to include investment trusts and 'other' packaged investments giving market exposure. This 'other' group includes structured deposit products that were previously sold in large volumes by highly unqualified bank staff. The new rules also make it a condition for independent advisers to consider this new wider range of products for their clients.

- *Raised professional standards for advisers*: this includes adherence to a code of ethics, continuous professional development and higher minimum qualification levels. The entry level is now at level four on the Qualification and Credit Framework (QCF). This is described as equivalent to the first year of a degree course, though it's not said which degree subject that statement is based on!

- In any event, the new qualification requirements are certainly much higher than what went before – as pointed out in government debate in 2011 when the Treasury Financial Secretary, Mark Hoban, said:

  The current minimum financial adviser qualification is at the same level as a diploma in shift management at McDonald's – whilst the products that are being sold by IFAs are infinitely more complex and long lasting in their effects than a Big Mac.

- *Improved the clarity of adviser charging*: which effectively outlaws the payment of commission on investment product sales.

So the RDR addressed a number of concerns about the FS industry and the last point, on commissions being banned, may be of particular interest to many people. But don't get too excited about it.

Why banning commissions hasn't changed much...

Commissions for advice and product placement have simply been replaced by fees or, as it's known in the industry, 'Client-Agreed Remuneration' (CAR). These fees must now be more explicitly disclosed and separately charged for, but they can still be taken from your investment products, if you prefer to pay that way.

So, in some ways, very little has changed.

What the FCA wants us to understand here is that financial advice is not a free service. But you know, it never was – it was just positioned that way by less honest advisers. Good advice – technically robust and tailored to our personal situation – costs money, and it is now a bit easier to see what's being charged for it. Good advisers have always been clear about their charges, and it remains up to you to make sure you're only paying a fair level of fees for the work being done.

Whether the RDR initiatives clear out all the bad or overcharging advisers remains to be seen. More clarity is fine, but we've had a lot of clear information on commission costs for many years – and we've mostly ignored it!

In 2005 the FSA introduced a 'menu of charges' initiative to encourage us to shop around for better value on investment products and associated advice. The idea was that advisers should tell you the maximum amount they would receive in commission at the start of your first meeting – a bit like a menu outside a restaurant, which means you can walk away if you feel the prices are too high. Then in 2006 the FSA introduced a 'Treating Customers Fairly' initiative, which was meant to ensure that all advisers and product provider firms:

- made the fair treatment of customers a key part of their corporate culture
- only sold products designed to meet our needs
- provided clear information and kept us informed before, during and after the sale
- gave only suitable advice that took account of our circumstances.

For you as a customer, this should have ensured that:

- you received the expected level of performance from both the investment product and any associated services
- you did not face unreasonable barriers if you wanted to change the product, switch provider, submit a claim or make a complaint.

What's more, for some considerable time, financial advisers have been obliged to follow the FSA's principles for good business, which include: acting with integrity, acting with due skill, care and diligence and observing proper standards of market conduct.

Now, these are all fine words, initiatives and obligations, but clearly they've had only a limited effect on the less professional parts of the adviser community, thus making the new RDR rules necessary. Perhaps the most interesting thing about this problem of 'high commission paid to advisers' is that the amounts have been disclosed to us, **very clearly,** for the **past 30 years!** The regulations on the marketing of investment and pension products compelled the providers to disclose this information to us, initially only in our *post-sale* cooling-off notices, and then in our *pre-sales* illustrations of benefits. And for more than twelve years the rules have further compelled providers to point out, in plain English, all the 'nasties' in their products – giving clear warnings about potential investment risks and any ongoing financial commitments we have to make. These warnings are contained in the 'Key features' document for life policies (including investment bonds) and personal pensions. The equivalent document for collective investment funds is called the 'Key investor information document.'

Also, any projection of future values on regulated investments must adhere to certain limits on growth rates *and* must display the total effect of all charges: adding up adviser charges, product charges and fund management charges. So whilst we can welcome improvements to the regulation of the investment industry, the fact is that we've had every chance to object to high commissions and high product charges for very a long time.

There's really only one conclusion we can draw about those 'key facts' and other regulatory warnings – *we just don't bother to read them.*

And why don't we bother?

Well, I really don't know. I guess a lot of us can't be bothered with small print. And a lot of people don't like dealing with percentages and tables of numbers – despite the fact that these tables can show just how hard our investments will be hit by charges.

My personal view is that it comes back to the fact that we're simply too trusting as a nation and that it's just not British to haggle ... unless we're on holiday! I believe there's some evidence that Americans drive a harder bargain on price for investment products than we do. Whatever the reason, we clearly need to understand that the 'regulator' will *not* protect us from investment risks or from high product charges.

Get irate!

- The market for regulated investment advice has changed. The FCA knows that its predecessor (the FSA) was slow to resolve mis-selling and will act more quickly in the future. The clamp-down on bad advice, with more and bigger fines being imposed, has already begun.

- Charges for advice/commissions have been disclosed for decades – they're just more clearly disclosed now.

- Entry-level qualification standards for advisers have been raised, but these changes don't guarantee higher investment returns or high quality advice or fair value charging. So you still need to take care when entering into risk-based investments. And remember that views about 'market value' differ widely, even amongst the most highly qualified advisers.

- It's always been possible to negotiate a better deal with financial advisers – at least those who are independent. We just need to leave our British reticence behind and pluck up the courage to ask. Savvy investors already do this.

Coming up next

There's no doubt that good financial advice can save you a lot of money in unnecessary tax. But in recent years some advisers got carried away with this sort of planning. More 'aggressive' tax avoidance schemes have backfired and cost their investors dearly. So, next we'll look at those issues - and how some smart thinking can save you a lot of tax without breaking the law!

Chapter 8
The taxman and the troubled tax advisers

The scary tax traps to avoid without resorting
to aggressive tax schemes

In this world, nothing is certain except death and taxes.

~ Benjamin Franklin

You may have come across that quote from Benjamin Franklin and it's worth taking some more of his advice before we talk about tax matters. (And don't worry, we won't go into all the grisly detail on that stuff). Franklin's ideas can help us make better decisions as individuals – and our politicians could benefit from his age-old guidance too!

Franklin was an intellectual powerhouse, a leading US politician, author, printer, satirist, political theorist, scientist and inventor; he invented the Franklin stove, the carriage odometer, the lightning rod and bifocal glasses! Passionate about liberty (coupled with responsibility, thrift and hard work), he formed the first public libraries in the USA. He's also credited with securing France's help to the Americans in the War of Independence against the British – although we might question whether the French needed much persuasion!

In his book *The Way to Wealth* (1758), Franklin compressed 25 years' worth of maxims from his best-selling annual publication *Poor Richard's Almanac*. His advice for a better way of life had two main themes: industry (hard work and commitment to the cause) and thrift (the careful management of time and money).

The benefits of thrift were promoted by Prime Minister David Cameron in the aftermath of the financial crisis in 2008-09 – and 'thrift' is certainly a more attractive word than 'austerity' to describe a plan to pay down debt.

In the heady, debt-fuelled consumer boom years up to 2007 we might have scoffed at Franklin's ideas for a better way of life, but thrifty ideas are very modern thinking – at least for now. Here are some of Franklin's maxims which, I'm sure you'll agree, are as relevant today as they were when he wrote them 260 years ago:

Early to bed, and early to rise, makes a man healthy, wealthy and wise.

Diligence is the mother of good luck.

Little strokes fell great oaks.

There are no gains, without pains.

Dost thou love life? Then do not squander time, for that's the stuff that life is made of.

Beware of little expenses; a small leak will sink a great ship.

When the well's dry, they know the worth of water.

What maintains one vice, would bring up two children.

When you have bought one fine thing you must buy ten more, that your appearance maybe all of a piece. (Shopaholics and brand victims take note.)

The borrower is a slave to the lender.

Employ thy time well if thou meanest to gain leisure.

What wonderfully solid and simple advice about money and life.

Franklin's more famous quote, about the certainty of death and taxes, is also borne out by history as we've now had over 200 years of taxation in the UK.

Our bicentenary of income tax was in 1999, a time of 'celebration' for our taxman who's held various different names over the years (most of them not repeatable here). The official name, since the merger of the Inland Revenue and Customs and Excise offices, is Her Majesty's Revenue and Customs. Or, more simply, HMRC.

Did you know that income tax was first introduced as a temporary measure in 1799? For 200 years before that, the government's main source of revenue was through *land tax.*

> Many would argue that land taxes should be reintroduced today – and there's certainly an argument that they're fairer than taxing work.

William Pitt the Younger (Prime Minister from 1783) introduced 'certain duties upon income' to finance the war against Napoleon. Those were tough times for England, with a rising national debt, a starving army and mutiny in the navy (due to disgusting living conditions), all of which prompted the introduction of income tax in support of the war effort. The tax only lasted until 1802 and was abolished by Henry Addington who had then taken over as Prime Minister during a short-lived peace with the French. When war broke out again, the tax was brought back in 1803, only to be abolished again in 1816, a year after the Battle of Waterloo. It was finally introduced permanently by Sir Robert Peel in 1842.

Robert (Bob) Peel was perhaps more famous for establishing the Metropolitan Police Force at London's Scotland Yard in 1829 when he served as home secretary. The thousand new police constables were nicknamed 'Bobbies' amongst the locals and 'Peelers' amongst the criminal fraternity.

Pitt's original income tax introduced the idea of progressive rates and was levied at just 2 old pence in the pound (1/120 or 0.83%) on incomes over £60 (about £5,000 in today's money). The rates then increased up to a maximum of 2 shillings (10%) on incomes of over £200 (£17,000 p.a. today), and the tax raised £6 million (of an expected £10 million) in its first year. Fiscal forecasting was clearly a great deal more challenging back in those days, as we'd not yet invented computer-generated spreadsheets!

Nowadays we're hit on all sides by one form of tax or another, and as we all know, the rates are much higher than in the past. Today, you'll very often pay tax:

- **when you earn your money** – through income tax and National Insurance

- **when you spend it** – through value-added tax (VAT) and various other forms of excise duty. These taxes now form a large part of our fuel and alcohol costs

- **when you buy a house or other investments** – through stamp duty and stamp duty land tax (SDLT)

- **when you make profits on your investments –** through both tax on the income from your investments (regardless of whether you receive or reinvest it) **and** on your capital profits when disposing of assets. This second layer is called capital gains tax (CGT)

At the time of writing CGT does not apply to gains on your main home.

- **when you die** – through inheritance tax (IHT) which applies on the value of your estate if it's over a certain size. Note that in some situations there can also be inheritance tax payable on certain gifts made *during* your lifetime.

And, unfortunately IHT does apply to the value of your home.

Which way are tax rates heading?

Well, in the UK (in the tax year to 5 April 2014) we paid total taxes – to HMRC and local governments – of *five hundred and eighty thousand million pounds.*

About 45% of this was as income tax and National Insurance, whilst just less than 20% was VAT. Less than 10% was corporation tax (this may not come as a surprise given all the news in recent years of large companies avoiding paying tax altogether). The remaining 20%+ was collected from more than 20 other taxes including: fuel duties, business rates, council tax, CGT, IHT, SDLT, stamp duty on shares, tobacco duty, duty on wines and spirits, beer and cider, air passenger duty, insurance premium tax, landfill tax, betting taxes, vehicle excise duty, bank levy and environmental levies. Add in other sources of revenue and the UK Government received around £625 billion in 2013-14.

That's an incredible amount of money.

Unfortunately, the Government's total managed expenditure in the same year was about £720 billion. It's fair to say that this is spent on vital public services (including education, health, pensions, public order, defence, transport, industry, agriculture and housing), but the question is whether it's all spent wisely.

These are scary numbers but scarier still is the fact that we spent c. £50 billion just to pay the interest on our debt. And that's more than we spent on *either defence or public order!*

> If you want more detail or for the latest government 'tax and spend' numbers, go to the Office for Budget Responsibility's website www.budgetresponsibility.org.uk

One thing to understand is that the current multibillion pound shortfall (between what we take in and what we spend) has to be borrowed. And that simply adds to the debt for future generations to repay.

Now, governments with high debt *need* economic growth. Growth is a wonderful cure for debt because it both reduces government spending (on unemployment and other welfare benefits) *and* it delivers higher tax revenues (as businesses make more profits and people earn and spend more). But of course, to reduce our total public debt we have to do more than just slow down the rate at which we overspend! You'll have heard the technical term for the **overspend** (the 'deficit') but many people (including some politicians) often confuse 'reducing the deficit' with 'reducing the debt' pile. These are two very different things – so let's clear up this confusion.

The difference between deficit and debt

Cutting overspending to zero doesn't reduce our debts. To do that we need to move from overspending (deficit) to underspending (surplus). And like many countries, we in the UK have a long road ahead before our Government's receipts exceed its expenditure.

A cynic might suggest that our Government has usually resorted to the unspoken (and highly risky) strategy of 'inflation stealth' to reduce its debt in the past. High inflation is sometimes described as another form of tax – to transfer wealth from those with savings to those carrying debts, including the Government. It certainly reduces the real wealth of people with bank account savings.

Economists would undoubtedly argue about whether the high inflation we've had in the UK in the past was deliberately engineered. The question is, does it work to eliminate debt and might the Government try it?

I guess the Government – in concert with the Bank of England – could decide to go soft on inflation and allow it to rise significantly **and** then remain high for a long time. Let's say the Government allowed inflation to race up to, say, 7% p.a., and then stay there for ten years. Now, 7% p.a. inflation compounded over ten years is equivalent to a doubling of prices. So, if this were to happen, then any debt repaid ten years from now would use money that only has half of today's value. Nice trick eh?

Unfortunately there are a great many problems with this approach. First, we'd all be a lot poorer unless our incomes had also doubled over that time. And those people on fixed incomes (like many of those with private pension annuities) would lose out heavily. Indeed for a number of years recently we did, on average, get poorer as earnings rose more slowly than prices. That was an unusual situation and we'd like to hope that such days are behind us – but we can't guarantee it of course. Then there's the risk that investors (the institutions both here and overseas from whom our government borrows) would lose confidence in our control of inflation. If this happened, our interest payments on borrowed money would increase substantially, making our debt burden worse, not better.

So, debt reduction by 'inflation stealth' is not a brilliant plan and we might therefore hope that it's **not** what our leaders are planning, at least not extensively. We would hope that they're seeking to support strong economic growth to help pull us out of this debt trouble.

Some economists argue that to achieve growth (and avoid a severe economic depression) at times like this, governments should support the economy with spending and investment projects. The thinking is that the private sector (that's us – the consumers and private businesses) has effectively gone on strike with *our* spending, so the government needs to step in and spend *for us*. This is certainly a good plan for avoiding the most severe ups and downs in an economy. But this plan hits a major stumbling block when, as a country, we're already deeply in debt when a recession hits – when we need the government to spend more. At these times it's difficult to argue for more debt to stimulate growth because we risk the same loss of confidence amongst our investors (our lenders) as with the inflation problem above.

In the worst case, we may be unable to source borrowings at a price we can afford – we'd be locked out of the bond (borrowing) markets. We'd then need to seek help from a *supranational* group such as the International Monetary Fund (IMF) who only lends funds to a country on the condition that it has a say in how a country's finances are run.

That's a really bad place to be – but it's worth remembering that it's somewhere the UK has been before (in the 1970s), and, at the time of writing, it's a place currently occupied by Greece.

Governments normally try to contain a growing debt burden and limit the pain of higher taxes or service cuts on future generations. Sound governments cut out wasteful spending without cutting useful front-line services unnecessarily. The buzz terms are 'thrift' and 'efficiency' savings rather than 'austerity' measures. But whatever we call government spending cuts, we know that they cause pain when people are displaced from work. And that pain can take a long time to fade. It takes time for an economy to adjust and for new, genuine and sustainable jobs to be created. It can also take a long time for people's feelings about job security to pick up enough to trigger a generalised increase in consumer spending and industry investment.

It may well be that the Government can help to stimulate growth with some targeted support for projects with large growth potential. And it should obviously focus its limited funds on sustainable industries – we don't need quick-fix job creation schemes that offer no valuable service and simply load more debt onto future generations. In the meantime, whilst (as they say) the economy rebalances towards new industries (and away from banking, for example), we're likely to face several years of heavy taxes to balance the books.

Indeed, our governments have pursued this course for some time. We already have the highest proportion of people paying higher rate tax for 20 years – and it's projected this could double over the coming years, from 4.6 million in 2014-15 to c. 9 million in 2033.

> This increase is caused by something called 'fiscal drag', the process by which tax allowances and thresholds are indexed only to prices – and so fall behind people's (normally) faster rising earnings. More detail here: http://budgetresponsibility.org.uk/wordpress/docs/FiscalDrag.pdf

You don't have to be a multi-millionaire to pay higher rates of tax either. In this tax year (2015-16) you'll personally pay *42% total tax* (including National Insurance) on taxable income above £42,385 p.a. And that ignores any student loan repayments you might have.

> It also ignores the stinging 13.8% rate of National Insurance that your employer (if you have one) pays on a large part of your earnings.

But here's the thing: this 42% rate of tax is LOW compared to the rates now hitting tens of thousands of middle-class Britons with children.

Are you paying 70% tax?

Did you know that the loss of child benefits, where **one** member of the household earns between £50,000 and £60,000, can result in an **_effective marginal tax rate of over 70%!_** This 'effective' marginal rate applies to a family with four children – it's only 60% if you have two children!

Once your income goes above £60,000, your effective marginal tax rate drops to 40% again and (officially) it stays at that rate until your income reaches £150,000 p.a., at which point the 45% rate starts.

But there's actually another kink in the income tax system if you earn over £100,000 p.a. At this point your effective tax rate spikes back up to 60% on your earnings up to £121,200. This is because once your earnings go over £100,000, you start to lose the tax-free band of your income – the personal allowance (PA), which is currently £10,600. The PA is lost at the rate of one half of 'total taxable income' above £100,000, so it's all lost if our total income reaches £121,200.

(£100,000 + £21,200 [2 x £10,600])

Of course, losing your tax-free allowance on **half of** your income above £100,000 (and up to £121,200) pushes that amount (which was previously tax free) into the 40% tax band. So you suffer an extra 20% tax on that extra income which is already being taxed at 40%.

Result? **A marginal tax rate of 60%** (20% + 40%).

Okay, now I'm really sorry about all those numbers but I hope you've got the key message here. Hard-working middle-class Britons are actually paying tax (at the margin) at rates of 60% and even over 70% in some cases. **That's mad!**

These rates of tax are really not what you'd expect in the UK. They're more like what you'd expect to find in France, under its Socialist government. That said, even the French only imposed such **_penal tax_** rates on people earning over €1 million – and they've now given up on them altogether. They found, not surprisingly, that these rates caused talented people to leave their country – and that they failed to generate much tax!

But these 70%+ tax rates in the UK (brought in under a Conservative-led coalition!) are not the highest rates we've suffered.

In the 1966 song 'Taxman' by George Harrison (the opening track on The Beatles' album 'Revolver') we hear about the obscene levels of tax that applied under Harold Wilson's Labour government at that time. Do you remember the lyrics, or the music that went with them? Try googling 'taxman' by the Beatles and have a listen.

George Harrison's idea for the song came to him when he realised that they were giving **most** of their money away in taxes. And they certainly were hit hard: most of their earnings would have been in the top tax bracket so they were liable to a **95% rate of super tax.** Their song of complaint that they received just £1 for every £19 they handed over to the 'taxman' was really no joke!

Amazingly, that extraordinary rate of tax is the not the highest ever applied in the UK.

In 1974 the top rate of tax on **earned** income was raised to 83%; with an investment income surcharge of 15% on top, the total marginal tax rate on investment income reached 98%. And that was just short of the **highest ever** rate of tax in the UK that peaked in the Second World War at **99.25%.** Indeed, the top rate of tax was around 90% throughout the 1950s and 1960s.

Let's be clear, the top tax rates in those days were abusive, and it's really no surprise that we suffered the same kind of 'brain drain' of professional people from the UK in the 1970s as some poorer European countries are suffering today. Nor should we be surprised that such government aggression towards taxpayers spawned a huge tax avoidance industry. I think any reasonable person would want to hear about legal ways to trim back their tax bills, when faced with those sorts of rates.

Of course times have moved on, and the core rates of tax are much lower today than they were in the 1970s, despite those high spikes in our marginal tax rates at certain income levels as described earlier. And it looks like public opinion has now hardened against tax avoidance, even by legitimate means – perhaps with the exception of charitable giving.

The dangerous game of tax avoidance

You may recall a media frenzy in 2013 about a possible limit on tax relief for the wealthy giving large sums to charity. The Government backtracked on this proposal quite quickly after substantial criticisms – and it seems sensible for it to have done so. After all, when people give to charity they give 100% of that money to a good cause. If they hang on to it and pay tax on it, then only the taxed part goes to the public good cause.

But the main event regarding tax avoidance in recent times has been the swathe of high profile celebrities (comedians, TV personalities, pop stars and sports stars) who've been exposed as having used aggressive tax avoidance schemes to cut their tax bills. There were, allegedly, some multi-million pound earners who'd used such schemes to achieve tax bills lower than those of their house cleaner – and that's clearly not right.

These rich tax avoiders found their reputations damaged as the media dragged their stories into the open. Most investors in those schemes were professionally advised and so they might have had only a limited understanding of what they'd invested in. But this is no defence against the taxman's challenge to these schemes, and in many cases the claims for tax relief are being rejected. Investors are being forced to hand back tax relief that they've already enjoyed and this could push some into financial ruin.

So it was a hard learning experience for some celebrities and other wealthy people, and there was little public sympathy for them. The public was genuinely angered by this. The episode also raised questions about the rules of play with tax in the future. Until recently there was a clear divide between tax evasion and tax avoidance, and this still applies, but now there's a middle, fuzzy ground!

Tax evasion is the illegal practice of failing to declare and pay tax that is due. Ignorance of the law is no defence and penalties include fines or, in extreme cases, imprisonment. Examples of tax evasion include: renting out property and failing to declare the income; selling that same property at a gain and failing to declare the profit; putting cash into an offshore bank account but failing to declare the untaxed (gross) income.

Legitimate tax avoidance (or planning), on the other hand, is the legal practice of arranging our financial affairs to minimise the tax we pay. For example, spending money to develop a business (for example, to train an employee) is a legitimate business expense and this avoids tax on profits. Alternatively, we might save money in an individual savings account (ISA) or a pension to avoid tax – perfectly legitimately. Tax reliefs on these savings vehicles are designed by government!

The new, fuzzy middle ground comes in the form of HMRC's General Anti-Abuse Rule (GAAR) that provides the taxman with new powers to attack what they see as 'aggressive tax avoidance'. The army of clever tax avoidance experts is in retreat; their services in the design of schemes that simply avoid tax are no longer required. And their efforts to protect existing investors in such schemes from the taxman are failing. Investment schemes that are not government-approved and serve no useful purpose other than tax avoidance are being closed down. They may have worked before (according to the letter of the law) but they're not within the spirit of it.

Now, this whole area of aggressive tax avoidance is complex and there are ongoing battles between HMRC and tax advisers to the wealthy. We can't cover the issues in depth here but you can find out what HMRC are seeking to attack by going to their website at www.gov.uk/government/publications/tax-avoidance-general-anti-abuse-rules

What we can say is that there are plenty of legitimate ways to save tax on your savings and investments including ISAs, Pension plans and other products. I'd certainly encourage you to look at the tax benefits of pensions, which after recent rule changes are one of the most tax efficient investments possible for a great many people.

Get irate!

- HMRC is on the warpath regarding aggressive tax avoidance schemes.

- If you need advice in this area – perhaps because of investments you've already made – then speak to a qualified tax expert.

- You may want to consider taking a second opinion and consider a complaint if you feel that a tax avoidance scheme was misrepresented to you in the first instance. The Financial Ombudsman Service (FOS) has upheld claims against advisers over the advice given on tax avoidance schemes.

- Straightforward, popular, government-approved savings and investment products remain useful for saving tax and are far more useful than many people think. You won't be attacked for sensible planning to reduce your taxes.

Coming up next...

Having said that pensions are a wonderfully tax efficient investment for many people, it's really quite curious how some advisers sell them. It's almost as if they want to put you off buying one even if you need it.

Let's look at that now.

Chapter 9
Naïve number crunchers

How to cut the headline cost of your pension in half

Money frees you from doing things you dislike. Since I dislike doing nearly everything, money is handy.

~ Groucho Marx

© Copyright Paul Claireaux

We've already seen why some financial advisers tend to underplay the risks and overplay the potential returns from stock market-based investment: they're wedded to a model of risk that doesn't work.

Yet an extraordinary thing happens when those same advisers help us with our pension planning. Suddenly they throw away their optimism and become ultra-cautious about our finances. And given that our retirement fund is the second biggest investment (after the home) that many of us make, we should get to grips with what's going on here.

If you make a 'finger in the air' guess at the income you'll need in retirement, the chances are that you'll come up with a figure of around two thirds (just over 65%) of your current earnings. There's really not much logic to this 65% guess. It's just a number that advisers sometimes suggest – based on a rough estimate of your current expenditure less the cost of your mortgage – if you have one. The assumption is that you'll plan to pay off your mortgage by the time you retire. A 'two thirds' target pension is also a throwback to the maximum income available under the defined benefit (DB) pension schemes of yesteryear.

I could distract you with a hundred pages of technical pensions jargon at this point, but I don't think you'd thank me for that! However, it will help to define DB pension schemes in simple terms and to compare them to the more common DC (defined contribution) alternative. For more detail about pensions and other savings boxes, go to my blog at www.paulclaireaux.com

These notes should suffice for now.

Defined benefit (DB) pension schemes

These pensions are those which ... well ... define your benefits! For example, a typical DB scheme will define a pension promise of, say, 1/60th of your earnings for each year of service (this is called the 'accrual' rate). So, someone in such a scheme with 40 years' of service would become entitled to a pension of two thirds (40/60ths) of their earnings.

These schemes have largely disappeared from the private sector of industry because of the very high costs to employers. They remain available in the public sector although many schemes are undergoing changes to reduce their costs for **future pension** accruals.

It's important to understand that existing benefits already earned under those schemes are not normally affected by these changes. So whatever pension you earn up to the point of any change, you get to keep – a point often missed by those protesting against change.

Defined contribution (DC) pension schemes

Most private sector workers will save for their retirement with some kind of DC pension scheme. These include personal pension plans (PPPs), stakeholder pensions (SHP), self-invested personal pensions (SIPPs), group money purchase plans (GMPPs) and small self-administered schemes (SSAS).

With DC pension schemes it's the – yes, you guessed it – contributions which are defined! Or, to put that another way, the final pension outcome is unknown. What you get out depends on a host of variables, including: the amounts you (and your employer) put in, the effects of inflation and investment returns on the 'real' value of the pension fund over the term to retirement, and the pension annuity rate you can obtain when you get there.

You can often influence your potential investment returns (and your exposure to investment risk) by selecting from a range of investment funds. But you can't control those investment returns or future interest rates. So, unlike DB pensions, DC pensions offer no guaranteed level of pension income.

In the past, many insurance-based pension providers did offer guaranteed minimum rates of investment growth on DC pensions using with-profits funds. And one insurer in particular (Equitable Life) was extremely successful in selling with-profits pension products that also promised a *Guaranteed Annuity Rate* (GAR) to convert the fund to pension. Unfortunately for investors in those products, as longer-term interest rates declined over many years, these promises became impossibly expensive for Equitable Life to fulfil and it became insolvent. The process of clearing up that debacle – and providing compensation to policy holders – dragged on for many years. Other leading insurance companies also sold expensive GAR-type pensions, but to a far lesser extent than Equitable Life, and were able to meet their liabilities and survive. However, the high cost of these mistakes has resulted in there being few (if any) income guarantees available on modern DC pension schemes.

With modern DC pensions you target the income level you want in retirement, regularly review your progress towards that target and adjust the amount you save to stay on track. To review your progress you'll need to use some sensible assumptions about those variables I've just mentioned – primarily, investment returns and annuity rates – and as we'll see shortly this is:

Where we go wrong with pension planning

We've just seen that a typical (standard) 'guess' at what you'll need as a pension income is about two thirds of your final earnings. But if you think about this a bit harder, and draw up a detailed forecast of your likely spending habits, you may well arrive at a much bigger number, perhaps twice the standard figure.

Yes, a target pension of 130% – of salary whilst at work – is quite common when people do this exercise! We'll call this the 'dream pension'.

How can this be? How could you need **more** income in retirement than you need whilst you're working? Well, quite easily, because when you retire, the time previously allocated to work might be exchanged for days out (including shopping trips) and for taking those dream holidays (that you've put off all your life) and otherwise generally having a good time. Whilst at work you may not have had the time (or the money) to do all this expensive stuff.

The trouble for most of us, is that a pension of more (30% more) than our final earnings really is just a dream. If we 'do the math', we'll see that funding such a pension would take up so much of our income now that we'd be in poverty throughout our working life! Very few people can save enough to build up that sort of pension income without it hurting their lifestyle (along the way) a great deal. That said, I can think of two groups of people who might make it:

- People who can afford to save an extraordinarily high proportion of their income. This would include some single people who have no expensive interests, hobbies or vices, **and** who don't take many expensive holidays.

149

- People who 'get lucky' taking enormous investment risks with their money, for example, people who buy heavily into property just as prices start rising, catch a boom in prices and then get out again before prices collapse. It is possible if you're lucky (or smart) with your timing, but as we're reminded with every property price crash, this approach has its own risks.

In any event, the issue for most of us is not that we'll fall short against that dream pension; it's that we're not even saving enough for *half* a dream pension. Let's look at why this is.

It's broadly true to say that DC pensions are far less generous than the typical DB pension which, if you stayed in it long enough, would provide that 'two thirds' pension at retirement. The average employer contribution to private sector DB pensions is around 16% of employee salaries compared to just over 6% for DC pension schemes (ONS, 2012). But, as ever, these broad statistics hide the more useful facts. That figure of 16% is just an average across all age groups in DB pensions. What's far more useful is to understand the **'effective' employer input** for you as an individual. And this depends on how close you are to retirement. The less time you have before retirement then the less time there is to invest the pension fund monies and so the higher the cost to build that 1/60th worth of pension.

For those very close to retirement, the effective cost of a DB pension can rise to **50%** (or more!) of their earnings, whereas for a very young worker it may perhaps only cost the employer **4%** (or less) of earnings, depending on the worker's own input. So you can see that the 16% average number is meaningless to us as individuals.

A key point to understand here is that, just because DB schemes are very generous (at least for middle-aged and older workers), it does *not* mean that the more widely available alternative (DC schemes) are bad value, despite what you might read in the press or hear from some union leaders.

DC pensions can be extraordinarily good value savings plans. Even a basic workplace pension will (up to certain limits) provide a 'matching' employer contribution of about 60% of your personal input. And many employers are more generous than this, matching 100% or more of your own payments. Translating this into simple (money box-like) terms, this means that a basic (60% matched) workplace scheme would enable you to build a pension fund of £1,600 for a net outlay of just £800!

Let's just be clear on how that works. The £1,600 is made up from:

1. Your personal input of £800, plus

2. Basic rate tax relief of £200 (giving £1,000), plus

3. The 'free' 60% employer payment on top.

This is a very nice deal – where else could you achieve that? It would be impossible to beat that with any other ordinary savings vehicle. And (whilst higher rate tax relief applies) a 40% taxpayer would enjoy £200 extra tax relief, taking their net personal cost down from £800 to £600.

> Note that if you're self-employed or a partner in business, then you don't enjoy these 'free' employer contributions. But you do enjoy tax relief at your marginal rate, which depends on your profits.

So, let's stop and take stock here. These DC pensions are clearly fantastic savings plans, yet every week we hear of another report telling us that we're not saving enough. Some reports suggest 20% of us don't save anything at all for our retirement.

Why don't people put a lot more into pensions?

There could be many reasons for this. Some may be reluctant to commit monies to a savings plan that they can't access before the age of 55. Others simply need to focus on paying down expensive short-term debt and building their short-term savings – their emergency fund – before they can attend to this longer-term savings challenge. But for the rest of us I think the problem comes largely from the way we look at this issue. We don't compare pensions with simple savings boxes as we've done above. We tend to look at the problem from the other end of the telescope – which wouldn't be quite so bad, except that we're using the wrong telescope!

In a nutshell, what we tend to do is ask someone (or use an online calculation tool) to work out how much we need to save to hit our target pension. Then, when the frightening number comes back, we end up doing little or even nothing about it. And it's true that the answer we get to this question is invariably frightening – *very* frightening. But it's essential to understand why this is so – and in many cases it's simply because **the number is wrong.**

The idea that we need to save every penny of our spare income to achieve a modest level of pension is not attractive to anyone – regardless of age. But tell that to a young saver – someone under, say, 35 – and you risk putting them off saving anything at all.

And here's the thing . . . these young savers are being misled.

Yes, I know, the word 'misled' is a strong one – conjuring up images of hard-nosed salespeople promising impossible investment returns – you know what I mean:

> *"Oh yes, this fund has consistently achieved **15% p.a.** growth over the past ten years and I confidently expect that to continue into the future ... blah blah blah."*

This is indeed misleading nonsense, but it's not what worries me here. With pensions I'd suggest that tens of thousands – if not millions – of people are put off long-term saving **not** because their adviser is over-optimistic but because they're over-*cautious!* And there are broadly two reasons for the frighteningly high and unaffordable pension cost estimates being given to people every week.

First, the calculations often use a cautious (aka 'low') assumption for the investment returns that you'll achieve on your pension fund. Second, they often assume a high cost to convert that pension fund into a pension income. This is because they assume that you'll want to remove any inflation risk to your pension once it comes into payment.

Now, you may think that taking this 'belt and braces' approach is a good thing when it comes to investment and pension planning, and sometimes it is. But when you're cautious on both these counts (investment returns and inflation risk in retirement), and when you project the numbers over very long timescales – as we do for younger savers – then you simply end up with a ridiculously high cost estimate. And these silly numbers can be found everywhere – including in nice neat tables, virtually every weekend, in the money sections of many newspapers! I'm sure you've seen the articles:

'Check the cost of funding your pension'

Take a good look at these tables next time you skim the money pages to see what I mean here. They're genuinely putting young people off from saving. Indeed, they're actually helping to make the much heralded pension time bomb a reality. For instance, here's what one leading newspaper told a 25-year-old that they need to save if they want to fund a relatively modest pension of £25,000 p.a. (in today's money terms) from the age of 60:

Ten thousand pounds

Yes, that's right – apparently the pension saving required by this 25-year-old is about £10,000 per year. And that's each and every year *and* increasing annually with inflation for the next 35 years.

What do you think a 25-year-old might do after reading that?

This is madness. It's like telling someone who wants to buy a car that the only car they can have is a Rolls-Royce. Yes, we might all like to have one of those cars but hardly anyone can afford to have one, including the Rolls-Royce sales reps!

My guess is that, after being told these costs, our 25-year-old might laugh it off and joke about it with their friends. Maybe they'd spend that month's savings on a 'bender' of a night out or on a good holiday, or maybe they'd go out and order a nice new car – anything to avoid thinking about the poverty facing them in later life.

So, this is no joke, is it? Because whatever our 25-year-old decides to do, it certainly won't involve any kind of commitment to serious saving for their later years. And what can be done about this? Well, how would it be if I told this 25-year-old that they could have that £25,000 p.a. pension income but for a fraction of the cost quoted in the newspaper – perhaps 70% less?

Let's be clear on this, before anyone accuses me of misleading you. Yes, it's true that if you pay in 70% less to a pension compared to your colleagues at work, then, all other things being equal, you'll receive 70% less back at the end. But this is not the point I'm making here. I simply want to prove that the papers are wrong – that our young workers don't need to save £10,000 a year into a pension to make it worthwhile. And that if we carry on telling them this they'll end up putting **nothing away at all**, which is how some people react today.

You're probably thinking this sounds absurd, right? How can the newspaper give one figure – sourced from a major pensions provider – and yet I can arrive at a number 70% lower?

It's actually relatively simple – I'm just doing two things.

First, I'm pointing out the difference between the headline-quoted costs of pensions in the newspapers and the amounts that actually come out of our pocket. So we can halve the cost versus the headlines very easily, as we've already seen. A £1,600 pension fund is built at an £800 net of tax cost to a basic rate taxpaying employee (with £200 tax relief and that 'free' £600 employer payment on top). And, with more generous workplace pensions, the cost to the employee will be reduced by more than half (versus the headline) at this stage.

Second, I further reduce the estimated pension cost by making more realistic assumptions for this younger person. We'll look at these one by one below:

1. Do not assume that you'll pay for inflation protection

The most commonly used product used to convert a pension fund into income at retirement is called a 'pension annuity' – and if you assume that when you retire you'll buy a 'level' annuity (i.e. a pension without inflation protection once it comes into payment), then you'll massively reduce your estimated pension costs.

I'm not suggesting you ignore inflation from now and throughout your savings years up to the point of retirement. You should, certainly, target a pension income in today's money terms. All I'm saying is that you could – for planning purposes – assume that your *pension income* will be level in payment from the date it starts. And it's perfectly fair to assume this because this is exactly the basis on which most people (including most financial advisers) buy their retirement incomes! We tend to buy *level* (as opposed to inflation-proofed pensions) quite simply because they cost significantly less to obtain the same starting income.

Now, the exact figures vary with our age and with long-term interest rates when we buy a pension annuity. But broadly speaking (for any given pension fund) an inflation-linked pension starts off at some-where between 30% and 50% *less* than the level income alternative that you *could* have had.

Let's think about that. If inflation were to chug along at, say, 3% p.a. during your retirement, it's obviously going to take a long time for your lower starting (inflation linked) income just to catch up to the 'flat' pension alternative. In fact, it will take about 17 years to catch up.

That's a long time, but wait – this would only mean that the inflation-proofed income had caught up to the *amount* of the flat pension alternative. For it to catch up with the *total* income received from the flat pension – bearing in mind that it would have delivered 17 years of higher income – would take about 12 more years. So, that's nearly 30 years in all, before the inflation-proofed income has paid out (in total) as much as the level pension.

If you reach retirement in good health and believe that you might live for another 30 years in retirement, or if it looks as though inflation might rise above the Government's low target rate (typically around 3%) then you might want to buy an inflation-linked pension at that time. That said, you'd still need to weigh up the relative value of having inflation proofing on your pension income versus a much higher starting income. Regardless of your health it would seem to me that age 90 is late to start thinking about touring the world!

And remember, all we're doing here is tweaking the assumptions we use in estimating the cost of our pension. We want to see if, with fair assumptions, we can make this pension saving game affordable. If we can then we might be inclined to start saving. You're not locking yourself into a decision about the shape of income you'll buy when you reach retirement. That can wait until you get there.

If your investments do well, or you manage to pile in some extra savings during your high-earning years and you end up with a very large pension fund, you can always choose to buy that expensive, escalating pension income when you retire. Alternatively, you might skip the annuity idea altogether, leave your funds invested during your retirement years and 'draw-down' what you need each year, assuming that the fund doesn't run out – a risk you avoid with an annuity. Or, you might choose to cash in ALL your pension fund under the new freedoms that came into force in 2015. Although if you do this you should take care to avoid unnecessary tax and work out where your retirement income will come from!

So, you'll have choices about what to do with your pension fund when you retire – but you don't have to worry about those whilst you're building up your funds.

2. Increase the investment return assumption

When calculating the cost of your pension, you could assume a higher risk/higher potential investment return on your monies. The default return assumption used by advisers and with online calculators is usually quite conservative. And it may be valid to take a higher investment risk/higher potential return approach when you're young and saving regularly over very long time periods. After all, what does it matter if markets are choppy in the short term? You might benefit significantly from short-term falls in the markets because you get to 'buy in' to your investments inside your pension at a lower average cost compared to a steadily growing market.

> Of course you still need your chosen markets to trend upwards over the long term and you shouldn't assume all stock markets do that at all times. That was the mistake people made with Japan in the late 1980s, as noted earlier. We still need to avoid markets on very high valuations.

Conversely, if you're nearing retirement – and depending upon what other investments you have – it may be more appropriate to *reduce* your investment risk and hence the return assumption you use in your pension planning. That would *increase* your estimated pension cost compared to a standard estimate – which is another reason to start planning at a young age.

3. Increase the annuity interest rate assumption

The annuity rates (used for converting a pension fund into pension income) assumed in projection systems are linked to the investment returns assumed in the pension build-up phase. So, by choosing a higher investment return assumption (point 2), your estimated costs for pension funding are *reduced* again through a *higher* assumption about the annuity conversion rate.

4. Lower the assumption about product costs

Product and fund charges vary enormously across the industry, but in good quality workplace schemes they'll typically be very low – perhaps 0.5% p.a. or less as an ongoing charge with little or no upfront charge. Some advisers (and online systems) may assume charges of 1% p.a. or more for the ongoing charge – and whilst this may not sound very different to 0.5%, it makes a big difference to your returns, and thus to your estimated cost of building a pension over the long term. So, you should both minimise the costs on your pensions and make sure that the projections you use reflect the actual charges on your pension – and no more.

5. Forget the traditional pension – just build an escape plan

By this point it's likely that we've already cut 70% or more from our newspaper headline cost of a reasonable pension. Simply by looking at our personal net costs (net of employer contributions and tax relief) together with the four steps mentioned above, we should have achieved this goal. But it is possible to cut the cost of our target income even further, provided we're happy to assume that the income we receive from our pension fund will 'step down' a few years after it starts. The idea here is to make an *escape plan*.

Warning...

This is *not* a traditional pension (level or inflation-proofed) in any sense. However, an escape plan could allow you to transform your life – perhaps with a new career later in life, and the opportunity to do more of what you enjoy. And a basic, low cost escape plan might just lower your anxiety and stress around this whole area.

You may want to start up a business or want a new career that demands a university degree that you don't currently have. How on earth can you use a pension plan to provide the income you'll need, to support yourself *and* your dependents, whilst you step off the treadmill of your current work to start something new?

Well, it may be possible for some people. One way of achieving this is to take the tax-free cash part of your pension fund (normally about 25% of the total) and simply spend it all to boost your income during your escape 'transitional' period. Let's look at an example.

Let's say you built a £240,000 pension fund (in today's money) by the time you're 55. This may sound like a big pension fund to build up, but it could be achieved at a personal net cost of just £150 per month (£5 per day) with savings starting from age 25. You can scale these amounts up or down in line with your affordability.

> I've assumed that: 1) contributions are increased each year in line with inflation, 2) you receive a 60% matched employer contribution, 3) you enjoy 20% personal tax relief, and 4) you enjoy real investment returns after charges of 5% p.a.
>
> The actual cost may be higher or lower than this, depending on how these factors turn out.

Current pension regulations would allow you take £60,000 as tax-free cash from this £240,000 pension fund, which you could use to pro-vide £20,000 (plus interest) each year (tax free) for three years. You could then use the remaining £180,000 in your pension (£240,000 minus the £60,000 taken as cash) to provide a pension income for life – which could also start at age 55 if you needed it – or you could defer this income until later if your resources allowed.

The £180,000 might generate about £11,000 of taxable income at age 55 (depending upon long-term interest rates at the time) but most of that would be tax-free if you didn't have other taxable income when you started drawing it and if the tax-free 'personal allowance' remained at or around its current level in real terms. So, you'd have roughly £30,000 p.a. tax-free total income (£20,000 from the cash fund plus about £11,000 from the pension) running for three years – which is surely enough to get most people started on a serious new venture.

By the way, you're not obliged to spread your 'tax-free cash' over three years. You could take it all out in year one if you like – and have about £70,000 to spend.

Of course, once you've spent the tax-free cash part of your pension fund, you'd fall back onto whatever income you could generate from the remainder – about £11,000 p.a. in our example. But if your plan has worked, by that time you'd have built up your business (or be established in that new career) to supply the extra income you need. Alternatively, you might simply accept a more modest lifestyle after an initial bout of higher income 'partying' funded by spending your tax-free cash. But factor in the arrival of your state pension as this could make up a lot of the shortfall from your private pension in later years.

> If you're several years away from your state pension and on target for a full record of NI contributions or credits, you might assume a state pension of around £8,000 p.a. (in today's money terms). For more details on state pensions – how they work, how much to expect and at what age etc. – see Appendix 4.

Now, you may recall that you can only normally access your pension funds once you've turned 55. This age limit is set to increase (to 57 from 2028) and then track along at 10 years before state pension age. So you may wonder if this escape idea is any use if you want to escape your current work at the age of, say, 50 or 45.

And I think it is. An escape plan could help you achieve a 'life change' at an earlier age – if that's important to you.

You could use your pension to target the cash you'll need for escape at age 55 but then use your other savings to pay for that escape at the earlier date you want. You can then replenish your savings from your pension tax-free cash pile later on. For example, you might use your pension cash to repay your mortgage when you're 55 or 60 whilst using the funds you'd otherwise planned to use to repay the mortgage to build your escape plan at, say, age 50.

Some may consider this last idea (the escape plan) to be an extreme way to cut the cost of achieving your target pension. It certainly isn't suitable for everyone, and if you use it then you must understand it only provides a front-loaded income, that is, an income that steps down in later years. So you need robust plans in place to supplement your income in those later years, either with a new career or a business, and/or from your state pension. But the escape plan can be a lifeline – a way out of your old work and into a new and potentially more rewarding life for your 'autumn years'.

I understand that many people will prefer to plan for a full stop to work, but the challenge is in building a pension fund big enough for this because it can be an expensive option. That said, the lesson you can take from this chapter is that it's not half as expensive as a lot of newspapers (and some advisers) say it is.

Get irate!

- These ideas can be applied by anyone with DC pension benefits, regardless of whether they are also entitled to DB pension benefits.

- DC pensions offer no certainty of pension outcome, so you need to review your funds and targets regularly, say, once every three or four years when you're young and more often as you approach retirement.

- Unfortunately very few people have done this with a sensible set of assumptions, and many are now reaching middle age with very few savings for retirement. Faced with the prospect of carrying on working at the same job for a lot longer, some people take big risks with their money at this stage of life in an attempt to build the funds they need in a much shorter timescale. This is a very risky approach to retirement planning.

- The traditional formula for pension planning is neither a pleasant nor viable option for many people. You do not have to work all your life – especially if you're unhappy with your work – just to build the funds to escape at 65 with an inflation-proofed income. There are other, less painful and more energising ways to achieve the income you need in our later years.

- Inflation-linked annuities will normally take a *very* long time to deliver the same amount of pension income as a level annuity, which starts at a much higher level.

- For younger people, with a long time to go before retirement, you only have to be 'slightly' too conservative in your assumptions (about investment returns or the type of pension you'll buy) to make your estimated pension costs unaffordable.

- You have a much higher capacity for investment risk (and therefore potential investment returns) where you're saving regularly over a long timescale – say, 10 years or more. The investment risk dynamics are very different to investing a lump sum for just a few years.

- Start your pension savings early to minimise the pain of funding a modest income.

- Adopt a strategy of lifelong learning to stand a better chance of enjoying lifelong earnings to supplement whatever your savings provide.

- You **can** cut the headline costs of pensions by more than 70%.

- You can cut them further using a step down 'escape' plan.

Coming up in the next chapter

Up to this point in this book, we've focused on problems in the 'regulated' side of financial services. Of course, there are a lot more crooks making misleading promises outside of the regulatory net. So let's start looking at those now – by exploring the 'wacky' world of trader training.

Chapter 10
Gamblers posing as investment experts

A mad form of gambling in which you risk
losing it all – and more besides.

Gambling: The sure way of getting nothing for something.

~ Wilson Mizner

Imagine you've seen an advert for an 'exclusive' big night out, with a £1 million *prize* competition.

The competition is to take place at a big hotel in the city and will take up only one hour of your time. The advert says that no special skills are required, and that all entrants will have an equal chance of success.

The catch? You have to pay a non-refundable entry fee of £1,000, in cash upfront. Naturally, your first thought is that this might be some kind of scam. But as you read on, you're reassured that, before parting with any money, you can investigate the competition for yourself. You can watch a 'live' event in progress and talk briefly with other contestants. Each competition is limited to just 1,024 participants on a first-come, first-served basis and you read that you should **'hurry to book now because places are selling fast'**.

So, simply out of curiosity you decide to register for the competition – after all, you can opt out if you don't like what you see. On the night, you're greeted by a smartly dressed, professional-sounding, attractive young lady who, as promised, escorts you straight to the competition hall with a dozen other new players for a view of proceedings.

> The use of the word 'attractive' above may sound sexist but the fact is, gambling is more prevalent amongst young males than other groups in society, so the providers tend to use attractive young women in their promotional activities.

You can see that the contestants are all happy enough. Most are smiling or laughing, some are cheering and everyone seems to be enjoying themselves. You lean forward to ask a group on a nearby table what they think of the game, and they all give a thumbs-up. So, satisfied with what you see, you return to the hotel reception with the other participants for the next game and you hand over your £1,000 cash entry fee. You're then given a copy of the competition rules and two pieces of equipment: an old penny coin and a spring-loaded coin-flipping device (old penny coins are much more fun to flip than new pennies as they're about three times as big).

The rules state:

- This competition takes place as a series of rounds in which all contestants use the device to flip their penny coin. The results are recorded by the facilitators.

- Those whose coin comes up 'heads' continue on to the next round. The remaining contestants must leave the hall by the back door.

- There will be as many rounds as necessary to eliminate all but one last contestant, who will receive the £1 million prize. If, in any round, all remaining contestants flip 'tails' with their coins, then they are all eliminated and there is no winner of that competition.

So now you know why everyone in that room was so happy. **They** were the only people left in the game! The losers had all been shuffled out of the back door, doubtless feeling pretty bad about their decision to bet £1,000 on the flip of a coin. They'd deliberately been kept away from you (in the hotel reception) whilst you made up your mind whether to play or not.

Anyway, it's too late to pull out now – you're in the game.

So, let's think through how this game would play out – it's simple enough to work out.

If we assume that all the coins are perfectly balanced we'd expect a 50:50 chance of heads or tails on each throw, and if the throws were distributed perfectly evenly on every occasion, we'd expect this game (with 1,024 contestants) to last for about ten rounds. There'd be 512 players remaining after round one, 256 after round two, 128 after round three, etc., all the way down to the last person.

Of course, given the random outcomes from coin tossing, this game may last a bit longer – or finish a bit earlier – than ten rounds. Either way the organiser wins. If they pay out £1 million they've got a profit of around £24,000 (1,024 players paying £1,000 each gives one million and twenty four thousand pounds in deposits, less the £1 million prize money) and if, as might be expected from time to time, the last few players in the final rounds of the game all throw a 'tails', then the organisers would make over £1 million.

You may be thinking this is a ridiculous story. No one would be stupid enough to take part in a game with such a high chance of losing his or her stake of £1,000. And I'd tend to agree with you – *but only if the players knew and understood the odds of losing before starting the game.* But remember, in this story, you didn't know the chances of losing upfront. You were just told that there was a very real chance of winning £1 million from a £1,000 stake, and that you were allowed to meet with the other 'happy' players (those still in the game) before committing to play.

Now, there are a great many ways to gamble our money away and the chances of winning (and thus the risks of losing) are very different with each game. If you place your bets on red (or black) at a French roulette wheel, you have about a 48.65% chance of winning (because 18 out of the 37 slots in the wheel are red and 18 are black). And if your colour comes up, then you simply double your money. This means the chances of losing to the house are on average about 2.7% (100% minus 2 x 48.65%) and so, if you hang around at that wheel for 100 spins and put down £10 each time, you can expect to lose about £27 by the time you leave!

Some might say that's a cheap price to pay for an evening's enter-tainment and you might get lucky and win. And yes, of course you might get lucky. Then again, you might be *unlucky* and lose a whole lot more – *perhaps hundreds of pounds* in this example.

Yes, some people do win gambles sometimes, and occasionally somebody wins the 'big money'. And it's the hope of winning that 'big money' that draws people into gambling and then keeps them hooked.

The hope of the 'big win' is also what draws people into other addic-tive games, including many computer games. They keep us playing by giving us just enough of a dopamine kick from our occasional wins to keep us interested, despite our far more common losses. And keeping the punter interested with the dream of a big win is also the popular formula in other entertainment businesses that dominate our atten-tion. Think about 'The X-Factor' or TV phone-in games (with those ridiculously easy-to-answer questions) and those allegedly low-cost 'bid to buy' websites. They're all playing the same game – selling a dream – and they all disappointment most of their customers.

The fact is that with games of pure chance you'll lose a lot of money to the house over the long term. This has to be the case or they'd go out of business – and that doesn't happen too often!

Obviously there's absolutely no skill involved in tossing a coin – so you'd think that no one would be daft enough to seek advice on how to do that. But there are some people out there running training courses in something similar. These 'trading strategy' teachers claim to be able to teach us how to read market patterns and how to set up trades in the markets to deliver big profits very quickly. And their systems tend to involve the use of spread bets.

What is spread betting?

Spread betting is sometimes marketed as an alternative to ordinary investing and you'll often hear it described using a less gambling-like word, such as 'trading'. I guess 'trading' sounds a lot more professional than gambling. 'Trading' is okay – many of us trade our products or services in our daily lives. We know about trading (buying and selling) things, whether it's a car or a piece of antique furniture.

But let's be clear. This is not what you're doing with spread betting – you're *not* buying and selling assets. Assets are things with value and many of them also produce an income. A spread bet is just that, a bet, and because there is no asset being bought or sold there's no Stamp Duty tax to pay and no Capital Gains Tax (CGT) on any profits you make. This alleged 'tax saving' is marketed as an advantage of spread betting when compared with buying a real asset – shares, for example – but this is an absurd comparison. Of course there's no CGT on a profit if you're not actually buying and selling an asset on which to make any profit! What's more, because there's no CGT on any gains, there's also no CGT relief (against gains elsewhere) on spread betting losses. *This CGT disadvantage is seldom made clear by all operators – and that's very* unfortunate given that **most people actually do lose** at spread betting.

According to the "White Paper on Spread Betting" (by Chris Brady and Richard Ramyar of Cass Business School) and similar research in Taiwan, around 80% of spread betters end up losing money, and even the 20% who win can't win consistently.

Losses on spread betting can be very significant, and gamblers using these products can and often do end up *losing many times more than their original stake.*

What?

Yes, let me say that again in case you missed it, using the language that spread betting companies are obliged (by the Financial Conduct Authority, or FCA) to use, right up front on their website:

Spread bets are leveraged products and **can result in losses that exceed your initial deposit.**

In other words, you can lose many times more than you put on the table to start with. So these bets can be much riskier than betting on horses.

Yes, I think that's clear now. Let's get back to our trading training seminar anomaly.

Why would anyone expect to 'learn' how to bet in a purely random game like coin flipping? And why would an alleged expert and experienced 'trader' be so keen to share their secrets? Surely all they have to do is sit at their computer and carry on trading, and very soon they'll become multi-millionaires?

You might think it's very generous of these traders to share their secrets with us – at their FREE seminars – but let's stop and think why they'd want to do that. I mean, if they really could teach everyone how to read the markets then surely they would attract students from everywhere – including the big investment banks? And if those students all took advantage of the market price imperfections – that they can allegedly see from daily price movements – then this would move the market and remove those same opportunities.

I assume that anyone day trading the markets will want to own some high-tech (high priced) software and PC equipment to access the price charts and jump on the opportunities before the rest of us see them. But surely the big investment banks can afford the biggest and best equipment – so, if there are killings to be made with very short-term trades, won't those big investors get to them before anybody else?

It seems to me that we are the last in the queue for quick trading gains – if there are any such (legal) opportunities at all. Hmm, I wonder ... is it possible that *some* of these 'trainers' in day trading just got lucky for a while, made some money and decided to stop betting and get into training whilst they were still ahead? Or perhaps they lost all their winnings (and more besides) on a last roll of the dice? Perhaps they're skint? Perhaps they're really gambling losers posing as winners. Perhaps they have to do the training workshops in order to pay back their personal losses on spread betting?

And some of the people I've seen promoting themselves as trading training experts really do look rather skint (I occasionally attend these events for research purposes!).

I guess it could be that these trader trainers are just so busy 'trading' that they forget about their appearance. They don't notice the need to buy new shoes when the old ones are completely worn out. I distinctly remember one man, with holes in his shoes and a horribly worn-out suit, telling one group of assembled hopeful traders (and me) about the fortunes to be made by 'trading'.

I'll never forget that presentation because the man assured us that spread betting was the only realistic way to double our money within a year. And he told us that we could achieve that whilst taking very little risk with our money.

Yes, that's right, we could all (every one of us there that evening) double our money. Here's what he said, word for word:

> Doubling your money each year is perfectly possible. Think about it: a doubling is only a profit of 100% (he was clearly very good with maths!) ... and that's equivalent to profits of just 6% per month compound.

And he's right too – arithmetically – 6% per month every month would indeed compound up to roughly 100% over a full year.

But where he's wrong (*and very wrong*) is on the important matter of risk. Those sorts of returns are not achievable without taking massive risks with your capital. What's more, the chances of achieving 100% returns in a year are very low indeed.

Just think about this. If it were that easy to double your money, then everybody would be doing it. In fact none of us would bother doing anything else!

The challenge facing us here is something called 'survivorship bias'. The losers in these games of chance have been hidden away (smuggled out of the back door of the hotel) and now all we can see are the winners, or rather, the 'survivors', left in the game. If we allow ourselves to be carried away with the dream of becoming one of those winners we will be lured into this game. So let's be very clear on this point. You can't get skilful at games of pure luck, however hard you try – or however much you spend on training courses! Yet, an astonishing number of people (including some intelligent people) miss this simple point and get drawn into this form of gambling.

Let me introduce you to Joe.

Joe is 33 years old and married to Naomi. They have a four-year-old son, Luke, with another on the way. They want to move out of their two-bed flat and buy a three-bed house for their growing family. They both have reasonably well paid jobs but their cost of living is high and they only manage to save modest amounts each month.

They don't yet have enough for the deposit on the house that they want – their savings account contains £4,000 and they need around £7,000 (to add to the small amount of equity they have in their current flat) to put down on the new house. The prices of the types of house they're looking at did fall a fair bit in the crisis of 2008-09 but have since started rising again – quite sharply. And now their savings are growing more slowly than the rate at which the required house deposit is increasing. They're getting frustrated that their chances of moving any time soon are slipping away.

One of Joe's footballing friends, Phil, has mentioned on several occasions how he's made 'big money' with some simple trades on the markets. Joe knows that Phil is not rich so he's obviously not making a fortune at this and Phil doesn't have children so perhaps he can afford to fritter away some of his spare income. And Joe suspects that this trading game might be risky, but he reckons there's no harm in checking it out. After all, it might just be the answer to building that £7,000 in double-quick time. Phil says his trading really isn't risky and that you can put stop losses on your trades – to limit losses – if you're nervous. They only cost a small percentage. Apparently it's easy to set up an account and get started for a modest sum and you can do all the trading online from home.

Joe decides to do some more homework before putting any real trades on. He finds out that spread trading is 'geared' and needs to know exactly what this means. There's a mass of stuff on the trading website but it's all rather dull and confusing. So, as he does when looking at most new things these days, he searches on YouTube for a short lesson and soon finds this basic training video which enhances his confidence. See here: http://bit.ly/Hpebd3

As it says on the video, "gearing is good"!

"So far so good," thinks Joe, "this might just be what we need to build those funds for the house. And that lady in the video clearly knows what she's talking about. She explained the concept very well."

So Joe sets up an account to start spread 'trading'. He decides not to mention this to Naomi as he doesn't want to worry her. In any event she might put the brakes on the idea – she can be a bit like that sometimes!

He decides to place a trade on the shares in a mid-sized fast growing engineering company that he's familiar with. He was thinking of buying shares in that company anyway and this seems like a great way to magnify his profits. He places his first trade as an 'up bet' at £20 per point. In this case a point is a 1p movement in the share price – which currently stands at 1,000p. (With spread betting you can make either up or down bets depending on which way you think prices will move).

> There are, naturally, charges (bid to offer spreads) on these accounts and the price needs to move by more than the 'spread' in prices (in the right direction) to start making any profit. But we'll ignore these charges in this simple example.

Joe's trading account informs him that in order to make this trade he must make a deposit (also known as an upfront 'margin' payment) of £4,000. This is based on 20% of Joe's initial 'total risk exposure' – that's fancy talk for the maximum loss on the trade. The maximum loss on this trade is calculated as £20,000, which is Joe's £20 per point bet multiplied by 1,000 (the maximum number of points the share price could fall if it collapsed to zero). And £4,000 just happens to be everything Joe has in his savings account with Naomi. He does think twice before going ahead, but after talking the idea over with Phil (over several beers), Joe decides to move their £4,000 into the spread betting account to cover his first trade. He puts a 5% stop loss in place to prevent any nasty losses, and then it's done – Joe's first trade is on.

Joe was planning to sell out of this trade once the price rose by about 10% to 1,100p. That seemed like a reasonable bet given that the price fell by nearly 10% yesterday. Joe believes it's common knowledge that prices always bounce back after big falls! He's also worked out that a 10% price move would deliver about £2,000 of profit (a 100 point move times £20 per point), and that this would take him and Naomi on their way to getting their new home. After setting everything up and reading around the site a bit more *(over a couple more beers)* Joe crawls into bed quite late that night and then struggles to get off to sleep. He's really quite excited about this trade.

Unfortunately, just before the markets open the next morning, the company on which Joe has placed his bet issues a profit warning and the price is marked down, a lot, at the open. Joe can't believe his eyes – the price has fallen like a stone. It's down 40%!

"Crikey," thinks Joe "that's bad, that's really very bad."

He takes a deep breath and starts to consider how he's going to break this to Naomi. Then he remembers, "It's okay. I have a stop loss on that trade at 5%. Thank goodness for Phil's advice on stop losses – we'll be fine."

Joe calculates that he'll be down around £1,000 (5% of 1,000 points x £20 per point) plus the charge in the spread. Whilst this is clearly not a good situation, it's also not a disaster.

Joe considers closing the account to prevent any more losses, but not for long. "What's the point of closing the account now?" he thinks, "that was simply the first trade and I got really unlucky. I'll soon make up for that loss on the next trade. Lightning never strikes twice in the same place – right?"

Just then, Joe gets a phone call. It's his account manager at the spread trading company and he's asking what Joe wants to do with his account.

"What do you mean 'Do I want to close my account?'" says Joe, "No, of course not, I want to put on another trade – do you think I give up that easily?"

The man on the phone tells Joe that he could close his account by paying in another £4,000. However, if he wants to place more trades, like before he'll need to add in another £8,000.

"What? How on earth can that be?" says Joe, "I put £4,000 in that account and with my 5% stop loss I reckon I'm down about £1,000.

There should be plenty left in there to place another trade."

"Well no, I'm sorry," says the man. "Unfortunately the price of the share you'd traded 'gapped' down overnight."

Joe isn't sure what "gapping" means so the man explains.

"Gapping is a sudden shift in the price from one level to another. It can happen during a trading day or overnight when markets are closed, which is what happened here. And when the market opened this morning the price was already 40% down. So yes, your stop loss sell order triggered but I'm afraid it did so at a much lower price than you were expecting."

"Hang on" says Joe. "Are you telling me these 'stop loss' things don't actually stop my losses when this happens?"

"Well yes," replies the man. "You see, you could have bought a 'guaranteed stop loss' and this *would* have protected you from this *gapping* problem. However, the guaranteed stop orders have higher charges – which eat into your trading profits – so not everyone goes for them … but obviously they're worth it in these situations. The details are all clearly marked on our site for you to read."

Joe is stunned and silent.

The man pipes up again. "So in the meantime you just need to pay us £4,000 to close down your account – or pay in, say, £8,000 if you wish to continue trading."

Joe only now realises how stupid he'd been.

To begin with, he'd thought that he was only risking about £200 (5% of £4,000) – but then, when he did the sums he figured he'd lost perhaps £1,000 worst case – because of the five times gearing on his return. But now, because of the price gapping, it turns out that he's lost £8,000 in just one night. Their precious £4,000 of savings had all gone on this mad experiment and worse still, he's now in debt to this spread betting company for another £4,000.

What is he going to tell Naomi?

Okay, so that's the end of another one of my 'extreme' stories – designed to make a critically important point.

Please make no mistake, this sort of thing does happen. The price of even leading company shares can gap by this amount. For example, on the night of 21/22 November 2011, the share price of the holiday company Thomas Cook Group fell by over 50%. That's a very big 'gap' to contend with – and the share price continued falling on 22 November, ending the day some 75% lower than the day before. But not all losses in spread betting happen this way. Some people lose their money slightly more slowly, at the rate of perhaps 5-10% of their money on each bad trade.

> This assumes no bad luck with 'gapping', that the bets are set with stop losses on the underlying asset price of 1% to 2%, and that the spread better makes a 20% margin deposit – i.e. 5 times gearing.

Either way, the fact is that a great many people do lose the sort of money Joe lost in our example – and some lose much bigger amounts with spread bets and similar types of geared financial instruments called *Contracts for Difference* (CFDs). Some people may only lose a few hundred pounds, some lose thousands or tens of thousands and some lose very big time. Only a very small number of people win over the medium term and there's no evidence – which I'm aware of – that any of those winners are anything other than lucky.

Sean Quinn was an Irish businessman, and in 2008 he was the richest person in Ireland. *The Sunday Times* Rich List estimated his personal worth to be €4.722 billion (£3.73 billion). According to the BBC, between October 2005 and July 2007 Sean Quinn had built up a 28% stake in the former Anglo Irish Bank using CFDs to gamble on the bank share price. And one might think that Mr Quinn (more than any of us) could afford to pay for the analysis he needed in order to make an intelligent bet on that bank's share price. However, the bank share price collapsed just the same and his bet went horribly wrong. And the resulting losses were in large part responsible for Mr Quinn's bankruptcy in January 2012.

So it doesn't matter how rich you are – you really can lose everything with this sort of gambling.

Get irate!

- Spread betting is not trading, it's an extreme form of gambling, and you can lose significantly more than your initial stake.

- Price gapping can make stop losses worthless. Guaranteed stop losses cost a lot more and therefore significantly reduce the chances of winning anything at all.

- On their own (without any offsetting assets) these betting instruments are highly dangerous. Some people will argue that small 'down bets' can be used to insure against losses where you have a significant holding in the underlying asset, but there are less risky ways of insuring your portfolio – using covered warrants.

- Spread betting has grown significantly in the UK in recent years. Figures for total account activity are difficult to obtain, but Wikipedia cites *The Times* as reporting that there may now be over one million spread betting accounts in the UK.

- Serious gambling addiction problems are far more prevalent (perhaps up to 15 times more) amongst spread betters than the general population of gamblers.

This and other important risk warnings about spread betting (and contracts for differences) can be found at the Money Advice Service site at:

www.moneyadviceservice.org.uk/en/articles/
spread-betting-and-contracts-for-difference

The original source of research is the 2007 UK Gambling Commission prevalence survey.

Some final thoughts on the wider problem of gambling

- 'Problem gambling' is gambling to a degree that compromises, disrupts or damages family, personal or recreational pursuits. Indicators of gambling problems include such things as: chasing losses, a preoccupation with gambling, a need to gamble with increasing amounts of money, being restless or irritable when trying to stop, using gambling as escapism, lying to people to conceal the extent of gambling, having tried but failed to cut back on gambling, having committed a crime to finance gambling, having risked or lost a relationship/job/educational opportunity because of gambling, and becoming reliant on others to help in a financial crisis caused by gambling.

- According to the NHS, there may be as many as **450,000 problem gamblers** (of all sorts) in the UK. The internet has made gambling more accessible, allowing more and more people to gamble from the privacy of their own home. This is thought to be one of the reasons for the increase in the number of women gamblers.

- There's a link between gambling and alcohol misuse. Many gambling addicts are addicted to alcohol. Depression and attempted suicide rates amongst gambling addicts are around double the national average. Gambling addicts are more likely to go to prison as a result of criminal activity – typically theft and fraud.

- Gambling can be successfully treated in the same way as other addictions. Cognitive behavioural therapy usually has the best results.

- GamCare www.gamcare.org.uk is the main support organisation in the UK, providing face-to-face counselling; it runs a free national telephone helpline for emotional support, information and advice, 8am-midnight, seven days a week: 0808 8020 133.

Coming up in the next chapter

The final group of (**external**) money monsters that you need to know about, are the criminal scammers – so let's get an up to date picture of their activities now.

Oh, and if you'd like to get to grips with the biggest money monster of all – the one who lives **inside** our heads – just grab a copy of my second book, *How We Mislead Ourselves About Money*.

Chapter 11
Scummy scammers

The many forms of the modern scammer
– and how to avoid them

Eighty percent of the population are really great, caring people who will help you and tell you the truth. The other twenty percent are crooks and liars. That's just how it is.

~ Tom Hanks

© Copyright Paul Claireaux

x

It's bad enough to lose a small percentage of your money each year because of a 'rhino' adviser's excessive charging. But this only becomes a serious problem if you ignore it. You may be able to remove unnecessary charges by moving your funds to a more reasonably priced service.

> Warning: Before you decide to encash any existing investments – in order to re-invest in new ones – make sure that you're not throwing away valuable features (such as investment guarantees) on your current holdings. Also, take account of any tax and product exit charges that could arise on selling.

Suffering a *large* percentage loss on your investment in a market crash is more painful, but this might also be repaired over time if markets recover *and* you remain invested. Indeed, if you invest regularly, then market dips can even work in your favour by reducing the average price at which you buy in.

Either way, your returns are determined by when you start investing, and if you start at the very worst of times, when markets are grossly overpriced, then your returns may be very disappointing. However, the pain of these losses is nothing compared to what you might suffer if you're caught out by a scam. First, there's the pain of losing your money – which might not be recovered at all – but then there's the horrible feeling of humiliation that comes from knowing you've been fooled.

Scams come in many different forms, but essentially they're all criminal activities to defraud us of our money. The regulators will try to find and prosecute scammers (if they're reported), and to recover fraudulently obtained funds, but there's no guarantee that they'll succeed.

Given that scammers operate outside the law, you cannot expect the Financial Services Compensation Scheme (FSCS) to bail you out from your losses if you get caught. You may lose everything that you put into these scams – this may sound obvious, but not everyone realises the lack of protection they have against these criminals. It's true that if your money has been stolen from your bank account, or your debit or credit card has been used fraudulently, then you should be able to get that money back. However, **you would be liable** for losses where your bank proves that you were grossly negligent – such as giving someone else your PIN code or leaving it somewhere visible to others in a workplace.

There are some situations where you may not realise that you've been scammed at the time. With identity theft, the first you might know about it is when you start receiving bills for things you haven't ordered, or demands for repayment of debts that aren't yours.

A key feature in most of the scams listed below is that the criminal will try to obtain personal information such as date of birth, current and previous addresses and, best of all, some proof of identity such as a passport or driving licence. With this information they can open bank accounts, order goods and take out credit cards or mobile phone contracts, and so on – all in your name. This activity will affect your credit rating, making it difficult for you to obtain any genuine credit until the issues are resolved.

The internet has made it easier for criminals to operate scams from remote locations, including those outside our national borders, and now many of the threats are online.

It's understandable then that regulators and security agencies would want to view the types of messages going through this channel. Delivering systems that respect our privacy and that allow completely free communications across so many online channels is a real challenge, but that's another debate.

The types of tricks played by scammers are constantly changing to avoid detection, so any list of scams will soon be out of date. However, it's worth being aware of the main risks to your money. You can find up-to-date information on scams on the Financial Conduct Authority (FCA) and Money Advice Service websites:

www.fca.org.uk/consumers/scams

www.moneyadviceservice.org.uk/en/categories/
scams-and-identity-theft

Here's a brief outline of the more common types of scam:

Face-to-face fraud

Whilst some door-to-door selling is perfectly legitimate there are, as the BBC's 'Watchdog' programme proves every week, plenty of criminals at work on the doorstep too. You may be pressured into buying things you don't need, including expensive but poor quality home maintenance or improvement work. These services, which often demand a hefty upfront administration fee, can include:

- energy-saving home improvements, such as a new boiler or roof/cavity wall insulation

- a survey that allegedly tests for rising damp in the outside walls of your house and invariably shows a need for expensive damp proofing work

- patio or driveway repairs or replacement

- roof cleaning or repairs to broken tiles.

Now, you may *need* some or all of this work to be done, but you should not be pressured into making any hasty decisions. If you feel like you're being put under pressure, then get a quote for the work from other suppliers and ask for references.

Spear fishing – the advance fee scam

In this scam you may receive an uninvited letter or email from someone. They may claim to be wealthy but suffering persecution for their political or other beliefs in some troubled part of the world. A lot of these scams have historically come from Africa (Nigeria in particular), but they could come from anywhere.

You are offered a significant fee, to be paid directly into your bank, simply for helping them to move their money out of their troubled country. They ask for your bank details – to enable them to make this payment – and this gets them started with identity theft. If you provide enough details they can start emptying your bank account straight away. Alternatively they'll ask you to send money to pay their 'legal fees' (or some other fictitious costs) that they claim they cannot pay from their own account for fear of raising suspicions with their authorities.

Of course, there are **no fees *for you*** in this scam. The only money involved is that which you transfer to the scammer or lose through identity theft.

According to the Money Advice Service, a similar scam has been operated out of China relating to payment from wills. *The Sunday Times* ran an article ('I Got Fooled By Sophisticated Computer Scam', 29 September 2013) which told of a Chesterfield man who very nearly got caught by this. He said that he *"prided himself on being an experienced and cynical investor."* Yet he became convinced that he'd been left US$8.5 million in a will by a distant relative in China and was on the verge of wiring the crooks £20,000 (to pay the costs of releasing his monies) before being saved by an eleventh-hour phone call from the FCA.

This man had even taken the trouble to check the validity of the offer with the US Securities and Exchange Commission (SEC) who had apparently replied that this all seemed okay. But it turned out that his email password had been compromised, allowing the scammers to view his correspondence, send emails from his account and block incoming emails. So the SEC reply would have been blocked and replaced with a fake reply – effectively telling this man to go ahead and wire the money.

I've no idea how the FCA managed to discover this scam and identify and contact the potential target in time, but what we do know is that *most people are not so lucky.*

Identity thieves deliberately target wealthy individuals and obtain personal information by various means over a period of time. Then, when they approach you with their offer of riches – whether by email or phone – they have so much information about you on file, that you're fooled into thinking they must be from a genuine organisation.

Keep your email password secure and change it from time to time.

Lottery and prize draw scams

This is similar to the rescue/advance fee scam in that you're asked for your bank details and, possibly, an upfront payment. The difference is that this time your payment is supposedly required to release your lottery or other big draw 'prize' winnings. Alternatively you may be asked to call a special telephone number to claim your prize. This turns out to be a premium rate line and the call takes an extremely long time to complete – by which time it costs far more than the prize, if you receive anything at all. You might even be asked to prove your identity before receiving your prize by providing passport or other details that are then used to steal your identity.

Money mules

In this scam you're offered a fee to allow someone else's money to pass through your bank account. You'll be given a plausible but false reason for agreeing to this whilst what's really happening is an attempt to launder dirty money – the proceeds of crime – through your account.

Criminals attempt to clean up/launder their dirty money by passing it through a series of legitimate accounts. This thwarts the police's efforts to find the real (illegitimate) sources of the money. If you allow your account to be used in this way you can be convicted of money laundering. The maximum penalty is 14 years' imprisonment.

Interestingly in the UK, we treat the proceeds of crime as those monies obtained from acts that would be criminal if they had taken place in the UK – so, for example, under UK law, the proceeds from a bull fight in Spain would constitute 'dirty' money.

Boiler room and 'pump and dump' share scams

'Boiler room' describes the 'high pressure' and illegal selling of shares or other investments. You'll be promised high profits on your money provided that you act quickly, before the share price 'takes off'. Sometimes the company whose shares are being touted does not exist at all, but you'll be sent fake share certificates to persuade you that the investment is genuine, whilst your funds clear into the scammer's account.

Alternatively, in a 'pump and dump' scheme the scammers hold real but virtually worthless stock that they sell ('dump') at inflated ('pumped up') prices on to unsuspecting buyers. The scammers are able to push up the stock price by driving a buying frenzy based on false stories about the company's prospects. Once the scammers have dumped their stock, the misleading stories end and the price collapses as all the recently conned investors realise their mistake and rush to sell their shares.

According to the FCA, *"victims of share fraud lose an average of £20,000 to these scams, with as much as £200m being lost in the UK each year. Even seasoned investors have been caught out, with the biggest individual loss recorded by the police being £6m."* It makes sense to check the FCA's register and deal only with firms that are authorised. You can also learn to be a **scam smart** investor here: http://scamsmart.fca.org.uk/

Ponzi schemes

In these schemes you're offered a low-risk investment promising much higher returns than bank savings alternatives, whilst still giving you access to your capital if you need it. What's more, the promised high returns are actually delivered to the early participants in these schemes – who are so pleased that they then become the unwitting promoters of the scam to their friends and family. In this way a network of new and highly trusting investors grows rapidly by word of mouth. The money that you pay into these schemes **may** be invested in various assets or it might simply be left on deposit at a bank. Either way, it's only the organiser who's certain of getting a high return – as he takes what he wants directly from his investor's funds!

In the early stages of the scheme, the investors who need a regular income – and those who withdraw their capital may receive the promised high returns. These monies are simply paid out from the money paid in by all the other investors – so depleting the scheme's funds below what's been paid in. But by making these payments, the scammer maintains the illusion of the fund working as promised. In this way, the Ponzi scheme is kept going for as long as new investors (victims) can be found to offset the withdrawals. And if the 'proven' returns are pitched at a sufficiently attractive level – whilst still being believable – then very few people will want to withdraw their money. They will want to earn the high returns and so will leave their money invested in the scheme. Low levels of withdrawals keep the scheme running for longer.

At some point, like a chain mail letter, the scheme collapses in on itself. This can happen when the flow of new investors dries up or an event may trigger more requests for withdrawals than the rapidly vanishing fund can meet. The financial crisis of 2008 was supposedly the trigger that exposed Bernard Madoff's multi-billion dollar Ponzi scheme.

At the end of these schemes there may be no funds left to pay the remaining 'trusting' investors – normally the majority. However, if regulators catch such fraud early enough they can suspend the fund whilst it still has some value, and then allocate what's left more fairly across all investors.

The Madoff scheme must have been particularly well hidden within Madoff's accounting systems because he managed to obtain funding support from several global banks and other institutional clients – in addition to more vulnerable private clients. This suggests that these scams are either very difficult to detect, or that regulatory oversight is inadequate.

Just remember that it's not possible to deliver high investment returns and risk-free early access to your capital. If that's what you're being promised, then walk away.

Missed call fraud

Here's where you receive a telephone call that stops after just one or two rings. Then when you call back – on what turns out to be a premium-rate telephone number – you're kept holding for as long as possible whilst the scammers generate an income from your phone bill.

Phishing

With phishing, you receive a fraudulent email out of the blue from someone claiming to be a representative of a large organisation – such as your bank, credit card company, HMRC or PayPal, the payment service. You're advised that for some, very reasonable sounding reason, you need to log on to your account. You're provided with a link from the email that takes you straight to a well-designed fake copy of your provider's website, where you enter all your account details.

To avoid being caught out, whenever you log on to a site where security is important (for banking, other investments and communications such as email, Facebook etc.) look for the 'locked padlock' icon in the browser window and make sure that the site's web address begins with 'https'.

A fake website can also give itself away by requesting more information than is usual when you log on. If your bank asks you to supply your user name, password, PIN code and card number, then alarm bells should be ringing in your head, and you should be ringing your bank! This scam – to phish for personal details – may also be attempted by telephone contact. If you're suspicious, say you will phone the caller back and then check the number they provide – with your bank – before doing so. You should also make sure you have a dial tone before calling anyone back – some clever scammers know that by staying on the line they can escape being caught in this way.

Pharming

Pharming is the high-powered version of phishing – and more difficult to detect because it doesn't offer any clues. There are no unexpected emails or telephone calls inviting us to provide our personal details. This scam simply takes you to the fake website directly, despite the fact that you've typed in the right web address! To achieve this, the scammer must somehow install malicious software onto your computer or infect the server (the remote computer) through which your internet service is provided. Common anti-virus software cannot protect us from this latter type of system corruption but you can make the same checks as outlined above to ensure that you're logged on to a secure website.

Online auction fraud

In these scams you're taken in by fake buyers who send cheques or promise a money transfer for goods that you send off in good faith, only to find that their payment bounces. Scam sellers also prowl the auction sites selling flawed or non-existent goods. Some excellent notes about online shopping and auction scams are available by searching 'online shopping scams' at www.actionfraud.police.uk

The fake virus hoax

Here's where you're called by someone claiming to be Microsoft Windows Support (or some other genuine sounding organisation), and asked if your PC is running slowly. Most of us will say 'Yes' to this question because our PCs do run slow if we fail to attend to basic start-up program management. You're then told to look up a particular file on your PC. You're advised that the information you read back on this file means your PC needs urgent attention before it crashes altogether, and you're helped to purchase some expensive and completely unnecessary software. By using your bank or credit card on a non-secure system, you then expose yourself to identity theft at the same time.

Finally, the scammer may request that you follow instructions to download other software, or follow some further instructions in order to provide their 'technicians' with remote access to your PC. Then they're able to scan your PC's files for more confidential information, such as passwords.

Dating fraud

You're lured in to this scam, often via a dating site, with the promise of romance with a very attractive person who is normally based overseas. When the scammer believes they've hooked you romantically, they start making requests for money. You may be told that the money is to help an elderly or sick relative or that it's for your 'date', to pay for their travel costs to visit you. Not surprisingly, they don't show up!

New job and 'work at home' scams

This is similar to the dating scam, but here the promise is about a new career (often overseas) rather than romance. You're asked to pay heavy fees upfront for training and other materials, accommodation and arranging visas. The sad truth is that the promised job doesn't exist.

Then there are the 'work at home' scams where it's promised that you can earn easy money from the comfort of your home. Again, large upfront fees are charged to register for the scheme, but then sales 'leads' or products turn out to be worthless and your registration details are used for identity theft.

Vehicle fraud

Various scams exist around the sale of cars. You might be sold a stolen car or one that's been illegally repaired after having been 'written off' as beyond repair after an accident. Or you might be sold a vehicle on which a hire purchase agreement remains outstanding. Such cars do not belong to you, even if you've paid for them! They belong to the finance company until all the payments have been made, which means you might end up paying twice for the car.

You can find a useful guide of the pitfalls around buying used cars at:

www.theaa.com/motoring_advice/car-buyers-guide/cbg_usedtips.html

Health scams

There are health scams promising miracle cures for everything – from baldness, cancer, impotence and acne to being overweight, and so on. Signing up for a course of drugs or other treatments can commit you to large regular payments. These fake treatments, if they arrive at all, may have little or no effect, or may actually damage your health. Always talk to your GP or local pharmacist who'll tell you whether the product you're thinking of buying is safe and effective. Never stop taking a prescribed medicine or start taking a new medicine without speaking to your GP first.

Land banking

In land banking, a company will divide a piece of land into small plots and sell it to investors at a significantly higher price than it paid for it. The plot is promoted on the basis that it will obtain planning permission for residential development in the near future, at which point, you're told, it will soar in value. Many of these plots are located in areas protected from building development including agricultural land, green belts, nature conservation and special scientific interest areas. Some plots are simply too small to build on.

The Financial Conduct Authority (FCA) estimates that land banking schemes have cost UK investors as much as £200 million.

Misleading property promotions

Some property developers looking to raise funds for new developments – whether in UK commercial or residential or overseas holiday resorts – will promote the potentially high rental returns on their investments without being clear about the risks to that income or to your capital. They'll talk about 'guaranteed' or 'secure' (or some other reassuring word) levels of high income. A good many of their adverts would be deemed 'unfair' by the regulator for packaged investments, but property development adverts appear to be escaping regulatory attention.

Misleading property investment educational seminars

Watch out for high-cost seminars that promise a complete education on how to become a property development expert. Some of these courses are simply one-sided promotional events that provide little information about the significant downside risks of 'highly geared' property investment. They may be little more than a series of introductions to a supplier's finance and property development services.

'Highly geared' property investments use borrowings for a large proportion of the property purchase price. This means that potential losses are many times larger than the deposit paid.

Many of these 'get rich quick with property' educational seminars are incredibly misleading – and the fact that some are promoted under the names of famous personalities is no guarantee of quality. For research purposes, I've attended seminars promoted under TV personality Martin Roberts' name and others promoted by Rich Dad™ Education – which claims to be approved by best-selling author Robert Kiyosaki. What I found was that the speakers at both of these FREE seminars made grossly unbalanced and misleading statements. Their overhyped messages offered no valuable ideas, they were clearly just 'teasers' to get us to buy their expensive weekend property seminar. Here are just a few of the misleading statements taken from a Rich Dad seminar, shown below in italics – with my observations in square brackets.

State pensions are useless and because of the way they're structured (with couples getting less than twice that of a single person) you need to get divorced just before retirement in order to get more state pension!

[This is a completely misleading interpretation of UK state pensions from someone who admitted he wasn't qualified to comment or advise on pensions.]

*Private pensions are a waste of time – you'll just work hard and pay in for 50 years to end up with little or nothing in return. 'You're **not** going to get a pension'* he shouted several times throughout the evening.

[This is nonsense as we've already seen – although we've also seen that to maximise your benefits, you do need to start early on your savings and make sure you obtain any 'free' employer contributions.]

It doesn't matter if you don't have any money to get started on your property portfolio – you can simply raise the deposit you need on a series of credit cards!

[Good grief, use a credit card to start investing? The examples we were given – showing how to turn credit card debt into riches – all assumed big (15% plus) short-term price increases on the properties. Clearly such gains are very rare – or we'd all be making them every week. There was no balance to the presentation to show what might happen to the investor if the property they'd bought on credit fell in price instead of rising. *The answer is that such an investor would be 'wiped out' financially and potentially bankrupted.*]

Pension scams

These warnings apply to people with 'defined contribution' (DC) pensions.

Most people working in the private sector will save for their retirement with a DC pension scheme of one sort or another. These include personal pension plans (PPPs), stakeholder pensions (SHP), self-invested personal pensions (SIPPs), group money purchase plans (GMPPs) and small self-administered schemes (SSAS).

With DC pensions your contributions are defined so, unlike 'defined benefit' pension schemes, there's no certainty on what you'll get out. That depends on a host of variables, including the amounts you (and your employer if you have one) put in, the effects of inflation and investment returns on the 'real' value of the pension fund over the term to retirement, and the pension income rate you can obtain when you get there.

Pension scammers will use all sorts of tricks to grab a slice of your pension fund:

- If you're under 55*, some scammers will offer to help you release cash from your pension early – without telling you that you may suffer a tax charge of 55% (yes you could lose more than half of your fund in tax) if you encash your pension funds early – unless you have a right to do so under your pension scheme or special permission due to ill health.

> You can normally access your pension funds from age 55 although it's been announced that this age will rise in the future to remain ten years before state pension age. So, for example, that means it'll probably have risen to age 57 by around 2028.

- Other scammers will try to tempt you to invest your pension fund in some investment with a 'promised' high return. Such investments are invariably 'stuffed' full of charges to pay the seller and very high risk – so your risks of losses would be very high.

- Or, they'll try to tempt you to encash your pension so that you can invest in some 'dodgy' fund in your own name (outside the pension wrapper).

Now, whilst it's true that recent changes to pension rules may allow you (if you're over 55) to encash your pension fund, this does not necessarily make it a good idea. So please, think carefully before encashing it. You may:

- lose a valuable feature, such as a guaranteed growth rate on your funds or a guaranteed pension income rate

- risk running out of the money you need for income in later life, and

- pay an enormous amount of **unnecessary tax** – because most of an encashed pension fund is normally taxable at your marginal rate.

So what should you do if you're approached with some 'interesting' ideas about what you could do with your pension?

Well, take your time about this – it would be a rare situation if you had to take rushed decisions in this area. And talk your situation through with someone from one of the free government guidance services:

- The Pensions Advisory Service (TPAS) or

- Pension Wise (some Citizens Advice bureaux will offer face to face Pension Wise sessions), check online for details.

They should be able to help you spot a nasty scam before it happens. If you'd prefer a recommendation on whether to encash your pension or where to invest the funds, then take advice from an FCA regulated adviser – and it's worth shopping around to find the right adviser for you.

Application form scams

We're now programmed to 'Google' most questions we face in life, but it's a big mistake to trust all the information we find on a Google search – as a lot of young people discovered to their cost when they searched 'driving licence application' over the past couple of years.

A lot of the bogus 'check and send' websites have now been closed down but you may still bump into one if you're not careful. Their *value-added* service for driving licence (and other) applications – promises to get your application correct before you send it in. The fact that these sites exist at all may suggest a human tendency to abdicate responsibility to others – but clearly it's **our** personal responsibility to check our applications. By using these sites you could pay as much as three times the normal price for your driving licence – and not receive those promised checks of your application of course!

It's humiliating enough to get caught by this scam (and lose that unnecessary checking fee) but the biggest risk here is the potential for identity theft. Giving away your personal details (postal address, email, etc.) allows criminals to start building a file on you to scam you again in the future – perhaps by applying for credit cards or phones in your name, or to simply start emptying your bank account.

Get irate!

- Do not give away **any** personal details – postal address, email, credit card number, or anything else – unless you know exactly who you're giving it to and that they're trustworthy.

- Treat **any** offer that looks 'too good to be true' with extreme caution and, unless you're a sophisticated investor, stick to FCA-authorised investment funds to gain better protection.

- Buy good quality internet security software and keep it up to date.

- Use the latest version of your internet browser, as it comes with fixes for recently detected security vulnerabilities.

- Change your email password regularly and make sure it's a robust one – with a random mix of letters and other characters – not your name followed by 1234!

- If your email account is overflowing with rubbish, get a new email address and only tell the people (friends and suppliers) that you want to be contacted by. Good email services will allow you to filter out what's important versus promotions or junk.

- Check that all websites you use for financial transactions are legitimate. You can find guidance on how to do this here: www.actionfraud.police.uk/thedevilsinyourdetails-online

- Do not respond to uninvited offers from strangers, and report anything suspicious to www.actionfraud.police.uk

- Do not succumb to pressure selling or allegedly time-limited offers. If you need repair/renovation works done around your home, get quotations from well-established tradespeople and ask to see evidence of their work.

- Ask a trusted family member, friend or your coach to help you spot scams early.

Coming up, in the final chapter . . .

We've now looked at most of the big enemies to your money. So in the final chapter let's explore how to find 'good quality' help on money matters

Chapter 12
Getting the right help

... and saving money on advice

*You can spot the 'extrovert' accountant. They look at **your** shoes when talking to you.*

~ Anon

© Copyright Paul Claireaux

By this point, you should know a lot more about the *external* enemies to good money management. Of course, we all carry our own *internal* money enemies in our minds – and you can learn about those and how to deal with them, in my second book *How We Mislead Ourselves About Money*. Beyond that, you could learn **how to plan your own financial freedom – in 5 simple steps** in a book of that title that I'm planning for late 2015. You can get progress updates on that book at www.paulclaireaux.com

But let's finish this book with some thoughts on what to do next – and who the best person might be to help you.

The first thing to do is relax!

Yes, I do think there's value in sitting back and reflecting on the ideas we've talked about in this book. Better still, go for a long walk in a park or the countryside to ponder your financial life plans. The natural environment tends to give us a better perspective on life's challenges. Rome really wasn't built in a day and you won't build the funds you need for the future in a day either – despite what those spread betting trainers might tell you!

So slow down and take a measured approach to planning your longer term money. Yes, it's important to get on with this but don't 'panic' about the issue now, just because you read about it today. Sleep on it and start work on it at the weekend or whenever you can allocate a good slug of time to start dealing with it properly. Just don't make that 'sometime' never!

If you'd like more **ideas for achieving more with your money and in your life** – then register at my website www.paulclaireaux.com and the ideas will be sent straight to your inbox.

You might like to review the key ideas in this book by looking at the 'Get irate!' summaries at the end of each chapter. It's well known that we get a better grasp of new concepts when we re-read them. You might also like to highlight the key points that are most important to you – and you'll benefit enormously by writing some *notes* too – on the issues and actions you identify as you make your review.

We're all challenged by money issues of one kind or another at various points in our life. But we can reduce the stress they cause by writing them down and working on them. They don't go away if we ignore them – they just get bigger and that makes us feel worse. So, *please*, for your own sake, start writing that list – even if it's only a list of questions you want to ask of a financial coach or planner. You could also explore some other sites with useful information and ideas around money and investments. Here are just a few to get you started:

For general information and ideas

The Money Advice Service (MAS)

www.moneyadviceservice.org.uk provides a wide range of useful and free information and financial planning tools. It's overseen by the Financial Conduct Authority (FSA), so there's a good chance that the information is up to date and technically correct!

The Royal London Money Manager

Just one example of an insurance group backed site offering free access to a clever cash flow planning tool and various information guides. The information on the site is backed by a strong team of technical experts. Visit https://planner.royallondon.com/Login/

Candid Money

www.candidmoney.com is run by Justin Modray (a former independent financial adviser) and contains a lot of useful guides and a truly vast selection of calculators. There's also a tool that allows you to compare the charges on leading (self-invested) investment fund platforms, including Self-Invested Personal Pensions (SIPPs), at www.comparefundplatforms.com

Warning notes

Watch out for those numbers coming out of any online calculation tools – especially the pension versions. They tend to follow an ultra-conservative approach (we looked at this in Chapter 9), which can make the estimated costs of achieving your goals look horribly expensive.

Your challenge – like everyone else's – is to find a reasonable balance between saving for your future (and for your loved ones) and having money left over for some fun today. Excessively cautious calculations or expensive investment or pension products will not help you with this. So, 'sense check' what you're told you should save for your financial goals against the look-up charts on my blog at www.paulclaireaux. com You'll be able to see what funds you might achieve just by saving the equivalent of the price of a cappuccino each day. You might be surprised at how much you can achieve by saving so little – over the long term.

If you decide to select your own products and funds, then please do your homework. The 'self-invested' investment and pension products compared at Candid Money – and widely trumpeted by the media as our saviours – are not your only choice, and they're not ideal for everyone. Indeed, that wonderful prefix 'self-invested' – which many companies use to market their products – can be misleading. The fact is that virtually all investment and pension products allow us to 'self-invest' in funds of our choice – albeit that the fund range varies from provider to provider. The key point is that if you don't need a vast choice of funds – and frankly most people don't – then it's not worth paying extra for it.

The leading insurance companies and fund houses offer some great products at keen prices – so ask your financial adviser about those too. And check that any information guides you rely on for decision making are up to date. Some sites are very poor at keeping their material current.

For guidance on making a complaint or compensation claim

If you believe you've been mis-sold a financial product or you've held one that's gone wrong, then you can go to:

- The *Financial Ombudsman Service* (FOS) www.financial-ombudsman.org.uk This organisation can help you to settle complaints with financial service (FS) providers.

- The *Financial Services Compensation Scheme* (FSCS) www. fscs.org.uk This is the 'compensation fund of last resort' for customers of authorised FS firms. The FSCS may pay out compensation, up to certain limits, if a firm is unable to pay claims against it, usually because it has stopped trading or has been declared in default.

Finally, I recommend that you find a good financial planner or coach to help you draw up a good plan – one that connects your money to your goals in life.

Using a coach and saving money on financial advice

What type of financial advice or guidance would be best for you? This depends on various factors including the complexity of your personal financial situation *and* that of your wider family.

It's often forgotten that even moderately wealthy parents or grand-parents may be able –and keen – to help younger generations with their finances, and they can usually do so in a very tax-efficient way – especially where inheritance tax might be an issue on their estate. Take professional advice in this area.

The right choice of adviser or coach will also depend on your current knowledge about personal finance *and* the size of your wallet! It's a sad fact that many regulated financial advisers' charges are well beyond the reach of ordinary investors and savers. Advice charges have been trending higher for some years now, driven by a shortage in the supply of advisers and by our tolerance of the overcharging 'rhino' who's been hiding his charges in the products. Highly expert, specialist financial advice is now charged out at anything between £200 and £500 *per hour!*

On the other hand, if your advice needs are modest, then you should be able to find a good quality generalist adviser for £150 per hour or less. Yes, I know, this still sounds like a lot of money, but it's a great deal less than the thousands of pounds that used to be taken out of our investment products in commissions, and it's a fair price to pay if you obtain good quality advice and save thousands of pounds in reaching your goals over the long run. And you can do quite a lot to reduce the fees you're charged for advice – just as you might do with an accountant or solicitor – by making sure that you don't 'spend' too much of the adviser's time.

You can reduce the time you spend with an adviser by:

- **Learning the basics about investments and pensions**

    Doing this saves on the 'education' time your adviser needs to give you. Some advisers are happy to spend hours demonstrating their immense knowledge of how investments and pensions work. But at £250 per hour, can you really afford to listen?

- **Documenting your financial information clearly in a standard format**

  This will save your adviser time on basic 'data gathering'. A useful starter 'fact find' form is available from the Money Advice Service at:

  www.moneyadviceservice.org.uk/en/articles/
  complete-a-money-fact-find

  Or you can ask your prospective adviser for their 'fact find' form. Either way, you can get started on it before you meet up and start paying for advice.

- **Building your own outline financial life plan**

  This sets out your (current) financial goals for *your* life and those who depend upon you. It's true that things will change over the years, but having an idea of what you want to achieve with your money at this point in time will allow a planner to estimate the cost for each part of your plan.

- **Completing an attitude to investment risk (ATR) questionnaire**

  One example from Standard Life (a leading UK investment company) is available here: www.standardlife.co.uk/c1/ guides-and-calculators/assess-your-attitude-to-risk.page

  Your attitude to risk (ATR) assessment will give your planner a starting point from which to determine your 'capacity' for risk (CFR) on each investment or savings plan that you're considering.

If you're prepared in these ways you stand a good chance of agreeing a better price for any (regulated) investment advice you may need. Good advisers are keen to work with clients on this 'better prepared' basis because it makes their work easier too. You can draw up your outline plan either with your financial adviser or with the help of a good financial coach. This type of work – giving guidance on your options, running some rough cost estimates and helping you map out and connect your life goals to your money – is **not** regulated advice. So, you can get this help from whomever you want.

That said, this first stage of financial planning is critical, so get help from someone who's both trustworthy and financially savvy. And I'd suggest that they should have some other skills and abilities too.

What to look for from a financial life coach

They should be able to:

- **Sit quietly and *genuinely listen* to your concerns and ideas** – rather than talking *at you* with their pre-conceived ideas! Very few people can genuinely listen in this way but it's essential. A good coach acts like a sounding board and lets you explore **your** big challenges and your ideas for your life by talking them through. This helps you focus in on those things that you *really want to achieve* for yourself and your loved ones.

- **Help you understand your money** and your options for building funds.

- **Challenge you to consider how you'll pay** for your important life goals

- **Help you assess whether your financial life goals are realistic.** In some cases it simply won't be possible – using reasonable investment assumptions – to achieve your goals with the funds and spare income you have available. So in this case, your planner should help you explore which of your goals you might adjust and how. For example, you might need to revise down your plans for a *super high* pension income if that's not affordable. Or, you could plan to work a bit longer, and perhaps plan towards doing more work that you enjoy in your later years.

- **Support you in achieving your goals.** This could involve helping you form new habits to, say, cut out unnecessary expenditure or supporting you to develop new (or increased) sources of income by, say, going for that promotion at work or starting a new business.

Most people find life goal planning to be the most valuable part of the whole financial planning process. And because you can use a coach for this planning it can cost less than doing similar work with a regulated adviser. Some financial coaches are extraordinarily good at this work – like Simonne Gnessen at Wise Monkey Financial Coaching www.financial-coaching.co.uk who also trains others in this gentle art. I've personally trained with Simonne.

Unfortunately there are, as yet, not enough really good financial life coaches available in the UK. An increasing number of regulated financial advisers are taking lessons in coaching but few are able to combine their technical work with high quality coaching at a modest price. So be careful about what you're signing up for. Some advisers position life planning in a way that demands 15 hours or more of discussions over several meetings – which, at £200+ per hour means £3,000+ in fees just to get your financial life goals sorted out. And whilst the very wealthy might be happy to pay that, it's too much for the rest of us ordinary mortals.

Whoever you choose for coaching and mentoring on money issues should have a firm grasp of the hard technical issues (about money, tax, pensions, investments and life assurance) as well as having strengths in those 'softer' coaching areas we looked at above. I'd suggest that they should hold a Chartered Insurance Institute Diploma in Financial Planning (or equivalent) as a minimum qualification – although the balance of hard and soft skills you need from anyone helping you sort out your money will depend on your situation.

It's also a good idea to have a 'getting to know you' type of meeting with any potential adviser or coach – just to make sure you can both get along – before you commit to any ongoing work. A good coach will also want to have such a 'personal chemistry check' meeting up front.

One benefit of working with a financial coach (as opposed to a fully regulated financial adviser) for your initial planning work is that you can rest easy about their agenda. You know that they won't try to sell you any new investment, pension or life assurance products. And they won't have any interest in transferring your existing plans into new ones – even if it looks like this might be advisable. So their whole approach is geared totally towards helping you improve your situation across the board – and to make a better connection between your money and your life.

When you've done some sensible outline planning – and then only if you need new products (which you may not) – you can decide how to buy them. You might research the market and buy the products yourself, or you can work with a regulated financial adviser at this stage. My general recommendation would be to go through a regu-lated adviser for this second stage of plan checking, refinement and product purchase. A regulated adviser *should* be able to help you to find a suitable product and an independent adviser has the potential to find you the best deal from the whole market of providers.

Now, as we've said, there are still a few rhinos out there – so you need to be on your guard and choose your product adviser wisely. A good coach may be able to help you assess a potential regulated adviser (if you need one) and show you how to secure 'improved' terms. Many advisers will discount their fees for 'introduced' clients who are well prepared for advice.

The product purchase stage of financial planning

If your financial planning reveals a need for some kind of investment, savings or pension product then I'd suggest you use a regulated advice service (as opposed to a DIY approach) at this (product purchase) stage of the process.

Even if you think you know what you're doing, it's still worth getting a quick second opinion from an adviser or coach. A DIY approach may save you a little in fees but that's not a given: a good adviser will find you the best terms and you'll struggle to compete with those terms by going direct. Also, you won't have any recourse to a complaints and compensation procedure in the unfortunate event that you mis-sell yourself an investment product! My experience is that very few people really know what they're doing when it comes to investments and pensions; if you do, then you're the exception to the rule.

And the really big question to answer about taking a DIY approach is this: who are you going to leave in charge of your money – and presumably the family's money – if you meet with an untimely death or you lose your mental capacity? You should think this question through – before it's too late.

Types of financial advice and guidance

For very basic financial guidance – on matters such as budgeting, debt reduction and simple bank-type savings concepts – it may be worth talking to the Citizens' Advice Bureau (CAB) which offers a free, confidential and impartial advice service around the UK, in person or over the phone.

I'm not aware that their advisers are required to have experience or qualifications in long-term investments or pensions, but they're certainly helpful people and may point you in the right direction. They also have a useful self-help library on all kinds of issues at www. adviceguide.org.uk

If your questions relate to pension planning – or about pensions you already hold – then some Citizens Advice bureaux offer face to face Pension Wise sessions. Learn more about Pensions Wise at www. pensionwise.gov.uk Alternatively, you can find out more information about pensions at The Pensions Advisory service at www.pensionsadvisoryservice.org.uk

All of these services are free but bear in mind you'll only be given information: you'll also want to receive a recommendation about what you should do. For that you'll need advice from a regulated adviser.

Regulated financial advice – and its many forms

Basic advice

This is typically a scripted service (available online or from a call centre) which aims to help you check your suitability for a specific type of product that you're already thinking of buying. That might be an ISA or stakeholder pension savings plan for a self-employed tradesperson, for example.

The bottom line here is that **you** are responsible for your product choice.

The script does not undertake a full review of your circumstances, but instead simply follows a defined 'decision tree' process – until the conversation reaches the end of a branch. Some branches end with a recommendation to invest in the product, whilst in many cases the recommendation will be that you seek out a full advice service.

Full advice services

This is a far more comprehensive service based on a complete review of all your goals, finances and other circumstances. These services are divided into two broad categories – **independent or restricted** – which we'll look at in a moment. Both types of adviser should operate to a high professional standard – introduced under the Retail Distribution Review (RDR) early in 2013. This means they must:

- hold reasonable minimum qualifications. The new entry level for advisers has been set at level four on the Qualification and Credit Framework (QCF), said to be equivalent to first year degree level

- undertake continuous professional development

- agree their advice charges with you (the customer) – rather than simply taking whatever commissions are paid, and

- adhere to a code of ethics.

Both adviser types must also follow the FCA's general principles for good business. These principles have been in operation for some time and include acting with integrity, acting with due skill, care and diligence and observing proper standards of market conduct.

Independent Financial Advice (IFA) service

Advisers in this category can recommend an investment arrangement from a very wide list of product types *and* from any regulated investment provider in the market. That breadth of product choice will certainly be valuable to some people in some circumstances. However, it also places a greater burden of work upon the adviser: they have to maintain research and expertise across a wider group of products including investment trusts and exchange traded funds. This in turn adds upward pressure on fees in this sector. Whatever the cause it's fair to say that good independent advice is difficult to find at an affordable price for many middle Britons. You can reduce these fees by reducing the time you spend with an adviser as outlined earlier in this chapter – and if your investment product needs are straightforward you should try to negotiate the lowest fees possible. But, if you cannot find an IFA service to advise you at a reasonable price, you may want to explore what's available under a restricted advice service.

Restricted financial advice service

Advisers in this category may be restricted in either, or both, of two ways:

- First, in terms of the advice and product types they cover – for example, an adviser who specialises in just pension income advice and only sells those products (annuities and income drawdown etc.).

- Second, and more commonly, they may be restricted by the range of product providers they can access – either being tied to just one provider or restricted to a limited panel. St James Place is an example of such a firm.

This second restriction on its own is less of an issue than it was in the past due to the wider availability of fund choice (from multiple investment houses) inside most leading investment and pension products. That said, if you need a particular fund, product or product feature that a restricted adviser can't meet, then you'd be better served by an IFA service. Also, some restricted adviser firms are quite prescriptive about their adviser charge rates, and you may find that you have little or no room for negotiation. This inflexibility can also apply to some independent firms, so it can pay to shop around if you're well prepared and want to negotiate a better price for advice.

Just to confuse matters further - some firms in both (independent and restricted) categories may not be 'permitted' to give advice on certain matters. The FCA deems some advice areas to be particularly high risk to investors and places additional safeguards around them – such as demanding that advisers hold additional qualifications and that they follow set guidelines in their analysis. Such restrictions apply, for example, to advice on transferring pensions out of occupational defined benefit (DB) schemes into lifetime mortgages – previously known as equity release schemes – used to boost income for the elderly.

How to find an adviser

Your accountant or solicitor may have an 'in-house' IFA service in addition to their core services. If not, it's likely that they can introduce you to one – though this should not prevent you from finding your own if you prefer. Your bank, stockbroker or private bank will almost certainly have a broad range of advice services on offer – including regulated financial advice – which are likely to be pulled together under the marketing title 'wealth management' or something similar. These services may be either independent or restricted, so check which type you're dealing with and make sure it's what you're looking for.

Wealth management services are generally targeted at clients with wealth or income above a certain level – for example, it may only be available for those with net assets above £250,000 or an annual income above £100,000. These figures vary enormously, so check the limits. But don't be fooled into thinking that a service will be fantastic just because it's exclusive to the very wealthy or high income earners. Some of the worst value services are sold to the wealthiest people!

If you prefer to search out your own adviser rather than taking a referral, then the following sites can help. You can input the type of advice you're looking for and they'll return a short list of advisers in your geographical area:

- www.thepfs.org/yourmoney/find-an-adviser
- www.financialplanning.org.uk
- www.unbiased.co.uk

Questions to ask your prospective adviser

The unbiased site offers a handy checklist here: www.unbiased. co.uk/value-of-advice/adviser-checklist

And the really important questions to cover are around:

- **Type and range of services** (IFA or restricted; scope of advice and specialisms – savings, investment, protection, mortgages, pensions, tax, trusts and estate planning; initial advice process; ongoing support and reviews)

- **Personnel** (who would you be dealing with, their knowledge/ qualifications and experience – and how they advise – face-to-face or phone/Skype)

- **Fees** (the amounts and shape – initial and ongoing – you'll be charged).

I'd suggest that you press (firmly but without being rude!) on the question of fees, and perhaps ask how the adviser believes their *fees compare to other advisers of similar abilities.* It's also sensible to understand how those fees break down between initial and ongoing fees, and to see the breakdown of each element.

In short, what are you paying for, and how much is it?

If you want investment advice on a reasonably large sum – as opposed to just setting up a savings plan or putting life assurance in place – then you may want to dig deeper into a major theme we've discussed in this book.

We know that in the recent past – by which I mean twenty years – there have been some major booms and busts in the stock market. And these have resulted in *severe investment losses* for many investors. Some advisers had no sense of any problems in markets as these crashes approached and, given that markets have recovered since, some appear perfectly happy to brush these incidents off as those 'one-off storms' that we can ignore. So, you might want to explore your adviser's competence in this whole investment management area, and pose these types of questions:

1. Did they see any stock market problems back in 1997-99 or during the next bull run in 2004-07?

2. If not, then why not? (The overvaluations were pretty clear on any fundamental valuation basis – for example, that CAPE measure.)

3. If they did, can they give evidence of what they saw and what they did to protect their clients?

4. And what about now? What's their view on the prospects for the core assets (shares, commercial property and bonds) right now?

5. How is their view reflected in their risk-graded investment portfolios?

6. Who decides upon asset allocations, or is this outsourced?

7. What proven abilities does the investment manager have, what research capabilities do they have to stay on top of the latest issues for investors?

8. How do they approach asset allocation decisions?

9. How often are those portfolios adjusted?

10. How will my money be kept in line with them as they change?

Okay, I know, this is a fairly heavyweight set of questions if you're not familiar with investments. And I can understand that some people may not be happy to engage in a conversation around them. However, if you simply ask the questions you'll at least get an idea (from whether the adviser starts stumbling or shaking in their shoes) of whether it's worth pursuing the conversation or making a sharp exit!

> But do not equate a confident answer with competence.
> There are still a few confident idiots out there, I'm afraid.

It may cost you a few hours of your life to interview a few advisers before deciding upon whom to use, but you might save your life savings.

You'll probably want to add some other factors to your adviser selection list – like whether you get along with the adviser generally – their personality, your chemistry with them, etc – but be careful here, especially when it comes to 'shared interests'. Choosing your adviser based upon whether your children go the same school, or whether you share a passion for golf, rugby, designer clothes, fast cars or anything else is not a good plan and could cost you dearly. Focus on their skills, qualifications, value for money and whether or not you can understand anything they explain to you – **these things are vital.**

Once you're happy that you've found the right regulated adviser to help you manage your money and buy any new products, then you can move ahead towards the necessary transactions. Just make sure that before you commit to any long-term investment, you read and understand **all** the risks outlined in the key features and other documents. If you get to the point of 'sign up' – and you haven't been told much about risks, then something's gone wrong with their advice process. So apply the brakes very firmly and politely request (nay, demand) that your adviser explain the risks to you – in full.

Get irate!

- A trusted, competent and fairly priced financial planner (or coach) can be of immense value in helping you review your finances.

- A good planner or coach should be able to help you draw up an outline plan that connects your money to your life.

- Some advisers are generalists and others specialise in certain areas, rather like the medical profession. So you may need more than one adviser, or a different adviser with a different specialism, depending on the complexity of your finances and your needs – which will change over time.

- Both 'independent' and 'restricted' advisers must agree their charges with you – but some are more flexible than others. Shop around if you feel that your adviser's charges look expensive.

- Some firms operate more robust investment advice processes than others. Ask the tricky questions and shop around if you're not happy.

A final thought . . . on testimonials

Most adviser firms will offer to share testimonials from other clients to demonstrate the satisfaction delivered through the quality of their work. But be aware that client satisfaction around matters of investment is often a function of relatively recent – past few years – market performance. So if we're sitting on top of a mountain-high stock market it should be easy to find a lot of happy clients to write out glowing testimonials.

Not so after a big market crash, so check the dates on those testimonials!

Also, think carefully before you decide to leave a firm of advisers you've been very happy with on all other matters, purely because of poor investment performance during a savage market crash. Give your adviser the chance to explain what's happened and why. The fact is that in some cases it's the client's fault that the losses are so heavy. Some clients will have presented an overzealous desire for high returns when they originally engaged their adviser. So it's not necessarily the adviser's fault that they followed instructions and placed the client into higher risk funds for higher returns – or that those funds got hit badly in a downturn.

> In theory, a full advice process should assess our capacity for investment risk as well as our attitude to it and so protect us from ourselves. But some advisers haven't yet embraced this rule. So, if you're still not clear on the difference between your attitude to risk and your capacity for it, look again at Chapter 4.

The bottom line here is that we need to recognise **and** take responsibility for our part in investment decisions. If we don't, then there's a very good chance we'll **repeat our past mistakes** of the past but with a series of new advisers.

Appendix 1
The riddles of risk

What links the financial crisis to forest fires and our personal fitness?

I guess there'll always be conflicts between the generations across a whole range of issues. Our hopes for the property and other investment markets are no exception.

Younger readers of this book – those yet to invest in property or the stock market – might be pleased to see prices crash from their current levels. They could then afford to get onto the property ladder – and their (stock market-based) savings and pensions would offer prospects of better returns. However, older people – or at least those who own a property and/or already have most of the funds they'll need for the future in stock market-based funds – may want prices to continue rising.

So everyone wants to know which way asset prices might move. Will they collapse again soon, or are we now in more stable times?

The answer is ... I don't know for sure ... and nor does anyone else.

Yes, there are some simple valuation measures – such as CAPE (see Chapter 3) – but it's also useful to understand what's been driving asset price booms and busts in recent years to get a better perspective on your current position.

In 2005, house prices and stock markets were booming when a relatively young man named Raghuram Rajan joined a group of older and allegedly wiser economists and politicians, at a celebration to honour the career of Alan Greenspan, the outgoing chair of the US Federal Reserve. Rajan had been invited to give a talk on his academic paper, *Has Financial Development Made the World Riskier?*, but what he said disturbed and upset quite a few people in the audience.

He argued that we might be heading for a financial disaster!

He pointed out that financial managers were being encouraged to take risks that, although they had a low probability of going wrong, would have very severe adverse consequences if they did.

Whilst these 'tail risks' were paying off, which was most of the time, they were delivering very generous compensation to the bankers, Rajan explained. But then he questioned how the banks would be able to find enough cash to keep financial markets working if the risks went bad. And he asked how they might unwind their losses in such an event so as to minimise the consequences to the real economy.

At the time, the response to Rajan's presentation was very negative. Justin Lahart, writing in the *Wall Street Journal* (January 2009), recounted that former Treasury Secretary Lawrence Summers, famous among economists for his blistering attacks, told the audience at the event that he found *"the basic, slightly lead-eyed premise of Mr Rajan's paper to be largely misguided."*

Summers was a top economic adviser to the Obama administration and US Treasury Secretary from 1999 to 2001 under former President Bill Clinton; he's also a past President of Harvard University.

Raghuram Rajan is a US economist who, in 2013, was appointed Governor of the Reserve Bank of India, where he faces a big challenge to stabilise their economy. He's also a Distinguished Service Professor of Finance at the Booth School of Business at the University of Chicago, and a Visiting Professor for The World Bank, Federal Reserve Board. He formerly served as President of the American Finance Association and was Chief Economist of the International Monetary Fund (IMF).

No one called Mr Rajan 'misguided' after the 2008 economic crisis. The world's financial system blew up precisely because of the risks he'd highlighted. Suddenly, his intellect was acknowledged and his views on the crisis were published extensively, including some interviews in the Academy Award-winning documentary film, *Inside Job*.

Inside Job exposes the tragic comedy of errors made by politicians, regulators and bankers in the run-up to the crisis. If you want to understand what happened, this is a great place to start – and it's entertaining too. I took my children to see it at a local cinema and they loved it – seriously! Another film in this genre is *The Flaw*, which takes its title from Alan Greenspan's admission (after the event) that the reason his central bank couldn't see the crisis coming was because they had a flaw in their models.

Macro-economics (the big picture issues) is a horribly dry subject but, as these films show, it became popular in mainstream media during the height of the financial crisis. And whilst most people's interest faded as the media moved onto to other news, it's being revived now (2015) with a new film called *Boom Bust Boom,* directed by Terry Jones (yes that's right, of Monty Python fame).

You can look up the trailers for all three of these films on YouTube.

So what were the main causes of the 2008-09 crisis?

And have they *really* all gone away now?

Well, it's quite clear that we, in the so-called 'developed' (but perhaps more correctly named 'overspending') western world, allow our econ-omies to blow up from time to time. So, there's really no reason to expect that the 2008-09 crisis was the last we'll ever face. The deep recessions associated with credit crises present a high risk to the integrity of our society – and the really big crashes have come along at intervals of about 35 years since the late 1920s. Some argue that 35 years is about the right amount of time to clear out a generation of bankers who made the mistakes and bring in the next generation to repeat them!

Our housing market has crashed roughly twice in each timeframe – every 18 years or so – and it's possible that it's the housing market bubbles and crashes that cause the economic collapse rather than the other way round. Of course, the causes of economic and market crashes are complex and vary from time to time and place to place. But in the UK at least, it does seem that property is often a large part of the problem.

A key difference, which made things very bad in 2008-9, was that the property boom in the UK coincided with similar booms across southern Europe and, more importantly, in the USA, which joined the property boom and bust game in a very big way.

So what were the really big mistakes leading up to the crisis of 2008-09?

Politicians have known for a **very** long time that rising income and wealth inequality pose risks to society. Indeed, as Rajan, reminds us in his award-winning book *Fault Lines*, it was **Aristotle** who pointed out that:

> *Although quarrels are more likely in an unequal society, striving to rectify the inequality may precipitate the very conflict that the citizenry wants to avoid.*

It seems that from the 1980s, politicians on both sides of the Atlantic were becoming increasingly attracted to the idea of making credit more accessible to those on lower incomes, to help them 'join in the prosperity' of rising property prices. By allowing banks to expand their lending on houses they could see that, for short bursts at least, house prices would rise. And with those rising prices would come a general feeling of increased wealth that should tempt people to spend more in the shops. And that's good for the economy – at least for a while.

It's all very logical if you're short-sighted enough, and remember, politicians are only in power for short periods of time so they like quick results. Remember also that during the 1970s and 1980s the manufacturing industries in the UK and USA were being decimated by competition from Japan and elsewhere in the Far East, so the opportunity to create some extra jobs in banking, construction and estate agency sectors was viewed as welcome.

We're only now re-learning the idea that selling houses to each other doesn't actually generate any wealth! The buzzword now is 'rebalancing' the economy – which is another way of saying we need to rely less on 'house selling and clothes shopping' and more on real wealth creation if we're to have a sustainable economy. Rajan points out that the idea of expanding home ownership gained momentum in the USA under the Clinton administration, which was very keen on the idea that low-income families should share in the prosperity from rising house prices. In 1995, Clinton wrote, in a preamble to a strategy document to expand homeownership,

> *This past year, I directed the HUD [Department of Housing and Urban Development] secretary Henry Cisneros ... to develop a plan to boost home ownership in America to an all-time high by the end of the century ...*

> *expanding homeownership will strengthen our nation's families and communities, strengthen our economy and expand this countries great middle class.*

The document went on to say:

> *For many potential homebuyers, the lack of cash available to accumulate the required down payment and closing costs is the major impediment to purchasing a home. Other households do not have sufficient income available to make the monthly payments on mortgages financed at market interest rates for standard loan terms. Financing strategies, fuelled by the creativity and resources of the public and private sectors, should address both of these financial barriers to home ownership.*

At this point we were still a few years off the development of the complex financial instruments that eventually blew up financial institutions around the world. Yes, those same clever mortgage bonds that promised to take the risk out of selling loans to people who couldn't afford them! However, the instruction from on high was clear and, as Rajan says, *"the course was set"*. A few years later, investment bankers had indeed developed a way to pull in trillions of dollars from investors around the world to support this new lending to low-income families. The *number* of loans to homeowners with bad credit and undocumented incomes between 2002 and 2007 ran into tens of millions – and an estimated total of US$3.2 trillion in such loans were made.

> One trillion dollars is one million piles of one million dollars! That's an extraordinarily large sum of money. And US$3.2 trillion is more than the UK's entire gross domestic product (GDP) – that's the value of everything we produce and sell over the course of a year.

The new 'securitised' mortgage bonds offered big benefits for the investment banks that packaged them *and* sold them onto institutional investors all around the world. They also offered big benefits for those selling the mortgages to customers for fat commissions. Many of the firms selling the mortgages avoided the risks of them going bad. Once they'd been sold, these mortgages were passed on to investment banks for parcelling up and selling on to gullible investors – mostly other banks and insurance companies around the world! Unlike traditional lenders, these mortgage sales firms weren't fussed about vetting applications to check the borrower's ability to pay.

Back then, we'd arrived in the age of the NINJA loans – mortgages for people with **No Income, No Jobs** or any other **Assets.** No joke!

The investment banks also thought they'd found ways to avoid the risks of the mortgages going bad. They were primarily interested in taking a fee for packaging the mortgages into bonds to sell on. And even where they held some of these bonds on their own books they were able, or so they thought, to cover their risks at very low cost with a type of insurance contract called a Credit Default Swap (CDS). Unfortunately, when the mortgage bonds started collapsing in value en masse, the providers of the CDS insurances – like the world's largest insurer AIG – were effectively bust, so the mortgage bond holders went bust as well.

The disaster was made a lot worse by the incompetence of the ratings agencies. These firms (Standard & Poor's, Fitch and Moody's) were supposed to do all the hard analysis of these mortgage bonds – to report on their riskiness to potential investors. But another unfortunate situation had already developed which gave these agencies a conflict of interest and prevented them from doing their job properly. Traditionally, these rating agencies had earned their income by selling subscriptions for their analysis work to the buyers of the bonds. But then the USA Securities and Exchange Commission (SEC) decided that the ratings were too important for access to be restricted in this way. So the ratings agencies switched to charging the issuers of bonds for their rating analysis.

And that's rather a ridiculous idea when you think about it. I mean, how could a rating agency possibly offer robust and objective views on the security of bonds when their fees were being paid by the very firms trying to sell those bonds?

Better ratings make it easier to sell more bonds at better prices.

The Financial Crisis Inquiry Commission (set up by the US government to investigate the crisis) said, in January 2011, that:

> The three credit rating agencies were key enablers of
> the financial meltdown. The mortgage-related securities
> at the heart of the crisis could not have been marketed
> and sold without their seal of approval. Investors relied
> on them, often blindly. In some cases, they were obli-
> gated to use them, or regulatory capital standards were
> hinged on them. This crisis could not have happened
> without the rating agencies. Their ratings helped the
> market soar and their downgrades through 2007 and
> 2008 wreaked havoc across markets and firms.

Economist Joseph Stiglitz said,

> I view the rating agencies as one of the key culprits....
> They were the party that performed the alchemy that
> converted the securities from F-rated to A-rated. The
> banks could not have done what they did without the
> complicity of the rating agencies.

There's no doubt that rating these mortgage-backed bonds was big business for the rating agencies whose own revenues and share prices rocketed through 2007. Apparently, the rating companies earned as much as three times more for grading these complex products than for ordinary corporate bonds. And they competed with each other to rate particular mortgage-backed securities issued by investment banks, which arguably contributed to even lower rating standards.

Here's a quote from author Upton Sinclair (1878-1968) which seems to sum up this situation nicely. He said:

> It's difficult to get a man to understand something when
> his job depends on not understanding it.

So much for the regulatory doziness around the ratings agencies – but doziness extended well beyond this issue: in the USA, the UK and elsewhere in Europe. In the run-up to the crisis we'd collectively allowed the capital reserves of our banks to become wafer thin.

> Capital is the money that the banks (like any other
> business) should fall back on, rather than relying on
> taxpayer bailouts, when they make bad investments in
> loans or other securities.

Some other countries, notably Canada, were less affected by the crisis – at the time in any event, which may, in part, be down to the fact that their banks had higher capital requirements. We're also told that their lending was much more risk-averse than either the UK's or the USA's. Some argue that this was one reason we recruited a Canadian (Mark Carney) to head up our own central bank. However, others suggest a timing advantage, pointing out that Canada's housing market has since followed others into a boom and their banks are not in such great shape now. Either way, a group of leading academics are now calling for capital in our banks to be increased many times over, from about 3% of their assets to as much as 25%. That's a massive change and whilst it seems unlikely that the regulators will push the banks to hold this much capital, they are insisting on more. Apparently the bankers are not so keen on this but, as Mark Carney has pointed out, it's the banks with the highest capital that increased their lending the most (or shrunk it the least!) after the crisis. So a better capitalised banking system seems to be good idea, however you look at it.

I think we need to listen more carefully to the experts pushing for less risk in our banking system – their arguments are compelling. Their advice is that the world's banking system remains in a dangerously fragile condition – and little has been done to fix it, despite the damage it caused in 2008-09.

For a neat video which explains more about this, look up 'Anat Admati: The Bankers' New Clothes' on YouTube.

Another potential problem with our banking system is that we allowed our investment banks to become reconnected to retail banks. After the Great Depression in the 1930s a law was passed in the USA (the Glass–Steagall Act) that, amongst other things, limited the investment banking activities of ordinary commercial banks. The Act was repealed through the Gramm–Leach–Bliley Act of 1999 (GLBA), and some argue that this permitted Wall Street investment banking firms to gamble with their depositors' money, held in affiliated commercial banks.

Others argue that Glass–Steagall had already been watered down by various re-interpretations of the Act since the 1960s, and that by the time it was repealed there was nothing left to it. Some, including Bill Clinton, have even argued that allowing commercial banking firms to acquire securities firms (and securities firms to convert into banks) actually helped mitigate the financial crisis! It seems that the jury is out on the extent to which this issue contributed to the crisis.

Finally, we allowed the market in those insurance contracts – Credit Default Swaps (CDS) – on the dodgy mortgage securities to grow exponentially, with very little oversight or regulation. The Commodity Futures Monetization Act (CFMA) of 2000 (signed into law by Bill Clinton on the advice of Larry Summers) exempted derivatives like these from oversight and regulation. Incredibly, it took until August 2013 – several years after the crisis – for the US Securities and Exchange Commission (SEC) to start winning cases to hold bankers to account for their misbehaviour in the run-up to the crisis. Although, even now they only seem able to scapegoat individuals rather than find more widespread corruption.

You may recall the case of the self-styled 'fabulous' Fabrice Tourre (a former Goldman Sachs trader) who was found guilty by a New York court of misleading investors.

According to a Financial Times report on this case ('SEC Elated After Claiming Tourre's Scalp', 2 August 2013), "Mr Tourre hid from investors the fact that Paulson & Co – a hedge fund run by billionaire John Paulson – helped select the mortgages." Those mortgages were to be used to create a new investment product and the hedge fund manager's plan was to bet against it!

You really couldn't make this up!

If you want to learn more about the characters in the crisis – get hold of Michael Lewis' best-selling book, *The Big Short: Inside the Doomsday Machine*. It offers insights into the murky world of hedge funds which bought these insurances purely as best against those subprime mortgage bonds blowing up.

It's often thought – and we were told this by our politicians many times – that the financial crisis was a problem started in and caused by the USA. Clearly their subprime lending spree was at the centre of things – but as US Treasury Secretary Timothy Geithner pointed out in 2011, our light-touch financial regulation here in the UK was also "deeply costly" in the years leading up to the crisis. A 450-page report from the Financial Services Authority (FSA) into the UK's biggest bank failure – that of Royal Bank of Scotland (RBS) – shows just how our 'light-touch' approach to regulation played its part.

The *Financial Times* reported in December 2011 that:

> The FSA allowed the bank to run high risks with low stocks of capital and liquid assets and left it vulnerable to a loss of investor confidence.

> The FSA supervisory team grew concerned in 2005 about how fast RBS's commercial property portfolio was growing and they considered imposing a cap on the level of lending. But in what the report calls "an opportunity lost", the watchdog instead urged the bank to improve its stress testing and review its risk management. Quite incredibly – it also let Sir Fred Goodwin, RBS chief executive, water down the official FSA letter to the bank that raised the issue "in a way that reduced the force of the message to the RBS board."

> In 2007, RBS told the FSA it was 96 per cent confident that £4bn in capital would cover all of its risks. All of the other big UK banks submitted plans that met a much higher 99.5 per cent confidence level. When the FSA told RBS to use the tougher standard, the calculations suggested the bank needed an extra £3.1bn in capital. But rather than force RBS to nearly double its stock of capital, the FSA supervisors – worried that such a big change "takes some explaining why we so massively underestimated the capital impact of the risks facing the group" – decided to split the difference and told RBS to add just £1.7bn to its capital.

Bear in mind that these 'confidence' levels are arrived at using the same flawed model of risk discussed in Chapter 2, on 'dangerously trained pilots'. So capital cushions – even at the 99.5% confidence level – are woefully short of what's required in an extreme event in the 'non-normally distributed' world of risks. That is, in the real world.

This lenience may have been linked to lobbying of the FSA by RBS and other banks, to reduce the amounts they were forced to set aside for expected losses when calculating capital ratios. The FSA adopted the more lenient treatment in December 2007 and this boosted RBS's reported capital stocks by £840 million. In July 2007, the bank told the watchdog that it had been miscalculating its liquidity ratio and had fallen short of the requirements for the previous sixteen months. Rather than bring an enforcement action, the FSA wrote a letter to the RBS group treasurer reminding him of its "expectations concerning the accuracy of regulatory reporting".

Lord Adair Turner became chair of the FSA in September 2008. This was after the damage had already been done, but he defended the actions of the regulator on the BBC's Andrew Marr show on 15 February 2009, saying that other regulatory bodies throughout the world, which varied in structure and lightness of regulatory touch, also failed to predict the economic collapse.

This reinforces the issue, **in my view,** that both our banks and our regulators misunderstood risk. And in an interview with *Prospect* magazine in December 2011, Turner suggests that politicians had been too respectful of financiers. Here's an extract from the article:

> ... Turner said there was "a pervasive influence of assumptions about the City on the UK political dynamic. There was a belief that light-touch regulation, or limited-touch, would make the City bigger, and that the City was a source of employment and tax revenue. And therefore there was clear pressure on the FSA at times to say, 'Go easy on the City.' The FSA never used the phrase 'light-touch,' but politicians did, and they did it in speeches which were directed at the FSA."

Which politicians? "Oh – ministers right at the top. Prime ministers, Chancellors of the Exchequer, made speeches of that sort, in the last government."

There was also pressure for the regulator to be an advocate for the City, he said. Regulators "mustn't do crazy things that will necessarily harm [the sector]. But the moment you introduce an idea that they are part regulator and part, as it were, sponsor, spokesman, for an industry, that's dangerous, that's confusing."

The result was that London became a centre for some of the most damaging financial activity. One example was AIG Financial Products, which specialised in issuing credit default swaps (CDS), a form of insurance against borrowers failing to meet their debts. In the run-up to the crash, the Mayfair-based AIG FP issued over $2 trillion worth of derivatives. Activity that enhanced the spread of the global crisis.

"Well, AIG Financial Products in Curzon Street was actually regulated by the French," said Turner. "It was the French regulator. There is a major issue here about clarity of who is responsible. If you set up in London, as a branch of a European legal entity, then the single market rules are very clear that the local regulator has only limited control over what you do."

Isn't this all fascinating?

Our politicians blamed the Americans, and whilst they accept some fault, the Americans also blame us for our soft regulations. Meanwhile, keeping quiet in the background, we have the French, who were apparently not properly regulating their London office of the American-owned insurance company AIG, which was right at the centre of the financial implosion. If those insurance contracts had been priced correctly, things might have been very different.

Whoever was to blame – and it appears the list is long – what we do know is that we allowed our banks to expand so fast that when the crisis hit they'd become Too Big To Fail (TBTF), and so they had to be bailed out.

The worry now is that the banks are still too big.

And the really big issue is that the bad debts of the banks were passed to us – the taxpayers – when we bailed them out. How much of our money we get back depends largely on how those banks perform – and some are doing better than others. Most informed commentators now argue that we've gone as far as we can, that our government doesn't have any more scope to borrow more for another round of bailouts.

Government debt is now at very high levels and has not yet started falling, despite all the talk of austerity.

So, are our banks now too big to save?

I've not seen much comment on this question lately but an article in the *Financial Times* in November 2011 suggested just that: *"Europe's largest banks have become too big to save"*, and it went on to say:

> The one inescapable conclusion we must all draw from the recent financial crisis is that the so-called *"global systemically important financial institutions"* (GSIFIs) are not only too big to fail and too big to save, but most importantly, they are also too big to manage. The risks they run are too complex for the small group of managers at the top of any one of these mammoth organisations to fully grasp, for regulators to supervise and for investors to understand.

Whether or not any of our banks actually do fail will depend largely on the extent of their bad lending and how that's revealed in the coming years. The unthinkable consequences of their failure certainly seems like a big incentive driving our government to keep property prices propped up with schemes such as 'Help to Buy'.

It's useful to remember what happened in Cyprus when its banks became insolvent. They did receive bailout help but only once they'd agreed to some real pain for their depositors. People holding more than the protected deposit amount ended up taking losses of around 60% on their money.

Yes, that's right – the depositors took losses of 60% on money they thought was safely tucked away in the bank.

Could bank depositors lose money here?

Well, in the USA the failure of banks (and bank-type institutions) is quite common. IndyMac was just one example, rescued by US regulators in July 2008. It was a top ten mortgage loan provider in the USA and relied heavily on large, uninsured deposits to finance its lending spree in the riskiest loans during the boom times.

The US deposit guarantee scheme at the time only covered deposits up to $100,000 (about £65,000), and those holding more at IndyMac had to accept losses of 50% when it went bust. The federal government decided to prevent a broader panic by later raising the deposit insurance threshold to the current $250,000.

UK depositors have lost money that's unprotected in foreign banks, including those with branches in the UK, like BCCI in the 1990s, from which depositors lost millions.

We haven't had a UK bank failure in which investors lost money for some time, but we should not be complacent about this. It might well have happened in 2007 with Northern Rock, but on this occasion the Government stepped in to guarantee all deposits, regardless of size. It seems likely that this was a one-off reprieve for large depositors to prevent a more generalised panic. The larger depositors there can count themselves lucky. The bank was relatively small and that guarantee could be made, but we shouldn't rely on any extra safety nets being pulled out next time. The extra safety net at the 'Rock' has since been removed so their depositors now only enjoy the same level of investor protection as others.

The UK deposit protection limit is £85,000 per person per authorised institution until 31 December 2015 and £75,000 from 1 January 2016 until further notice. (It's revised occasionally to stay in line with the Europe wide limit of 100,000 Euros.)

Prior to the 2008 crisis, the rules around bank deposit protection were more complicated, and seldom explained to depositors. At that time, few people were aware that only about £35,000 per person (per banking group) was guaranteed safe in the event of a bank failure. But now you'll have noticed that the new (higher) limit is clearly visible on all bank marketing material and within their branches. The Government is clearly keen to ensure that it's not forced to provide another 'mega' safety net to depositors, in the event of the next crisis.

More information on bank deposit protection is available from the Money Advice Service website at:

www.moneyadviceservice.org.uk/en/articles/
compensation-if-your-bank-or-building-society-goes-bust

And at:

www.fscs.org.uk/protected

The **essential point to remember** is that the protection applies at bank **group** level. It does not apply to individual bank brands. So you might hold less than the limit (£75,000 from January 2016) in various different banks – and think all your money is safe. But if you hold more than the limit across a banking group, then that excess is *not* covered.

A banking group can include several different bank brands. For example, the Bank of Scotland group covers ten different banks:

> The Bank of Scotland
> Bank of Scotland private banking
> Bank of Scotland / Germany
> Bank of Wales
> The AA bank
> Birmingham Midshires
> Capital Bank
> Halifax
> Intelligent Finance
> Saga
> St James's Place Bank

And for example the **Nationwide group** licence covers four building societies:

> Nationwide Building Society
> Cheshire Building Society
> Derbyshire Building Society
> Dunfermline Building Society

Up-to-date details on all the banking groups are available here:

www.fca.org.uk/consumers/complaints-and-compensa-
tion/how-to-claim-compensation/banking-and-saving/
banking-and-savings-brands

So, do I think we're about to hit another banking crisis?

I have no idea. That sort of detail is really only available to senior bankers - and even they struggle to spot the problems coming. All I'm saying is that it *could* happen, and if it does, you need to make sure that you're ready for it. Holding a lot of money in one banking group is a very dangerous thing to do.

Okay, but was the crisis all the fault of government regulators?

Well their poor regulation did allow our banks to grow too big and become *too big to fail,* but there were plenty of other factors at play too. Remember, it wasn't regulatory failure that drove asset prices into the stratosphere. It wasn't the regulators who encouraged the banks to chase after us to take out more mortgage loans.

There was also something else going on. Something that distorted the banks' views of the risks they were running. And that thing generally became known as the 'Greenspan put'.

Alan Greenspan was chair of the world's most important central bank, the US Federal Reserve, between 1987 and 2006. This was the period in which we saw the greatest build-up of asset price bubbles (in property and stock markets) in history. A 'put' is a type of derivative security, which works like an insurance against a fall in an asset price. If an institution holds a lot of money in shares, for example, but doesn't wish to sell them, they might buy a 'put option' to protect their funds for a time against the risk of a significant market fall.

The nice thing about the Greenspan put was that no one had to pay for it! The US central bank under Alan Greenspan, and our own Bank of England, seemed to adopt a policy of taking the risk (aka, moral hazard) out of banking by lowering interest rates every time asset prices started falling.

> Lowering interest rates can push up the prices of assets. Investors take their money out of cash deposits and other short-term 'safe' securities and buy more risky assets in search of higher returns.

Let's think about that.

Would you borrow money to invest in risky assets – whether they're houses or shares – if you knew that someone would step in with a cushion to prevent you from getting hurt if prices started to crash? Yes, of course you would. That's a one way bet and this is exactly what investors worldwide did for years after the crisis – whilst interest rates were held at or close to zero.

This is a 'game' that's been going on for the best part of thirty years in our developed economies. At every sign of trouble – small recessions or stock market pull-backs – we've had a nice reduction in interest rates to get the growth party going again. You might think that's a sensible policy – to protect the economy from downturns, or, as Gordon Brown used to say, with monotonous regularity, *"Put an end to boom and bust!"* – and, yes, it does sound like a great idea until we start to understand how a healthy economy really works.

One way to think of an economy is as a living organism, like our own body. It won't thrive on being protected from every single challenge in the world, any more than our muscles or bones get stronger if we lay in bed all day. We might think it's nice to avoid the minor pain of regular work or exercise, but if that's our approach to life we'll simply become so weak that we collapse, catastrophically, when faced with the next strain. Individuals, businesses and whole economies need to work, they need to compete against others to get strong. They can't deliver real and sustainable growth if we wrap them in cotton wool and bail them out every time they mess up. They just get weak and fail.

In *Ubiquity: Why Catastrophes Happen*, Mark Buchanan shows us several examples of systems that can seem perfectly stable at one moment before suddenly collapsing altogether the next. And, I think his best example for thinking about the management of economies, is that of a vast wooded forest.

In their natural state, in the absence of humans, forests are still damaged by occasional fires triggered by lightning. These burn off a random patchwork of areas, clearing them of old wood and allowing space and light in to support the growth of new saplings. But from 1890 the US Forestry adopted a 'zero tolerance' policy on fires, (including those sparked by natural causes) and tried desperately to protect the forests from every fire whatsoever. As Buchanan notes:

> *One of the unintended consequences of this program was that the forests began aging. Old trees were not*

replaced by younger trees, and the natural evolution of the forest's materials changed. Deadwood, grass and twigs and brush, bark and leaves accumulated.

By suppressing these fires the fire service drove the forests into a highly unstable state – what Buchanan calls a **supercritical state.**

The protected woods built up an enormous fuel load of downed and standing dead trees and limbs, flammable underbrush and grass … such that a single lightning strike or cigarette butt could explode into a mass fire.

To see how these fires look when they explode, look up *'Texas Wildfires 2011(Worst in TX history)'* on YouTube.

Now, I cannot say that this particular disaster in Texas was caused by forest mismanagement over the years, but this video certainly gives us a graphic image of a large natural system exploding from a supercritical state. And there's very little we can do to stop these enormous disasters once they take hold. We might decide to focus our relatively puny human effort in protecting certain assets in some places, but for the most part we can only stand in awe of their power as they burn themselves out.

If we think of economies in this way we can see how our political and banking leaders, both in the USA and elsewhere, were very confused about what they were doing in the decades leading up to the crisis. They *claimed* to believe in free markets and believed that only a light-touch regulation was required because the market participants would work in their own and our best interests to develop thriving industries. Free markets should have burned off the dead wood and provided the environment for new saplings to sprout – right?

Well maybe, but at the same time as letting the banking markets loose, our leaders manipulated down the price in one of the most important markets of all – **money.** By constantly lowering interest rates they tried to protect markets from the pain of competition and small recessions. So the dead wood accumulated – in industry and particularly in the banking sector.

In his book, *Antifragile,* Nassim Taleb reminds us how economies act like many other natural systems. Taleb coined the term 'Antifragile' to describe the property of systems that benefit from modest amounts of harmful **stress or volatility.** Examples of that modest stress would include physical exercise, food abstinence for humans and occasional business failures for economies.

Of course most systems have limits to the amount of stress they can bear, and this will vary with their current condition. It would **not** make sense to ask a 50-year-old obese person, who smokes 40 a day, to set off on a marathon. But some modest increments in exercise would, over the long term, have highly beneficial effects. Taleb also notes that in these antifragile systems, **the very large unexpected events are generally negative in their affect, whilst strengthening takes a lot of time and effort.**

This is quite evident in our economic system. The banking system and our whole economy pretty much collapsed overnight in 2008, and we're only now learning that economic recoveries can take many years.

So I think there's a question here for our leaders. Will they continue trying to extinguish every small problem in our economy, or can they accept that these are just necessary changes in building a stronger economy?

Getting the balance right is never easy, but I think most people would agree that we've been getting it wrong for a very long time. Right at the centre of this problem has been the use of the wrong mathematical models for predicting risk. As Taleb says in *Antifragile*:

> An annoying aspect of the Black Swan problem – in fact the central and largely missed point – is that the odds of rare events are simply not computable.

The term 'Black Swan' comes from Taleb's earlier book, *The Black Swan: The Impact of the Highly Improbable* in which he describes the risks posed by surprising events. The discovery of black swans was a major surprise at the time – as everyone assumed all swans were white.

Market prices – in stocks or property – do not vary in line with the normal distribution model that many experts are still using today.

So, what can we predict about stock market prices in the short term?

Not much... all we really know is that the frequency of price movements – relative to the size of that movement – seems to follow an inverse cube power law.

Sorry, I've gone mathematical here. Inverse power law... what does that actually mean?!

Well, in simple terms, it tells us that very large movements occur far more often than the traditional (normal distribution) models suggest. Mark Buchanan, in 'Power Laws and the New Science of Complexity Management', points out that financial market drops of 10 per cent in a single day should – according to a normal distribution – occur only once every 500 years. Yet they've been shown to occur about once every five years!

This is not a trivial error in the system being used.

That said, even applying a power law we find that the chances of very big events – whilst more likely than under the standard model – are still very rare. So what's the big issue? Let's remember that these probabilities are determined using very large samples of data – perhaps over 100 years' worth or more – whereas I'd suggest that **we** are more interested in investing over shorter periods, albeit up to 20 years or so. And the fact is that markets do behave very differently to the expected probabilities over shorter periods. Their very large movements (like those of earthquakes and aftershocks) tend to collect around very short periods.

So, for example, we had two large (c. 50%) falls in the UK stock market within the last 15 years. This is far more than would be expected, whichever model you use.

When markets get overvalued, a big crash is far more likely – just as a big forest fire is more likely if we light the match when the forest is in a critical state.

The valuation (forest dryness) starting point *really matters.*

It's extremely risky to ignore the starting point in terms of valuation and to simply use average returns from the past to predict future returns. Yet this is what many financial advisers do, and this is how banks assessed their risks on those mortgage securities.

Anyone who's studied statistics at all – in science or marketing – will be familiar with the simple rules of thumb used with the Guassian (normal) distribution to estimate probabilities of deviations from the average return. And this model is fine where you're working with data that obeys that model of returns. This applies primarily to systems in which the events are entirely independent of each other, like laboratory experiments. However, in many living systems the outcomes are not independent of each other. They are interdependent, which means that each part affects what the others are doing. The Guassian model doesn't work here, but the power law very often does, and it's remarkable just now many natural and social systems are distributed according to these power laws.

In their paper 'Why Guassian statistics are mostly wrong for strategic organisation', Bill McKelvey and Pierpaolo Andriani list 55 different systems in which the frequency of events compared to the scale of those events follows an inverse power law. They include: networks in the brain, tumour growth, traffic jams, galactic structure, earthquakes, bush fires, asteroid hits, mass extinctions, casualties in war, social networks, size of villages, towns and cities, salaries, wealth and sexual conquests!

> In case you're still curious . . . an inverse power law simply states that one quantity A is 'inversely' proportional to some other feature (B). This is written $A \sim (1/B^n)$ So, for example, scientists have discovered that the number 'N' of earthquakes reduces in proportion to the square of their size (the energy 'E' that they release) and that's written as $N \sim (1/E^2)$ or, in plain English, there are lots of small tremors but a very small number of really big earthquakes. And that's quite similar to the distribution of stock market movements.

The other thing about systems which follow 'power laws' is that the 'average' (size of something for example) is quite meaningless. 'Averages' provide no insight whatsoever into what the future might hold.

Nassim Taleb, talking about his book *Antifragile* during a visit to Bristol, used a grisly but powerful analogy to make the point.

Imagine you're looking for a room for Grandma at a residential home. The manager tells you that, amongst the many positive features of their home, is the fact that the rooms are kept at a nice, comfortable 20°C on average.

Sadly, Grandma dies shortly after moving in, and only then do you find out that the temperature in the room – whilst indeed being 20°C "on average" – actually fluctuated wildly each day between freezing point and 40°C!

Taleb acknowledges that his central message, *that we measure risk incorrectly*, is really not new. It's based largely on the thinking of Benoit Mandelbrot who proved, as far back at the 1960s, that markets don't work in the way we've been assuming that they do.

> Mandelbrot is famous for being the father of fractal geometry. If you're not familiar with this, then look up *Fractal Zoom Mandelbrot Corner* on YouTube – and be prepared for it to mess with your mind!

If your adviser believes that markets are correctly priced at all times and that risk is perfectly measurable using a normal distribution model, then I recommend that you send them this link to a wonderful interview with this humble genius mathematician – here at: http://bit.ly/ZOTAly

The really crazy thing about our problem with risk management is that we've understood it for a very long time. We've simply chosen to ignore the facts in the hope of grabbing more growth by allowing absurd levels of lending in the short term.

But where are we now? How is our economy set and how 'fairly' is property priced? We should probably have a view on this because it's this highly geared asset class that so often gets our banks into trouble.

The worst of the house price crash in the USA *appears* to be over. We can't really say for sure but at least their values did get back to around their long-term average levels in real terms – *although they've been rushing back up again recently.* In the UK we remain a long way above our long-term average valuations – relative to incomes. The bottom of the last housing market crash in the UK was around 1996, since when we've enjoyed (if that is the right word) the greatest boom ever in house prices. If the 18-year cycle had held good, then we might have expected to see this boom finish with a crash around 2014. A further leg down in prices would certainly look likely given price/earnings valuations at the time of writing. You can get updates on this from my site at www.paulclaireaux.com

Then again, with interest rates held down at their lowest level for around 400 years (and with our central banks having distorted free markets with wholesale purchases of government debt) it might be a while before we see forced sellers of property this time round. We'll only really know what sensible levels for house prices look like when mortgage interest rates are back at more normal levels – and bear in mind that could easily mean two or three times its low point in recent years.

Let's be under no illusion. Escaping from our predicament of having too much debt (both government and private), is not going to be easy. You only have to look at recent problems in Greece to see that.

For a long time, from the 1980s through to around 2007, it seemed that we'd found the secret to lifelong riches without having to do much work ... or add any value to society. That generation – sadly it's my generation – got it wrong. People took out additional mortgages on their homes simply to spend the money! They treated their homes like an ATM whilst others were buying as many properties as they could to make big 'geared' gains.

Those days are gone and now we have a long road of debt repayment ahead. Our central bank's plan appears to be to suppress interest rates for long enough to get the economy back on its feet. Of course, there are uncertainties around the sort of economy we've created and whether we've kept too many zombie businesses alive and protected with ultra-low interest rates. Are we developing enough sustainable new businesses to take up the slack of high unemployment? And do we have enough well qualified people to take those jobs if they're created?

A big risk is that some groups of workers become tired of receiving below-inflation pay increases and we get more industrial unrest that starts a wage-driven inflationary spiral. At or before that point, our international investors (those who lend to our companies and government) might push our interest rates sharply higher, regardless of what the Bank of England does. This would deter businesses from making the investments we want, and would make our government finances even worse – forcing more cutbacks.

I'm sorry if all this sounds gloomy – it's just a fact that our economy remains in a fragile state. We're not out of this 'tinder dry forest' just yet. What's more, it seems that the UK is playing the same mistaken games with house prices that blew all these problems up in the first place. We're using taxpayers' money to get more people who can't afford houses to buy them. The various schemes collectively labelled 'Help to Buy' have the potential to create another house price bubble before the last one has properly deflated.

As for offering any precise predictions on when we might see the bottom of our house price cycle – or the next stock market decline – all I can say is that **it's really only possible to recognise a bottom after it's gone past you!**

Just be careful what you buy right now. And finally ...

If you're buying a retail investment product, a personal pension, stocks and shares, ISA, investment bond, etc., then please read the warning on the key features document. It will say something like this:

> *Past performance is no guide to future returns. The value of investments can go down as well as up. You could get back less than you invested. All investments should be regarded with a long-term view.*

Please take this warning seriously.

Appendix 2
The nutty economics Nobels

Some financial advisers promote their investment service as 'robust' because it's based on the ideas of a particular Nobel Prize winning economist. The trouble is that they don't tell you about the ideas of the **other** Nobel Prize winner of the same year.

In 2013 there was, for a change, some excitement in the economics profession as the Royal Swedish Academy of Sciences awarded Nobel Memorial Prizes in Economics to two economists, Eugene Fama and Robert Shiller. Their separate studies had been central to the debate about the behaviour of asset markets. So far, so boring you might think, but this was an astonishing decision because these guys' theories were completely at odds with each other.

As Professor John Kay pointed out (*Financial Times,* 15 October 2013) this was *"like awarding the physics prize jointly to Ptolemy for his theory that the Earth is the centre of the universe and to Copernicus for showing it is not."*

> Sadly, John Kay then pulled his punch in that article, saying, *"actually, it is not as bad as that analogy suggests"*, and went on to explore the different ideas of the Nobel winners.

But what this proved (five years after the 2008 crisis) was that the economics profession was as *unclear* and confused as ever about how markets for assets work.

The Academy might argue their award to Professor Shiller proved that they accept the idea of economies being driven by real humans (rather than those 'rational robots' of orthodox theories) and that human behaviour is confused, irrational and, most importantly, herd-like after all. But if this is so, why would they make an award **at the same time** to Eugene Fama, the father of efficient markets theory?

This is all very curious when, according to the *New York Times* (14 October 2013), Professor Shiller **himself** wrote, in his book, *Market Volatility*, that the assertion that stock prices were rational was *"one of the most remarkable errors in the history of economic thought."* And even more surprising when we note the work of another Nobel prize-winning economist, Joseph Stiglitz, who wrote a paper – with Stanford Grossman in 1980 – entitled *'On the **impossibility** of informationally efficient markets'*! Their argument – in simple terms – was that we cannot assume everyone to be both rational and irrational at the same time.

The idea of efficient markets is a very compelling one.

If market participants acted rationally (at least on average) in buying and selling securities, then this activity might deliver correct (fair) prices. But then again, if markets were perfectly priced at all times, it would be 'irrational' for any active manager to spend effort and money seeking out the imperfections in it.

That's quite a paradox!

So, markets can only be efficient pricing mechanisms for securities to the extent that we have enough active managers *ignoring the efficient markets theory* and getting on with the work of analysing which securities are best value to buy! To use a classic 'supermarket queues' analogy – if we all assumed that the queues system was perfect, then we'd all stand quietly and obediently in our queues, refusing to take advantage of any empty checkouts that become available.

That happens to be very British, but quite dumb, behaviour!

A brilliant summary of the different ideas from these two Nobel winners was provided by Gavyn Davies (a widely respected economist) in the *Financial Times* (20 October 2013). Davies reminded us that in the Fama explanation, investors are supposed to be *pessimistic* about future returns when prices are high, and *optimistic* when prices are low.

Why so?

Well, according to Fama, most of the variation in asset prices is determined by changes in risk appetite. When our risk appetite is high, we accept high asset prices because we accept a low expected rate of return to compensate for our risk. Likewise when our risk appetite is low, we let asset prices fall until their expected returns are high. Shiller, on the other hand – perhaps more in line with our experience – expects investors to be optimistic (bullish) at the top of the market and pessimistic at the bottom.

I'm really sorry if these contradictions from experts are messing with your mind but the truth is that both do have a case.

Fama's point is logical enough – for people who are informed about markets and who operate logically (as orthodox economics assumes). Think about it – if you have a big appetite for risk then you will buy risky assets at higher prices, despite their prospective returns being lower than they would be if you bought at a low point. You're accepting risks for a lower return – that's what having more appetite for risk is about.

But then Shiller makes the point that 'real' people don't 'compute things' that way. We go into risky assets at high points with a naïve hope for a continuation of those high returns. And there's empirical evidence for Shiller's view – in research by Robin Greenwood and Andrei Shleifer at Harvard ('Expectations of returns and expected returns', January 2013) – showing that investor expectations are highly positively correlated with past stock returns and with the level of the stock market.

In other words, we **wrongly** believe that past performance is a guide to future performance and we just love to buy in at the top of stock-market price cycles. That's certainly in line with the evidence we saw in *Chapter 4.*

What can we take from all of this confusion?

I'd hope that we can agree that it's beyond most ordinary investors' abilities (including mine) to create a portfolio of stocks that has a good chance of outperforming the wider market without being exposed to serious risks. And if the efficient markets idea persuades us to:

a) invest via diversified funds (which could be index trackers, active funds or both) and

b) steer clear of taking bets on the short-term movements in assets …

... then that's probably very helpful for most savers and investors.

However, I'd hope we can also agree that it's positively dangerous to conclude – as those 'perfect markets' advisers do – that the aggregate level of the stock market is correctly priced to offer good prospects for returns at all times. This would seem to be an especially risky view to take at times when prices for so-called 'risk-free' assets (like government bonds) are completely distorted (propped up) by central bank money creation – as they were for several years after the crisis.

Stiglitz and Grossman noted that completely efficient markets were logically impossible. And Daniel Kahneman (another Economics Nobel winner) has shown that we humans do *not act rationally* a lot of the time, while Robert Shiller himself has said that "*Mass psychology may well be the dominant cause of movements in the price of the aggregate stock market.*"

> This is why my second book is devoted to the psychological issues that surround our money management activities.

Some might argue that occasional irrational behaviours of market participants don't matter, because they're random in direction and therefore cancel each other out. They'll argue that it's the average 'wisdom of crowds' that we should be concerned about, and that in large groups we are *rational on average*. However, the 'wisdom of crowds' idea has problems of its own. Research by Jan Lorenz, Heiko Rauhut and others, outlined in their article 'How social influence can undermine the wisdom of crowd effect', shows that *a crowd view often produces very large errors* – and especially in settings that are heavily influenced by social networking and knowledge of other people's views and behaviours.

Such a setting sounds to me just like Wall Street or the City of London!

What is absolutely clear about markets is that an unquestioning trust in them is extremely dangerous. Huge damage is regularly inflicted on private investors who trust market prices at times of high valuation – such as the late 1920s, the late 1960s, the late 1990s or 2006-07. The whole world economy was brought to its knees by the belief that US house prices were fairly priced (and so couldn't fall by much) when in fact they were in an almighty and obvious bubble in 2004-5, as pointed out by Robert Shiller amongst many others.

Whatever any adviser tells us, the truth is that markets do not deliver nice, neat, average rates of return (even over the long term) regardless of when we invest. The concept is useless – as are those standard deviations of risk.

Here's the bottom line:

Markets (in stocks and houses) have very long cycles in which valuations shift from high to low and back again.

1. If you invest at a time of low valuation, then you have a better chance of enjoying high returns subsequently.

2. If you invest at a time of high valuation, then your subsequent returns are likely to be disappointing and very possibly negative.

Appendix 3
Investment assets
– the basics

We've touched upon issues of fund management throughout this book, but I've deliberately steered clear of the detail about various types of investment asset **and** how they might perform under different economic conditions. We cannot hope to deal with those questions in full in a book of this size. However there are some **basic** points worth noting in this area.

The three main types of asset

You can invest in many different types of asset including property (such as your main home or other properties) and 'alternative' investments (such as art, antiques, vintage cars, wine, gold bullion, stamps, etc.). But the ones you're most likely to encounter in popular retail investment products are:

Cash deposits

You can hold cash in a bank or building society account or as a cash fund within an investment product, such as a pension or ISA. Sometimes these cash funds within investment products are called money or deposit funds.

Some – allegedly 'cash' – funds are not entirely made up from cash deposits, which means that unlike bank deposits they can fall in value! And a key point to watch out for on these cash funds is that you do *not* enjoy investor protection in the same way as if you held bank deposits directly. Not all advisers are clear on this point – so take a second opinion if this issue concerns you.

More generally (at the time of writing, 2015) cash deposits offer very little interest return and are therefore considered unattractive.

However, they can be useful parking places for your funds when you're nervous about more risky assets.

Ordinary shares

Shares are sometimes called 'equities' and can provide you (or the fund you hold them through) with part ownership of companies. That ownership gives a right to any dividend income paid to ordinary shareholders – but note, not all companies make profits and pay out dividends consistently. Indeed, some never do. The value of a company's shares can rise and fall – sometimes violently. And in extreme cases, if a company goes bust, the share price will fall to zero – which is obviously very bad news for its investors. By holding an individual share, your potential losses are up to 100% of what you put in.

> But you cannot lose more than 100%! Unlike spread betting and other geared investments where you can lose many times your stake.

You can reduce your **'stock specific risk'** by diversifying your holdings. This means holding a range of shares. And to diversify properly you'd need to hold shares across a range of industry sectors. Just holding lots of *different* bank shares in 2007 would not have given much diversification! You can diversify even if you hold your shares directly – rather than through a collective fund – but the costs of dealing in many small shareholdings can be high. So if your total portfolio is modest in size, it's often less costly to diversify through a collective fund.

Diversification does *not* remove **'market risk'** – the risk that the whole stock market falls at once – and this risk can be significant, as we've noted throughout this book. But you would never expect to suffer a 100% loss on a well-diversified portfolio of shares. For that to happen, every company's shares in the whole market would need to become worthless – which would probably mean we've become a communist state. And remember, stock markets produce very different returns over different periods of time in both the short and long term. The UK stock market – measured by the FTSE All-Share index – produced:

- 26% p.a. average returns from the end of 1974 to Summer 1987
- 12% p.a. average returns from Autumn 1987 to January 2000

- Zero returns *and a 'bumpy ride'* from January 2000 to January 2013.

These numbers ignore dividend income – which, if reinvested, would have increased these total returns by somewhere between 2% to 5% p.a. (the actual boost depends upon the tax payable on your funds and on the start point of your investment. If you invest at a high point in a market cycle – when dividend yields are low – then the boost to your returns will be lower than if the dividend yield were higher.) These numbers are also **'nominal'**, which means they're not adjusted for inflation – which in the 1970s was very high indeed, in excess of 20% in some years. So inflation seriously reduced the **'real value'** of those high returns in the 1970s and 1980s.

But remember that money on deposit at the bank is also eroded by inflation and that 'nominal' (before inflation) returns on bank deposits are *generally* a lot lower than they are on shares – at least over the long term – provided you don't buy shares at a market top.

Bonds

Bonds are the securities issued by companies and governments when they want to borrow money. Bonds typically offer a fixed interest regular payment and then mature at a set point in the future when it's expected that the borrower will repay the original loan amount. Some (zero coupon) bonds make no regular payments (coupons), so the total return depends entirely upon the maturity value or the market value if sold earlier. Other (undated) bonds have no end date, so the total return depends on the regular payments and the market value when the bond is sold on.

Some types of bond offer inflation-linked returns on both the interest payments and return of capital. These are sometimes called 'indexers'. The UK versions of government bonds are called 'gilts', whilst company bonds are called corporate bonds.

If you buy a bond at launch (when it's 'issued') and hold it to maturity, then you'd expect to get your capital back. (This assumes that the borrower doesn't default.) However, if you buy bonds (in the open market) *after* they've been issued and/or sell them before they mature, then your capital is at risk. You might make a profit or suffer a loss, because prices will vary in the interim period. Collective funds* buy and sell bonds in this way and so their bond funds do contain some risk – the amount of which depends upon the type of bonds held in the fund.

The riskiness of bonds (the amount by which prices could rise and fall between purchase and sale) depends upon various factors, including:

- market expectations for future inflation and interest rates

- the time left to the maturity of the bond (aka duration risk) and

- the financial standing of the borrower. For example, as the markets began to question the solvency of the Greek government, its bonds fell sharply in value. UK Government bonds (gilts) are currently viewed as being very secure, but long-term gilt prices can still suffer badly if inflation expectations rise sharply.

A corporate bond is normally less risky than an ordinary share issued by the same company. This is because it's the shareholders who get 'wiped out' first in the event of a company going bust. If there are some assets left over in the company after priority debts are paid (such as those to the taxman) then the bond holders may receive some residual return. However, in an extreme case of insolvency it is possible to suffer a total loss on bonds – just as it is with shares.

The bonds described here (loan securities) should not be confused with capital investment bonds which are investment 'boxes' (aka wrappers) issued by insurance companies. The insurance bond 'box', just like a pension box, is simply used to hold our investment assets – of cash, shares and bonds.

Stock or bond markets in which prices have risen a great deal over a long period of time are called 'bull' markets, whilst those that are in a downward trend are called 'bear' markets.

Collective funds

This is a generic term for a whole range of retail investment fund products such as: unit trusts, open-ended investment companies (OEICs are similar to unit trusts) and the investment funds inside your pension or other insurance wrappers.

Remember that your total returns on all your investment products are reduced by charges for advice (if applicable) **and** fund management **and** for the product wrapper. Keep a lid on those charges.

Appendix 4
Don't ignore your state pension

It could be worth more than £200,000

Yes, I know, the state pension is a very boring subject – that's why it's here at the back of the book! But it's worth taking a quick look to **get the big picture** of how this thing works – because it'll help you make much better decisions about the rest of your longer term finances (and there's some good news in here too).

In Chapter 9 we saw how some advisers (and some of those online calculators) can make the cost of funding a decent pension look impossibly expensive. And we looked at what you can do to significantly reduce those cost estimates. I've also heard some advisers say that because the Government is constantly changing our state pension, there's no point in relying on it at all. Then, if you get some state pension it will come as a 'surprise' bonus! That's fine if you're incredibly wealthy but for the rest of us, our state pension will likely form a big slice of our income in our later years. And as we get older, it might very well grow to become a larger slice. Remember that state pensions rise with inflation, whereas few people have inflation-protected private pensions – they're too expensive.

Did you know that to provide the same (inflation-linked) income as the **basic** state pension, someone retiring today (2015) aged 65 would need a private pension fund of nearly **£180,000.** And to provide an income equivalent to the new **single tier** state pension (which starts from April 2016) they'd need c. £230,000!

What's more, insurers don't offer the same 'triple lock' inflation guarantee on private pensions as the Government does on state pensions. So even if we had the funds, we couldn't buy an income with inflation protection like the state pension. It's true that state pensions may be subject to more change in the future, but the big changes being made now should put them onto a sustainable footing. So, further changes *should be* relatively minor.

The current, complex, multi-layered state pension system is being replaced by a new, incredibly simple – and for many people higher – single tier state pension. For the first time in a generation, most people will be able to **understand** state pensions and this will help us with our planning.

Generally speaking, I think that our governments work to principles of fairness when they make changes to the law. And that applies to state pensions just the same as it does to the rules around public and private sector workplace pensions. One such principle is that *'what we've already earned we get to keep.'*

We'll see how this principle is being applied in the 'transitional' arrangements (as we move from the old state pension system to the new one) in a moment. But first let's clear up some confusion on this point that seems to be causing some industrial unrest of late.

In recent years there have been several public sector strikes called where the grievance has been either wholly or partly about how the Government is *'cutting our pensions'*.

That doesn't fit with the principle I've outlined above. So what's going on? Well, whether it's confusion or intentional misinformation it might be very useful (when the next strike is called over this issue) to ask the strike leaders to explain what they mean by 'cutting our pension'. What's happening is that pension schemes are being changed so that the rate at which scheme members build up their pension entitlement (their 'accrual') is being reduced – for future service.

There's a perception that pensions already earned – what people already have 'in the bag' – are being taken away. They're not. What is true is that older DB pensions (especially for older workers) cost significantly more than typical DC pensions – available to younger workers and new recruits. And it really wouldn't be fair to carry on giving over-generous benefits to the older generation . . . would it?

Getting back to state pensions – the bottom line is that they're very valuable:

Take them into account in your planning and you significantly reduce the amount you need to save for a good pension in total. And by making that 'pension cost' figure affordable, there's a good chance that you'll start saving for it *now* rather than putting it off until it's too late. The challenge is actually *understanding* state pensions – because they can be horribly complicated. A 2008 guide from the Department for Work and Pensions ran to 87 pages! This has since been replaced by a website that *looks* nicer but remains a minefield. See here:

www.gov.uk/browse/working/state-pension

There's a useful 106-page document to explain the thinking behind the new single tier pension and how it works, with examples of its impact on different people. See here: http://bit.ly/16I2Tzq

And here's a website dedicated to the new single tier pension: www.gov.uk/new-state-pension/overview

So there's no shortage of information but some of it is heavy going – so let's try to compress the key points into a few pages:

State pensions – in the good old days

State pension provision started in the UK under the Old-Age Pensions Act of 1908, which many regard as the start of our modern social welfare system. The weekly state pension commenced in 1909 at the rate of just 5 shillings per week (7s 6d for married couples) – **that's equivalent to roughly £27 (£40) in today's money.** It was paid to the half million or so pensioners who were eligible at that time – and eligibility back then was extremely limited.

First, you had to survive way beyond the normal life expectancy (about 50 years of age) because the old-age pension was **only given to people who reached 70!** Second, you had to be very poor. Your 'means' had to be less than £31 per *year* – that's about £3,300 p.a. today. And then only those deemed to be of 'good character' got a pension. So, this excluded those already in receipt of 'poor relief' and those classed as lunatics and people convicted of drunkenness (at the discretion of the court!) and anyone guilty of a 'habitual failure to work' according to their ability. It also excluded *anyone* sentenced to prison and ex-prisoners, who lost their entitlement for ten years after their release.

State pensions now (2015-16 tax year)

You may not think that state pensions are generous today, but clearly they're a lot better than they were in 1909 – and for a lot of people they're going to get better still in the future. They pay a lot more – relative to earnings – than when they started, **and** they start paying out from a much earlier age, *relative to your life expectancy.* Currently, state pensions consist of two elements: the basic state pension (BSP) and, for some, *an additional state pension* (more on these in a moment). Both are payable from state pension age. Entitlement is *not* means tested but it does depend on your record of National Insurance (NI) contributions and credits.

1. The current maximum *basic* pension is £115.95 per week per person.

2. Couples can therefore obtain twice this amount if they both qualify.

3. The maximum is given to people with a sufficient NI record of 'qualifying years' or who have 'credits' for the same.

4. Those with less than a full NI record will receive a proportion of the maximum basic state pension *(and you can boost your NI record with voluntary NI contributions – more on this later).*

5. Spouses and civil partners with less than a full NI record in their own right *may* be able to claim up to £69.50 per week based on their partner's NI record. Unmarried partners cannot do this.

6. Employees may be entitled to a top-up 'additional state pension' but the self-employed are not.

7. You can choose to defer your state pensions (both the basic and additional parts) in return for an increased amount –or take a lump sum instead. More on this later.

8. In April 2016, the current basic and additional state pensions are due to be replaced by a new single tier pension which will be worth no less than £151.25 per week. (The actual amount will be set in autumn 2015).

9. People who, under the current system, build up more state pension than the new version (by April 2016) will keep their higher entitlement.

The new single tier state pension (STP)

- The planned start date of April 2016 is one year earlier than originally planned.

- Existing state pension arrangements will still apply to those retiring before that date.

- A full STP (at least £151.25 per week) will require 35 years' of NI contributions or credits.

- The minimum qualifying period (of NI contributions or credits) to earn **any** STP will be 10 years.

- An NI record of between 10 and 35 years will deliver pro rata benefits. So a 25-year record would give 25/35ths of the full amount.

- STP can be deferred for an increased pension payment but there'll be no lump sum option as there has been with the basic state pension.

- Self-employed NI contributions will count towards the STP.

> We wait to hear whether self-employed NI will go up because of this increase to their state pension benefits.

- It will continue to be possible to pay voluntary NI contributions to buy more qualifying years.

- The 'triple lock' inflation protection is due to apply to the STP.

> But there's no certainty that such a generous (expensive) guarantee will continue indefinitely.

The transition to the new system

Everyone with an existing record of NI contributions or credits at April 2016 will be deemed to have earned a 'foundation amount' of state pension. This will be the **higher** of their entitlements calculated using the new rules and the existing rules. The foundation amount will be reduced if you've been 'contracted-out' of 'additional state pensions' in the past.

> Lots of people were 'contracted out' of part of the state pension. Their state pension entitlement was reduced in exchange for having NI payments reduced and redirected into private pensions. There's more on *contracting out* coming up.

Anyone with a foundation amount of less than the full STP can increase their state pension entitlement by 1/35th of the full STP for each further year of NI contributions or credits. Anyone with a foundation amount that's more than the full STP *will retain the extra benefits they've earned* but *will not accrue* any further benefits. The STP will accrue using our *personal* NI contributions. Unlike the state pension before 2016 you will not accrue benefits using the record of your spouse or civil partner, but existing inherited benefits will be recognised.

The nitty gritty...

Okay, so now let's take a look at:

1. How much state pension you might get – and when
2. Catching up – boosting your NI record
3. The inflation guarantee – how it works
4. What happens to your state pensions when you die
5. Should you defer taking your state pension?
6. Who gets a state pension and how do NI credits work?

How much state pension you'll get – and when

The maximum basic state pension is currently £115.95 per week but it's more useful to know what your personal entitlement might be based on your personal NI record. You'll find a quick calculator to estimate your 'basic' state pension entitlement at www.gov.uk/calculate-state-pension

Just bear in mind that this calculator doesn't estimate any additional state pension – so if you think you're entitled to that, then order a pension statement at www.gov.uk/state-pension-statement *This statement is not (at time of writing) available online.*

State pension ages (SPA)

These are on the move – upwards.

For men born *before 6 December 1953*, the current state pension age is 65. For women born before 6 April 1950, the state pension age was 60, but for those born between 5 April 1950 and 6 December 1953 the state pension age is being *gradually* increased from 60 to 65. A single state pension age for men and women will be achieved by late 2018. After that, it will be gradually increased to reach age 66 by October 2020 and then to age 67 by 2028. Any further changes will reflect changes in our life expectancy.

Yes, it's complex stuff – so it's worth looking up your own estimated state pension age using the Government's calculator. See www.gov.uk/calculate-state-pension

Catching up – boosting your NI record

If you reach – or reached – state pension age after 6 April 2010 but before 6 April 2016, you'll need at least 30 qualifying years to receive a full BSP. If you have fewer than 30 qualifying years you'll receive a BSP of 1/30th of the full amount for each qualifying year you've built up.

Currently you only need one qualifying year to start building up some BSP, but from 2016 you'll need ten qualifying years to earn any state pension at all – and 35 qualifying years for a full single tier pension.

> The rise to 35 years for qualification for the full pension may sound like a harsh change, but men who reached state pension age before 6 April 2010 needed at least 44 qualifying years to gain the full BSP and women needed 39 qualifying years.

You can check your record of qualifying years for basic state pension by contacting the Future Pension Centre at www.gov.uk/future-pension-centre (tel: 0845 3000 168). If you have a shortfall in your NI record of qualifying years, you can boost your entitlement by paying voluntary Class 3 (or Class 2 if you're self-employed) NI contributions.

> These contributions do not build entitlement to additional state pensions but do build entitlement to the new state pension.

You can normally make 'voluntary' NI payments to cover up to six years of gaps in your record. And if you reached state pension age on or before 5 April 2015 you may be able to pay in some extra years' voluntary contributions. More details here:

www.gov.uk/voluntary-national-insurance-contributions

Class 3 NI contributions are currently £14.10 per week or £733.20 for a whole year and it's really worth thinking about this cost in terms of value for money. One year's worth of NI payment delivers another 1/30th of the existing state pension (currently £115.95 per week or £6,029 per year) So for your outlay of £733.20 you get £225 more state pension *each year, every year for life with inflation proofing built in.*

That's an **incredibly good deal.**

> The deal on Class 2 contributions (for the self-employed) is even better – although I can't believe that will last for much longer.

Now, for those who've already done what they can to fill the gaps in their NI record there is one further option to boost your state pension. A new Top-Up Scheme will open in October 2015 to all pensioners who reach state pension age before the new state pension is introduced in April 2016. These new, voluntary **Class 3A** contributions will allow pensioners to top up their pension by *up to* £25 a week. However, bear in mind that this scheme is about five times more expensive than the Class 3 'catch up' scheme we looked at above!

The Government is currently quoting a cost of £22,250 for a £25 per week state pension top up for a 65 year old. More here: www.gov.uk/state-pension-topup

That sounds expensive but it could still be good value if you're healthy and likely to live for many years to come. Buying an inflation-linked annuity in the open market today would cost a great deal more. So, you might want to think carefully about using this Class 3A scheme versus the ordinary Class 3 top ups mentioned above.

The inflation guarantee – how it works

State pensions have traditionally been increased in line with an inflation index of one sort or other. But since April 2011 the basic state pension has been increased in line with the greater of:

1. Increases in national average earnings or

2. Increases in prices, measured by the CPI (consumer price index

or

3. 2.5%.

This is known as the 'triple lock' of guaranteed increases. For example the 2.5% increase in April 2015 was about double the rate of inflation.

What happens to your state pensions when you die?

If your spouse or civil partner is over state pension age when you die, they may be able to increase their BSP by using your qualifying years if they don't already get the full amount. If they are under state pension age when you die, any state pension based on your qualifying years will be included when they claim their own state pension. Although, for this to happen they can't have remarried or formed a new civil partnership by the time they reach state pension age. If you're single, divorced or your civil partnership was dissolved and you die after you've reached state pension age, your estate can claim up to three months of your BSP.

You can contact the Pension Service to check what they can claim. Visit www.gov.uk/contact-pension-service.

Should you defer taking your state pension?

It is currently possible to choose to defer your state pensions (both the basic and additional parts) in return for an increased amount. It will also be possible to defer the new state pension from 2016. You can defer in blocks of five weeks, and each five-week period of deferral gives a flat (non-compound) increase of 1%. This is equivalent to a 10.4% increase for a full year of deferment. Deferral of one year or more currently gives you the option of taking the increase as a lump sum, taxable in the same way as the pension. This lump sum option will not be available from 2016.

So is it worth it deferring your pension?

It depends.

Clearly, if you need the income as soon as you reach state pension age then there's no question. – Otherwise, it largely depends on how long you will live. Remember that if you defer for, say, one year, then you'll lose all of that year's pension. So you'll have to live for quite a few years enjoying your c. 10% increased pension to make up for that loss. The answer also depends on the rate at which pensions rise in future years. If inflation runs high, then you'll catch up on the amount you lost (during the deferral period) that much sooner.

Certainly if you take the state pension when it becomes available you might find something useful to do with it, even if you don't need it for yourself. You could give it away or spend it on children or grandchildren or save it somewhere tax efficient until you need it. And if it looks likely that inheritance tax (IHT) will apply on your estate it might be worth taking the pension and making regular gifts during your lifetime, as these can save IHT at 40% on the amounts given away.

So there could be quite a few factors to consider.

Who gets a state pension and how do NI credits work?

The precise amount of state pension you receive is based on your NI record of qualifying years during your working life. A 'working life' is from the start of the tax year when you reach age 16 to the tax year immediately before the one in which you reach state pension age. Working lives are longer now that state pension ages are rising. A 'qualifying year' is a tax year in which you received, or have credits for having received, qualifying earnings of at least the 'lower earnings limit' (LEL) – which is currently £5,824. Your earnings only qualify if you pay standard rate NI of the relevant class (Class 1 NI is payable by employees and Class 2 is payable by the self-employed).

It's worth noting that as an employee, you don't actually start paying NI until your earnings are above the primary earnings threshold (currently £8,060 p.a.), but you do start to accrue state pension entitlement once you earn more than the LEL of £5,824.

> Yes, I know, that's odd, but that's how it is

If you're self-employed you can opt out of paying NI if your profits are below £5,965, but doing so may be a false economy when you consider how just £2.80 per week in Class 2 NI payments builds up a very valuable state pension. You may be able to get National Insurance credits if you're not paying National Insurance, e.g. when you're claiming benefits because you're ill, unemployed, caring for someone or at other times, for example when you're on jury service.

There are many situations in which you can obtain NI credits. In some situations they're given automatically whilst in others you need to claim them. Find out more at www.gov.uk/national-insurance-credits

Potential benefits trap

A potential issue arises for parents of children under 12 because since January 2013, if you or your partner earns more than £50,000 p.a., then a tax will apply to progressively claw back your child benefit. For those earning over £60,000 p.a., the high income child benefit tax charge cancels the value of child benefit altogether. The person suffering the tax charge can avoid it if the child benefit is given up, but this could then result in that claimant losing their state pension accrual credits!

According to HMRC's site, it is possible to give up child benefit whilst retaining state pension accrual. But what if you've not yet applied for child benefit and you're not planning to – because of the tax charge? The Government's advice is to *"fill in the Child Benefit claim form to ensure you get National Insurance credits towards your State Pension."*

See here www.gov.uk/child-benefit-tax-charge/overview

If only the tax and benefits system were simpler eh?

The other 'grisly' bits

Additional state pensions

These remnants of various previous state pension systems will pass into history from April 2016. So it would be nice to forget about them and focus on the new (single tier) state pension of the future. But if you've been in work for a few years, these complex layers are still relevant because they determine whether your entitlement to state pension will be more or less than the new single tier amount when the changeover takes place in 2016.

Why did we have these 'additional' layers of pensions?

Well, it was recognised a long time ago that the basic state pension on its own was not enough for our needs in old age. In particular it took no account of people's different earnings levels throughout their lives. To deal with this issue an additional state pension scheme was launched in 1961. And this turned out to be the first of a series of additional schemes. Each change to the system since 1961 added another layer of state pension benefits using a different formula. The result is the highly complex system of today – which is one of the main reasons for the introduction of the new, simple, single tier pension from 2016.

The additional pensions – which gave extra pension benefits to *employees* but not to the self-employed – are outlined below.

The graduated pension

Introduced in 1961 this scheme provided a very modest accrual of additional pension until 1975. The maximum current entitlement arising from this scheme is about £12 per week.

State earnings-related pension scheme (SERPS)

This scheme enabled employed individuals to accrue a more substantial earnings related top-up to their basic state pension. The scheme was introduced in 1978 by Barbara Castle and is often referred to as the 'Castle scheme'. The scheme did not provide additional pension for those not working due to unemployment, sickness or home caring.

Those shortcomings were dealt with later with the state second pension (S2P).

The pension that accrued each year was originally revalued in line with national average earnings up to state pension age. More recently, the inflation protection has changed to a consumer prices index (CPI) basis, but it does not enjoy the triple lock.

SERPS benefits were calculated as a proportion of a **band** of earnings which started at a lower earnings limit (LEL) – roughly equivalent to the basic state pension (BSP) – and extended to an upper earnings limit (UEL), about eight times the lower earnings limit.

SERPS became very complicated when the rate of accrual was changed after the first ten years of the scheme's operation. At this point your total state pension entitlement could have been comprised of: a basic state pension, some graduated pension, and this layer – SERPS – which was itself built up in layers!

State pensions had already become impossible to understand.

The box below gives more detail about SERPS – just in case you're interested!

When SERPS was introduced in 1978 it provided accrual at the rate of 1.25% of band earnings for each tax year. The calculation took account of a maximum of 20 years (the best earning 20 years) of your working life to give a maximum 25% (1.25% x 20) of band earnings as an additional pension. This accrual rate applied to everyone with a state pension age before 6 April 1999.

For those with a state pension age after 5 April 1999, the accrual rate was reduced (from 1988) to give a maximum 20% of band earnings. And new rules also reduced the value further by averaging 'band earnings' over a working lifetime rather than over 20 years.

The result was that those with a state pension age after 5 April 2009 could only earn SERPs up to a maximum of 20% band earnings, whilst those with a state pension age between 1999 and 2009 enjoyed a mixture of accrual rates giving an average rate somewhere between 20% and 25% of band earnings.

In the event of our death, our widow, widower or surviving civil partner may be entitled to some of our SERPS pension. The amount they inherit ranges from 50% to 100% of our entitlement, with the exact percentage linked to our date of birth. The older we are, the more they inherit.

State second pension (S2P)

S2P is a similar earnings-related pension scheme to SERPS, and replaced SERPS for future accrual from April 2002. Individuals who were in both SERPS and S2P will thus have benefits under both schemes, and both will be paid at their state pension age.

S2P is more generous than SERPS for those with no earnings and for those on low to moderate earnings. It applies to:

- Those at work and earning more than the lower earnings limit (LEL)

- Carers with no earnings or earnings below the LEL in any year that they either receive child benefit for a child under 12, care for someone with a qualifying disability, or have an entitlement to Invalid Care Allowance

- Those entitled to long-term Incapacity Benefit or Severe Disablement Allowance, provided they've worked and paid Class 1 NI for 10%+ of their working life since 6 April 1978

- Registered foster parents claiming Carer's Credit.

S2P is not available to those at work earning less than the LEL *or* the unemployed *or* students *or* those caring for children older than 12 *or* the self-employed. In the event of our death, our widow, widower or surviving civil partner is entitled to 50% of our entitlement, regardless of our age.

The detailed workings of S2P (like SERPS) were changed several times over the years and this whole array of additional pensions is now beyond the comprehension of all but the most specialist of pensions gurus. Thankfully some common sense has now prevailed, and all these ridiculously complicated formulae are to be replaced with the new single tier pension (for future accrual) from 2016. If you've been working for several years, and provided that you've not been 'contracted out' of these additional pension schemes, then you may have accrued substantial benefits under them.

Whilst the *average* additional pension (on top of the basic state pension) being received in 2015 is estimated at around £35 per week, the maximum that could have been accrued by 2015-16 was £164 per week (over £8,500 each year). Add that to the basic pension to give a maximum total state pension of around £280 per week.

Few people have qualified for the maximum additional pension because the higher earners that might have done so have either been a) self-employed (which means they're not entitled to additional state pensions) or b) employed and *contracted out* of additional pension schemes. That said, when we add those *contracted-out* benefits to the basic state pension there are quite a few people in a very good position from the state pension system now. And remember that if, under the current system, you've built up a higher state pension than the new (2016) state pension – when it comes in – then you'll keep your higher entitlement.

Contracting out

For many years it was possible to contract out of these additional state pension schemes (SERPS and S2P) using either a defined benefit (DB) or defined contribution (DC) private pension arrangement. By contracting out, you gave up this additional element of your state pension in exchange for an alternative private pension funded using a rebate of the NI contributions that would otherwise have funded the additional pension.

Contracting out using a DC arrangement meant giving up a guaranteed additional state pension in favour of an uncertain amount of private pension. *(A private DC pension is uncertain because both investment returns and the pension annuity rate at retirement are uncertain.)*

Deciding whether or not to contract out each year required some complex and costly analysis of the issues and risks. What's more, this analysis (on average) gave very little benefit to the individual pension investor. Some people may have profited from the exercise whilst others have lost out. So, the option to contract out on this basis was withdrawn in April 2012.

Contracting out using a DB-type pension continues for now but will stop in 2016 when additional state pensions cease to be accrued.

If you are in a DB scheme, ask your pensions administrator about the plans for the scheme when contracting out stops. At that time both your own and your employer's NI payments will increase, and you may want to know if you'll have to pay in more for your DB pension accrual in the future. You may also want to take advice on whether the scheme remains good value for you at that time. For many people DB pensions will continue to offer very good value – but for some, the answer will be less clear-cut.

Pension credit

Pension credit is a non-taxable *means-tested* benefit, introduced in 2003 and designed to provide those over a qualifying age with a minimum level of income.

The *Guarantee Credit* tops up your weekly income if it's below £151.20 (for single people) or £230.85 (for couples). There is currently a second element to pension credit (the *savings credit*) designed to reduce issues of unfairness for those with modest incomes who've made savings for their retirement. Unfortunately this is being withdrawn from April 2016 so those with modest savings will be penalised relative to their situation today. It's also worth noting that the means test results in most forms of income, earnings and savings (capital) being taken into account. And that savings capital is 'deemed' to produce a high income regardless of what it actually produces.

The means test ignores the first £10,000 of capital/savings but then assumes capital above that amount produces income of £1 a week for each £500. In other words, the Government assumes you earn 10.4% p.a. income on your capital – now wouldn't that be nice!

The detailed operation of pension credit is devilishly complicated and with the withdrawal of savings credit in 2016 it's not worth covering in detail here. You can get an estimate of your pension credits entitlement at:

www.gov.uk/pension-credit-calculator

Read an overview of pension credit at:

www.gov.uk/pension-credit/overview

And find all the detail on pension credit at:

www.gov.uk/government/publications/
pension-credit-technical-guidance

The costs and complexities of the pension credit system – and the embarrassment it can cause to some people to claim it – are yet further reasons to introduce the new single tier pension (STP). The STP will pay a much higher amount than the current basic state pension and therefore take most people out of the means-tested benefit net altogether over time. However, the new single tier pension of at least £151.25 per week will *not be given to existing pensioners,* so many will continue to need the pension credit top-ups.

Appendix 5
Build a fund of £50,000 (or more) by saving the price of a coffee each day

You can use the chart in this section to estimate the funds you could build up **(in today's money terms)** simply by saving on a regular basis. It assumes you'll save just £3.30 per day (the price of a coffee) into a low cost savings vehicle (like an ISA) over various timescales. And you can see what higher contributions might produce, by scaling up. For example, for savings of £6.60 per day (£200 per month), simply double the result.

If you don't believe you have any capacity to save for the future – take a look here first:

www.moneyadviceservice.org.uk/en/tools/quick-cash-finder/calculators

How to use the chart

For each of your savings goals, read along the bottom axis to your timescale (in years) and then scroll up to the *appropriate** line. Then read across to the left hand axis for a rough estimate of your potential funds at the end of your savings term.

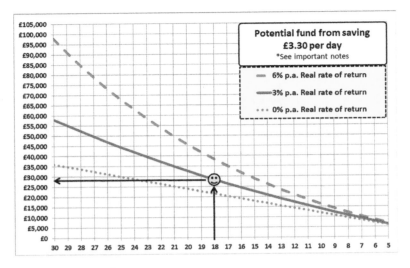

Here's an example

Let's say that 'Beau' is saving to help her new baby through university in 18 years' time. What fund (very roughly) could she expect to build over that time – with a £100 p.m. savings plan – and assuming that she enjoys moderate investment growth on her funds? We can follow the smiley face to estimate that she could produce nearly £30,000 (in today's money terms) towards the university fund.

That would be hugely valuable when that time comes.

Important notes.

The chart assumes that personal contributions rise each year in line with inflation. By showing funds in today's money terms, we've taken account of inflation between now and the end of your savings term.

Why is there such a wide range of outcomes?

For simplicity, there are just three lines on the chart. They show a wide range of outcomes because I've used a reasonably wide range of assumptions about 'real' investment returns. As you can see, different investment returns have a huge impact on our savings over the long term when compared to shorter-term saving.

Obviously, there are many more outcomes possible than those shown by the lines on this chart. Your outcome could fall somewhere in between these lines or outside them altogether if the growth on your fund is much higher or lower than the ranges we're using here.

Real rates of return (RROR) is just shorthand for returns above inflation – and the assumptions for the three lines shown are:

1. The top (red, dashed) line uses a high (6% p.a.) RROR after charges

2. The middle (green, solid) line assumes a moderate (3% p.a.) RROR after charges and

3. The bottom (orange, dotted) line assumes zero RROR after charges.

Which line should you use?

With longer-term saving of, say, 15 or more years to run to your savings goal, you might be happy to estimate your potential funds by taking a point between the top red line and the middle green line. For these savings terms where monies are invested regularly and wholly into higher return/higher risk (stock market-based) funds, there is a reasonable chance (though no guarantees!) of obtaining real investment returns of between 3% and 6% p.a. – provided that the charges on the savings plan are very low. For shorter-term savers a more conservative assumption may be appropriate. It all comes down to your attitude and 'capacity for investment risk' which depends upon various factors – which we covered in Chapter 4.

How have stock markets performed in the past?

Well, as I said in Appendix 1 we need to remember that:

> Past performance is no guide to future returns. The value of investments can go down as well as up. You could get back less than you invested. All investments should be regarded with a long-term view.

That said, we do know that the UK stock market produced total (including reinvested income) 'real' investment returns of about 5.5% p.a. on average over the past 50 years – and that this figure masks some huge variations. In some decades we've enjoyed real returns of nearly 13% p.a. whilst in others (as from the end of 1999) we've seen slightly negative real returns.

[Source: Barclays/Equity Gilt study 2015]

> Also the actual returns that you'll enjoy on regular savings plans (ISAs or otherwise) into risky assets can be higher or lower than the average returns on those funds over time. The returns from regular savings are dependent on the 'path' that fund prices take to their final point when we take our money out. This curious effect is sometimes called *pound (Dollar) cost averaging* which we'll explore in detail in my next book, *How We Mislead Ourselves About Money.*

Any assumptions you make about investment returns need to be 'reasonable' with regard to the potential performance of the assets inside your savings plan. You must accept that with greater 'potential' returns comes greater risk. So, if you choose to invest in cash deposits or other very low risk assets, you should *not* assume high (or perhaps any) 'real' returns. Your assumption for investment returns should also take account of the drag from charges on the savings product, on the funds inside it **and** for advice. These charges vary enormously between product providers and advisers – so make sure you take account of *all* charges being taken from your plan.

The BIG messages from this chart

- If you start saving whilst there's still a long time before your goals, then the most likely outcomes are good.

- If you wait until those goals are upon you, then the likely outcome is extremely painful.

The limitations of this chart

If you want to explore the cost of funding your income in retirement you'll need to add a couple more steps to this process. And if you have existing funds built up for your goals you'll need to take account of those. I'll outline how you can deal with both of these elements in a future book I have planned. If you'd like me to keep you posted on when that book will be available then sign up to my blog at www.paulclaireaux.com

Bibliography

The books, papers and articles listed below have provided inspiration and evidence for many of the ideas in this book. They offer excellent further reading, especially around the issues of economic theory, the fragility of our banking system, the impossibility of forecasting, human behavioural economics and the wider causes of financial crises.

Admati, A. and Hellwig, M. (2013) *The Banker's New Clothes: What's Wrong with Banking and What To Do About It*, Princeton, NJ: Princeton University Press.

Ariely, D. (2008) *Predictably Irrational: The Hidden Forces that Shape Our Decisions*, London: HarperCollins.

Ariely, D. and Loewenstein, G. (2006) 'The heat of the moment: The effect of sexual arousal on sexual decision making', *Journal of Behavioral Decision Making*, vol 19, pp 87-98.

Brady, C. and Ramyar, R. (2006) 'White Paper on Spread Betting', London: Cass Business School.

Buchanan, M. (2002) *Ubiquity: Why Catastrophes Happen*, New York: Random House.

Buchanan, M. (2013) *Forecast: What Physics, Meteorology, and the Natural Sciences Can Teach Us About Economics*, London: Bloomsbury.

Burns, D. (2000) *Feeling Good: The New Mood Therapy*, New York: Avon Books.

Burkeman, O. (2011) *Help! How to Become Slightly Happier and Get a Bit More Done*, Edinburgh: Canongate Books Ltd.

Burkeman, O. (2012) *The Antidote: Happiness for People Who Can't Stand Positive Thinking*, Edinburgh: Canongate Books Ltd.

Cain, S. (2012) *Quiet: The Power of Introverts in a World That Can't Stop Talking*, Portland, OR: Broadway Books.

Cooper, G. (2008) *The Origin of Financial Crises: Central Banks, Credit Bubbles and the Efficient Market Fallacy*, London: Harriman House Publishing.

Franklin, B. (1758) *The Way to Wealth*, Philadelphia, PA: Benjamin Franklin Paperback.

Graham, B. and Dodd, D. (1934) *Security Analysis*, New York: McGraw-Hill Trade.

Grossman, S.J. and Stiglitz, J.E. (1980) 'On the impossibility of informationally efficient markets', *The American Economic Review*, vol 70, no 3.

Hogshead, S. (2010) *Fascinate: Your 7 Triggers to Persuasion and Captivation*, London: Collins Business.

Ilmanen, A. (2011) *Expected Returns: An Investor's Guide to Harvesting Market Rewards*, Chichester: Wiley.

Kabat-Zinn, J. (2012) *Mindfulness For Beginners: Reclaiming the Present Moment and Your Life*, Louisville, CO: Sounds True.

Kahneman, D. (2011) *Thinking, Fast and Slow*, London: Allen Lane.

Kahneman, D., Knetsch, J.L. and Thaler, R.H. (1990) 'Experimental tests of the endowment effect and the coase theorem', *Journal of Political Economy*, vol 98, no 6, pp 1325-48, December.

Keynes, J.M. (1936) *The General Theory of Employment, Interest and Money*, London: Macmillan.

Lewis, M. (2011) *The Big Short: Inside the Doomsday Machine*, New York: W.W. Norton & Co.

Lorenz, J., Rauhut, H., Schweitzer, F. and Helbing, D. (2011) 'How social influence can undermine the wisdom of crowd effect', *Proceedings of the National Academy of Sciences of the United States of America*.

Partnoy, F. (2012) *Wait: The Useful Art of Procrastination*, London: Profile Books.

Peters, S. (2012) *The Chimp Paradox: The Mind Management Programme to Help You Achieve Success, Confidence and Happiness*, London: Vermilion.

Rajan, R. (2010) *Fault Lines: How Hidden Fractures Still Threaten the*

World Economy, Princeton, NJ: Princeton University Press.

Reinhart, C. and Rogoff, K. (2009) *This Time is Different: Eight Centuries of Financial Folly*, Princeton, NJ: Princeton University Press.

Samuelson, P.A. (1948) *Economics: An Introductory Analysis* (London: McGraw-Hill) [new edition 1998].

Shiller, R.J. (1990) *Market Volatility*, Cambridge, MA: MIT Press.

Shiller, R.J. (2000, 2nd edn, 2005) *Irrational Exuberance*, Princeton, NJ: Princeton University Press.

Smith, A. (1776) *An Inquiry into the Nature and Causes of the Wealth of Nations*.

Taleb, N.N. (2005) *Fooled by Randomness: The Hidden Role of Chance in Life and in the Markets*, New York: Random House.

Taleb, N.N. (2007) *The Black Swan: The Impact of the Highly Improbable*, London: Allen Lane.

Taleb, N.N. (2012) *Antifragile: How to Live in a World We Don't Understand*, London: Allen Lane.

Watts, D. (2011) *Everything Is Obvious: Once You Know the Answer*, London: Atlantic Books.

Watts, D., Salganik, M. and Sheridan Dodds, P. (2006) 'Experimental study of inequality and unpredictability in an artificial cultural market', *Science*, vol 311, 10 February.

Acknowledgements

The motivation for this book and all my educational work (to help people achieve more in their lives and to understand and manage their money better) has come from my challenging and questioning (and now adult) children: Harry, George and Edward.

As they started to grow up during the 1990s, each of them in turn came and asked me the same, simple question that I struggled to answer – namely:

'Daddy, what do you actually do at work?'

How do you explain to a five-year-old what a product development and marketing manager does? Never mind one who deals with investment and pensions products! So I explained that I was *'like the man who designed the toys we occasionally bought at the shops'*. That kept them off my case for a while!

Then, during my time as a key account sales manager (to our financial adviser business customers) I told my boys that I was like the *'person who struck deals with the bosses at the big supermarkets – to have my firm's baked beans displayed on their shelves.'*

The result was that my children thought I was both a toy designer and a baked bean salesman!

So I thought it might be a good idea – at some point – to provide them with the real story, to outline the benefits (and risks) of the industry and products I'd worked with. I also wanted to share my ideas on managing what I believe to be the greatest asset we'll ever have – ourselves.

When I started to tell other people that I was writing about all this stuff, they said it was something that they wanted to know about too. So thank you lads, this book is for you – but I hope it'll help a lot of other people too.

Some of the many other people I want to thank include:

- The hundreds of financial advisers that I've had the pleasure of dealing with over many years – many highly capable and some *less so!*

- My ex-colleagues in all parts of the business at Clerical Medical (CM) – in sales, marketing, actuarial pricing, fund management, project management, customer services, risk and IT.

I'm particularly grateful to ex-colleagues in CM's financial planning department – which most advisers will remember as the best technical support team in the UK over a number of years. These guys and gals were especially good at connecting the tax and pensions technical aspects of our products to the real customer needs that we served through financial advisers.CM was a good place to be during the 1980s and 1990s. It was a leading provider of pension and investment products, operating in the highly demanding Independent Financial Adviser (IFA) sector with a culture of honesty and high integrity.

Sadly, these were not the characteristics I recall most about the big bank that took us over – the managers of which were more concerned with fast growth than openness about the risks they were taking with their shareholders' money. Nor did they seem concerned about the risks they were exposing their borrowers to, with their hard sell/fat profit culture. The Halifax, which later merged with the Bank of Scotland to become HBOS, was a high volume seller of mortgages. It was their activity alongside other big lenders that inflated the UK house price bubble that burst and took them with it in the financial collapse of 2008. Thankfully I escaped that group – or rather their rescuer, Lloyds – in late 2010 after several attempts and tunnel digging. *I can confirm that it helps to say 'wibble' a lot! (That's a Blackadder reference.)*

So, perhaps *I should* thank that bank – for teaching me how **not** to run a financial services business and for opening my eyes to the personal and national economic disasters that come from greed, poorly regulated markets and a belief in perfect markets – that house prices only ever go up!

My thanks – for many of the insights shared in these pages – into human behaviour, economics and investments – go to the authors of the books and academic studies listed in the bibliography.

My particular thanks go to the following:

- *For helping me see the flaws in classical economics, investment theory and the dangers of the banking system:* Anat Admati, Martin Hellwig, Roger Bootle, Steve Keen, Mark Buchanan, George Cooper, Benoit Mandelbrot, David Orrell, Raghuram Rajan, Robert Shiller and Nassim Taleb.

- *For helping me see the irrationality and flaws in human behaviour:* Dan Ariely, Daniel Kahneman, Richard Thaler and Duncan Watts.

- *For helping me to see that humans can act rationally – even if it's not immediately obvious:* Tim Harford, Steven Levitt and Stephen J. Dubner.

- *For helping me to understand the machine that we wrestle with throughout our lives – our own minds – and for wonderful insights into the real meaning of happiness, motivation, leadership and personal performance:* Steve Peters, David Burns, Jon Kabat-Zinn, Mihaly Csikszentmihalyi, Manel Baucells, Rakesh Sarin, Kenneth Blanchard, James Prochaska, John Norcross, Carlo DiClemente, Tom Rath, Barbara Ehrenreich, Dan Pink, Susan Cain and Oliver Burkeman.

I thank my parents for a value they instilled in me from a young age – namely, 'if you want it then you'd better work and pay for it', and also for my father's love of engineering and science that fostered a passion for understanding how things work – and a lifelong search for truth and evidence.

I thank my brother, sisters and friends who, in different ways, have encouraged me to complete this work – including those who've found this project to be a source of great amusement!

I thank my cartoonist Noel Ford and my book designer Jane Smith, for their excellent work (and patience), and my editor Caroline Wijetunge for helping me make this sometimes 'grisly' subject easier to read, and for keeping me out of trouble – on issues of grammar *and* political correctness *most of the time.*

And finally I want to thank my partner Wendy, without whose patience this book series would never have been written.

Thanks to you all.

Lightning Source UK Ltd.
Milton Keynes UK
UKOW07f1612150116

266489UK00010B/77/P